WESTMINSTER ASSEMBLY'S SHORTER CATECHISM,

WITH WHICH IS INCORPORATED

A SCRIPTURE CATECHISM

IN THE

METHOD OF THE ASSEMBLY'S;

BY THE

REV. MATTHEW HENRY, V. D. M.

Carefully transcribed from the last London Edition of the Miscellaneous Works of that venerable author. The first complete American Edition; in which, the errors of the Press, found in the London Edition, are carefully corrected:

By the Rev. Colin McIver, V. D. M.

PRINCETON, N. J.:
PUBLISHED BY FRANKLIN MERRILL.

1846.

RECOMMENDATION.

The Scripture Catechism of the Rev. Matthew Henry, a new edition of which is now presented to the Christian Public, is a work calculated to be universally useful in increasing the knowledge and confirming the faith of all who will study it with diligence and prayer. Few persons who ever lived, could have produced such a work; if the numerous questions contained in it had been set down without answers, scarcely any one would have conceived it possible to furnish pertinent answers to the whole of them, in the precise words of Holy Scripture. Indeed, I have never looked into this Catechism without feeling an agreeable surprise, in observing the perfection of Scriptural knowledge which it manifests. Catechisms possess no authority but what they derive from the Bible; how important then is it, that those who adopt the Westminster Shorter Catechism, should be acquainted with the proof-texts, on which every doctrine rests? And where can we find these proofs so judiciously arranged, and so pertinently applied, as in this Scripture Catechism? I do therefore cordially recommend it to all pastors, parents, and others engaged in giving religious instruction to the rising generation.

A. ALEXANDER.

Princeton, N. J., Nov. 12, 1846.

THE AMERICAN EDITOR'S PREFACE.

THE assertion in the title page, that this is the first complete American Edition of the venerable Mr. Henry's Scripture Catechism, may, perhaps, be called in question, by some who may have seen a small volume, published in the year 1835, by Messrs. Griffin & Co., of New York, under the title of "The Catechism of the Westminster Divines; with Scriptural questions and answers, by the Rev. Matthew Henry, D.D., Author of the commentary on the Bible." But, whoever will take the trouble of comparing that volume, with the "Scripture Catechism" of Mr. Henry as published in his "Miscellaneous Works," will find, that the volume published by Messrs. Griffin & Co., is nothing more than a meagre collection of extracts from what was originally published by the venerable author.

In this edition, the typographical errors, found in the London Edition, are carefully corrected. The "Shorter Catechism," which Mr. Henry, in this work, has beautifully illustrated in the language of scripture, is here presented, in the very words of the Westminster Divines. This is here mentioned, inasmuch as, in the London Edition of this work, there are to be found some few deviations from the language employed by the Westminster Divines, though none of them are such as to affect the sentiment. Of the illustrative questions and answers contained in the London Edition, one only is, in this edition, omitted. This is done, under an impression which is believed to be well founded, that the question and answer here alluded to, was never written by Mr. Henry; but was, in some unaccountable way, interpolated into the London Edition of this work. If inquiry be made into the ground of this supposition, the reply to such inquiry must be, that the question and answer here referred to, considered in connexion, exhibit a palpable misapplication of a text of scripture, and convey an erroneous sentiment, which is flatly contradicted, in other parts of Mr. Henry's published works.

The Editor deems it unnecessary to add anything, commendatory of the following pages. The well established reputation of the author, is a sufficient recommendation to all the productions of his pen. May the Divine blessing accompany the publication of this Edition.

THE AUTHOR'S PREFACE.

WE are very happy (I know) in catechisms, which, to the inhabitants of this valley of vision, will be either the means of knowledge, or the shame of ignorance. The variety of these forms of sound words, while they all speak for substance the same thing, and are all built upon the foundation of the apostles and prophets, derogates not at all from the honour of the Christian doctrine, but rather (like the setting up of several candles in the same room) help to diffuse the light, and make it stronger. Many very excellent expositions we have both of the Church Catechism and of the Assembly's, and an ancient and profitable one of Mr. Ball's; and yet some encourage me to hope, that this essay, which is in a way not hitherto used, that I know of, will be found not altogether useless. Two things I aim at in it: one is, to put the catechism into such a dress, as to make it (if possible) both easy and copious, so as that it may not be an insuperable task to the learner, and yet may furnish him with plenty of useful knowledge. The bulk of it (which somewhat exceeds my first intentions) shows it to be copious; and yet I think it is made very easy, by breaking of it into so many short questions, and those answered by Yes or No, which the learner may at first content hmself with, the teacher, if he pleases, reading the proofs; and, by degrees, the learner, who is willing to take a little pains, and begins to be versed in the Scriptures, will find it no great difficulty to charge his memory with most of the proofs annexed, which the question oftentimes easily introduces, and which, by frequent use, will in time become familiar. I remember to have seen an Explanation of the Assembly's Shorter Catechism, (and I think it was the first that ever was published) by a great man, the Rev. Dr. Wallis, of Oxford, which was done by breaking the propositions of the catechism in short questions (as this) with Yes or No. That performance, though very short, was an excellent precedent, directing to a method of catechising, which has been of good use to enrich the understanding of the learners, without overloading their memories. The text subjoined here will shew that our Yea is yea, and our Nay, nay. To make this the more easy, the several sections under each article may be allotted to several catechumens.

But another thing I aim at, (and indeed the chief,) is to promote the knowledge of the scriptures. Divine truths, methinks, sound best in divine language; and the *things which God has revealed to us by his Spirit*, cannot be conveyed in a more safe and proper vehicle, than by the words which the Holy Ghost teaches, (1 Cor. ii. 10, 13,) which, though I would be far from superstitiously tying myself or others to, yet, I confess, I cannot but think they should be preferred. I have often observed how the evangelist rectifies a mistake which rose upon a saying of Christ's, only by repeating the word spoken, John xxi. 23. *He said not, He shall not die ; but, if I will that he tarry till I come, what is that to thee?* He said so, and no more ; add thou not to his words. We are directed not only to think, but to *speak, according to his word.* Isa. viii. 20.

It is especially profitable to acquaint children betimes with their bibles, and to shew them their religion there. *Timothy's Catechism* was the Scripture which he knew from his very infancy. 2 Tim. iii. 15. They who are ready and mighty in the Scriptures, will be thoroughly furnished for every good work, and thoroughly fortified against every evil work. What I have here endeavored, may, (I hope) prove a good expedient for this purpose, obliging myself to produce a text of Scripture for every question, it cannot be thought they should be alike apposite. Perhaps here and there one may be found that is *diverted* from its *primary* intention by an allusion only, (which I think is warranted by diverse of the New Testament quotations out of the Old,) yet I hope there is none *perverted.* Were we more conversant with the inspired writings, we should (as one of the ancients speaks,) " adore the fulness of the Scriptures. I have quoted the texts as concisely as I could, in hopes the diligent reader, who searches the Scripture daily, will be stirred up to look further into the places referred to, which he will often find very well worth his while. To that end, I have throughout added the book, chapter, and verse, which yet it is needless for them who learn by heart, to trouble themselves with.

The Author's Preface.

To the service of such ministers, governors of families, and other Christians, as shall see cause to make use of such a help, with an entire dependance upon the grace and blessing of God, for the acceptableness and usefulness of it, this small oblation is humbly tendered, by one who is earnestly desirous to increase in Scripture knowledge, and ambitious of the honor of being any way instrumental to propagate it.

MATTHEW HENRY.

Postscript to the Third Edition.

I am willing to take this opportunity to advise one thing more concerning the use of this Catechism, which I have found very beneficial, viz: That the learners be put in their answers to turn the question into a proposition, which they will easily do with a little direction. Example,—Is man a reasonable creature? Yes: man is a reasonable creature; for there is a spirit in man, &c. And this will lead them, when the question gives occasion for it, to make application to themselves. Again, is it your business in the world to serve the flesh? No: it is not *my* business in the world to serve the flesh; for we are not debtors to the flesh.

THE
WESTMINSTER ASSEMBLY'S SHORTER CATECHISM,

WITH WHICH IS INCORPORATED

The Scripture Catechism of the Rev. Matthew Henry.

---

1. *Q.* What is the chief end of man?
A. Man's chief end is to glorify God, and to enjoy him forever.

§ I.

1. *Q.* Is man a reasonable creature?
A. Yes: for there is a spirit in man, and the inspiration of the Almighty giveth him understanding. Job xxxii. 8.

2. *Q.* Has he greater capacities than the brutes?
A. Yes: for God teacheth us more than the beasts of the earth, and maketh us wiser than the fowls of Heaven. Job xxxv. 11.

§ II.

1. *Q.* Is man his own maker?
A. No: it is God that hath made us, and not we ourselves. Psalms c. 3.

2. *Q.* Is he, then, his own master?
A. No: there is a Lord over us. Ps. xii. 4.

3. *Q.* Is he his own carver?
A. No: should it be according to thy mind? Job xxxiv. 33.

4. *Q.* Is he his own end?
A. No: for none of us lives to himself, or dies to himself. Rom. xiv. 7.

§ III.

1. *Q.* Is it your business in the world to serve the flesh?
A. No: for we are not debtors to the flesh, that we should live after the flesh. Rom. viii. 12.

2. *Q.* Is it to pursue the world?

A. No: for we are not of the world. John xvii. 16.

§ IV.

1. *Q.* Is your happiness bound up in the creature?
A. No: for all is vanity and vexation of spirit. Eccl. i. 14.
2. *Q.* Will the riches of the world make you happy?
A. No: for a man's life consisteth not in the abundance of the things which he possesseth. Luke xii. 15.
3. *Q.* Will the praise and applause of men make you happy?
A. No: for it is vain glory. Gal. v. 26.
4. *Q.* Will sport and pleasure make you happy?
A. No: for the wise man said of laughter, It is mad, and of mirth, What doeth it? Eccl. ii. 2.
5. *Q.* Can the gain of the world make you happy?
A. No: for what is a man profited, if he gain the whole world, and lose his own soul? Matt. xvi. 26.

§ V.

1. *Q.* Is God, then, your chief end?
A. Yes: for of him, and through him, and to him are all things. Rom. xi. 36.
2. *Q.* Were you made for him?
A. Yes: this people have I formed for myself. Isa. xliii. 21.
3. *Q.* Were you redeemed for him?
A. Yes: ye are not your own, for ye are bought with a price. 1 Cor. vi. 19, 20.

§ VI.

1. *Q.* Is it your chief business to glorify God?
A. Yes: we must glorify God in our body and in our spirit, which are God's. 1 Cor. vi. 20.
2. *Q.* Must this be ultimately designed in all our actions?
A. Yes: do all to the glory of God. 1 Cor. x. 31.
3. *Q.* Is God glorified by our praises?
A. Yes: he that offers praise, glorifies God. Ps. i. 23.
4. *Q.* And is he glorified by our works?
A. Yes: herein is my Father glorified, that ye bear much fruit. John xv. 8.

§ VII.

1. *Q.* Is God your chief good?
A. Yes: for happy is the people whose God is the Lord. Ps. cxliv. 15.
2. *Q.* Does all good come from him?
A. Yes: for with him is the fountain of life. Ps. xxxvi. 9.
3. *Q.* And is all good enjoyed in him?

A. Yes: the Lord is the portion of my inheritance, and of my cup. Ps. xvi. 5.

§ VIII.

1. *Q.* Is it your chief happiness, then, to have God's favour?
A. Yes: for in his favour is life. Ps. xxx. 5.
2. *Q.* Is that the most desirable good?
A. Yes: for his loving kindness is better than life. Ps. lxiii. 3.
3. *Q.* Do you desire it above any good?
A. Yes: Lord lift thou the light of thy countenance upon us. Ps. iv. 6.
4. *Q.* And should you give all diligence to make it sure?
A. Yes: herein we labour, that whether present or absent, we may be accepted of the Lord. 2 Cor. v. 9.

§ IX.

1. *Q.* Is communion with God in grace here the best pleasure?
A. Yes: it is good for me to draw near to God. Ps. lxxiii. 28.
2. *Q.* Is the vision and fruition of God in glory hereafter the best portion?
A. Yes: for in his presence there is fulness of joy. Ps. xvi. 11.
3. *Q.* Will you, therefore, set your heart upon this chief good?
A. Yes: Lord, whom have I in Heaven but thee? and there is none upon earth that I desire besides thee, when my flesh and my heart fail, God is the strength of my heart, and my portion for ever. Ps. lxxiii. 25, 26.

II. *Q.* What rule hath God given to direct us how we may glorify and enjoy him?

A. The word of God (which is contained in the scriptures of the Old and New Testament) is the only rule to direct us how we may glorify and enjoy him.

§ I.

1. *Q.* Do we need a rule to direct us to our chief end?
A. Yes: for we all, like sheep, have gone astray. Isa liii. 6.
2. *Q.* Could we not find it out, of ourselves?
A. No: for man is born like the wild ass's colt. Job xi. 12.

§ II.

1. *Q.* Is divine revelation necessary to religion?

A. Yes: for faith comes by hearing and hearing by the word of God. Rom. x. 17.

2. *Q.* Is not the light of nature sufficient without it?

A. No: for the world, by wisdom, knew not God. 1 Cor. i. 21.

3. *Q.* Has God, therefore, given us a revelation?

A. Yes: He hath shewed thee, O man, what is good. Mic. vi. 8.

4. *Q.* Was there revelation from the beginning?

A. Yes: at sundry times, and in divers manners, God spake unto the fathers. Heb. i. 1.

§ III.

1. *Q.* Are the scriptures of the Old and New Testament the word of God, and a divine revelation?

A. Yes: for all scripture is given by inspiration of God. 2 Tim. iii. 16.

2. *Q.* Were they indited by the blessed Spirit?

A. Yes: for holy men of God spake as they were moved by the Holy Ghost. 2 Pet. i. 21.

3. *Q.* Were they confirmed by miracles?

A. Yes: God also bearing them witness both with signs and wonders. Heb. ii. 4.

4. *Q.* Do they recommend themselves?

A. Yes: for the word of God is quick and powerful. Heb. iv. 12.

5. Is not the Bible, then, a cheat, put upon the world?

A. No: for these are not the words of him that hath a devil. John x. 21.

§ IV.

1. *Q.* Was the book of scripture witten for our use?

A. Yes: whatsoever things were written aforetime, were written for our learning. Rom. xv. 4.

2. *Q.* And is it of great use?

A. Yes: for it is profitable for doctrine, for reproof, for correction, for instruction in righteousness. 2 Tim. iii. 16.

§ V.

1. *Q.* Are the scriptures the great support of our religion?

A. Yes: for we are built upon the foundation of the apostles and prophets. Ephes. ii. 20.

2. *Q.* Are they the standing rule of our faith and practice?

A. Yes: We must have recourse to the law and to the testimony. Isa. viii. 20.

3. *Q.* Are they the only rule?
A. Yes: for other foundation can no man lay. 1 Cor. iii. 2.
4. *Q.* Are they our guide?
A. Yes: for the commandment is a lamp, and the law is light. Prov. vi. 23.
5. *Q.* Do they shew us the way to Heaven and happiness?
A. Yes: for in them we think we have eternal life; and they are they which testify of Christ. John v. 39.

§ VI.

1. *Q.* Are the scriptures our oracle which we must consult?
A. Yes: what is written in the law? How readest thou? Luke x. 26.
2. *Q.* Are they our touch-stone which we must try by?
A. Yes: if they speak not according to this word, it is because there is no light in them. Isa. viii. 20.
3. *Q.* Are they the weapons of our spiritual warfare?
A. Yes: get thee hence, Satan, for it is written. Matt. iv. 10; Ephes. vi. 17.

§ VII.

1. *Q.* Is the written word a sufficient rule?
A. Yes: for the law of the Lord is perfect. Ps. xix. 7.
2. *Q.* Is it plain?
A. Yes: for the word is nigh thee. Rom. x. 8.
3. *Q.* Is the church's authority the rule of our faith?
A. No: for our faith should not stand in the wisdom of men. 1 Cor. ii. 5.
4. *Q.* May we depend upon unwritten traditions?
A. No: for we must refuse profane and old wives' fables. 1 Tim. iv. 7.

§ VIII.

1. *Q.* Will the written word be the rule of our judgment hereafter?
A. Yes: for we must be judged by the law of liberty. James ii. 12.
2. *Q.* Ought we, therefore, to be ruled by it now?
A. Yes: as many as walk according to this rule, peace shall be on them. Gal. vi. 16.
3. *Q.* And to be comforted by it?
A. Yes: for through patience and comfort of the scriptures, we have hope. Rom. xv. 4.

§ IX.

1. *Q.* Are the scriptures to be translated into vulgar tongues?

A. Yes: for we should hear them speak, in our tongues, the wonderful works of God. Acts ii. 11.

2. *Q.* And must we study them?

A. Yes: search the scriptures. John v. 39.

3. *Q.* And labour to understand them?

A. Yes: understandest thou what thou readest? Acts viii. 30.

4. *Q.* And must we rest satisfied with this revelation of God's will?

A. Yes: for if we believe not Moses and the prophets, neither would we be persuaded though one rose from the dead. Luke xvi. 31.

5. *Q.* Is it a great affront to God to neglect his word?

A. Yes: I have written unto them the great things of my law, but they were counted as a strange thing. Hos. viii. 12.

§ X.

1. *Q.* Must little children get the knowledge of the scripture?

A. Yes: Timothy is commended for this, that from a child he knew the holy scriptures. 2 Tim. iii. 15.

2. *Q.* And must their parents instruct them therein?

A. Yes: they must teach them diligently unto their children and talk of them. Deut. vi. 7.

§ XI.

1. *Q.* Must we all love the word of God?

A. Yes: O how love I thy law! Ps. cxix. 97.

2. *Q.* And must we meditate therein?

A. Yes: it is my meditation all the day. Ps. cxix. 97.

3. *Q.* And will this be to our own advantage?

A. Yes: for it is able to make us wise to salvation. 2 Tim. iii. 15.

III. *Q.* What do the scriptures principally teach?

A. The scriptures principally teach, what man is to believe concerning God, and what duty God requires of man.

§ I.

1. *Q.* Is it necessary that we have a faith concerning God?

A. Yes: for he that comes to God must believe that he is, and that he is the rewarder of them that diligently seek him. Heb. xi. 6.

2. Q. Can we have that faith without being taught?
A. No: for how shall they believe in him of whom they have not heard? Rom. x. 14.

3. Q. And have they not heard?
A. Yes: verily their sound went into all the earth, and their words to the ends of the world. Rom. x. 18.

§ II.

1. Q. Is not the knowledge of God a great privilege?
A. Yes: for this is life eternal, to know thee the only true God. John xvii. 3.

2. Q. Is it not the best knowledge?
A. Yes: for the knowledge of the Holy is understanding. Prov. ix. 10.

3. Q. Does the scripture teach us that knowledge?
A. Yes: for if we receive those words, and hide those commandments with us, then shall we understand the fear of the Lord, and find the knowledge of God. Prov. ii. 1, 5.

§ III.

1. Q. Do not the works of creation prove that there is a God?
A. Yes: for we understand by the things that are made, his eternal power and Godhead. Rom. i. 20.

2. Q. And do not the works of Providence prove it?
A. Yes: for verily there is a God that judgeth in the earth. Ps. lviii. 11.

3. Q. But do not the scriptures tell us best what God is?
A. Yes: for no man hath seen God at any time, the only begotten Son, which is in the bosom of the Father, he hath declared him. John i. 18.

§ IV.

1. Q. Are we all concerned to get the knowledge of God?
A. Yes: We should all know him, from the least even to the greatest. Heb. viii. 11.

2. Q. Must children get that knowledge?
A. Yes: I write unto you, little children, because you have known the Father. 1 John ii. 13.

3. Q. And must we all grow in that knowledge?
A. Yes: We must follow on to know the Lord. Hos. vi. 3.

§ V.

1. Q. Are we to believe what the scripture reveals concerning God?
A. Yes: for these things are written that we may believe. John xx. 31.

2. Q. And must we believe all that the scripture reveals?

A. Yes: believing all things which are written in the law and the prophets. Acts. xxiv. 14.

3. Q. Must we believe that which is not revealed?

A. No: for the things of God knows no man, but the Spirit of God. 1 Cor. ii. 11.

§ VI.

1. Q. Does God require duty of man?

A. Yes: for unto man he said, Behold the fear of the Lord, that is wisdom; and to depart from evil, that is understanding. Job. xxviii. 28.

2. Q. Is it enough to believe the truth revealed, if we do not the duty that is required?

A. No: for faith without works is dead. James ii. 26.

3. Q. Is it enough to do the duty required, though we do not believe the truth revealed?

A. No: for he that believeth not God, hath made him a liar. 1 John v. 10.

§ VII.

1. Q. Does the scripture teach us what duty God requires?

A. Yes: he hath showed thee what the Lord thy God requires of thee. Mic. vi. 8.

2. Q. And must we do the duty that the scripture teaches?

A. Yes: we must observe to do according to all that is written therein, and not turn from it to the right hand, or to the left. Josh. i. 7.

3. Q. Must this obedience always accompany faith?

A. Yes: for they which have believed in God must be careful to maintain good works. Tit. iii. 8.

IV. Q What is God?

A. God is a Spirit, infinite, eternal and unchangeable in his being, wisdom, power, holiness, justice, goodness, and truth.

§ I.

1. Q. Is God a Spirit?

A. Yes: for Christ himself has said, God is a Spirit. John iv. 24.

2. Q. Is he a pure Spirit?

A. Yes: for God is light, and with him is no darkness at all. 1 John i. 5.

3. *Q.* Has he a body as we have?
A. No: Hast thou eyes of flesh? or seest thou as a man seeth? Job x. 4.

4. *Q.* Can he be seen with bodily eyes?
A. No: for he is one whom no man hath seen, or can see. 1 Tim. vi. 16.

5. *Q.* Are not the angels spirits?
A. Yes: He maketh his angels spirits. Ps. civ. 4.

6. *Q.* Are not the souls of men spirits?
A. Yes: for he formeth the spirit of man within him. Zech. xii. 1.

7. *Q.* But is God a spirit like unto them?
A. No: for he is the Father of spirits. Heb. xii. 9.

§ II.

1. *Q.* Is God infinite?
A. Yes: for we cannot, by searching, find out God. Job xi. 7.

2. *Q.* Is he contained in any place?
A. No: for the heaven of heavens cannot contain him. 1 Kings viii. 27.

3. *Q.* Is he every where present?
A. Yes: for whither can we go from his spirit, or flee from his presence? Ps. cxxxix. 7.

4. *Q.* Can any hide himself in secret places that God shall not see him?
A. No: for do not I fill heaven and earth, saith the Lord? Jer. xxiii. 24.

§ III.

1. *Q.* Is God eternal?
A. Yes: From everlasting to everlasting thou art God? Ps. xc. 2.

2. *Q.* Had he beginning of days?
A. No: for he is the Ancient of days. Dan. vii. 9.

3. *Q.* Shall there be any end of his life?
A. No: for he is the same, and his years have no end. Ps. cii. 27.

4. *Q.* Is there with him any succession of time?
A. No: for his days are not as the days of man. Job. x. 5.

5. Can he die?
A. No: he is the only potentate, that hath immortality. 1 Tim. vi. 16.

§ IV.

1. *Q.* Is God unchangeable?

A. Yes: for he is the Father of lights, with whom is no variableness, nor shadow of turning. James i. 17.

2. *Q.* Is there any decay of his perfections?
A. No: for He fainteth not, neither is weary. Isa. xi. 28.

3. *Q.* Is there any alteration in his counsels?
A. No: for He is not a man that he should repent. 1 Sam. xv. 29.

4. *Q.* Is it well for us that he is unchangeable?
A. Yes: I am the Lord, I change not, therefore, ye sons of Jacob are not consumed. Mal. iii. 6.

§ V.

1. *Q.* Is God infinite in his being?
A. Yes: for he has said, I AM THAT I AM. Exod. iii. 14.

2. *Q.* Is he self-existent?
A. Yes: for the Father hath life in himself? John v. 26.

3. *Q.* Is he the best of beings?
A. Yes: for who is a God like unto him? Exod. xv. 11.

4. *Q.* Is he the first of causes?
A. Yes: for he is the Father, of whom are all things, and we in him. 1. Cor. viii. 6.

5. *Q.* Is he the highest of powers?
A. Yes: for he is the King of Kings, and Lord of Lords. 1 Tim. vi. 15.

§ VI.

1. *Q.* Is he a God of perfect knowledge?
A. Yes: for his understanding is infinite. Ps. cxlvii. 5.

2. *Q.* Can any thing be hid from him?
A. No: for all things are naked and opened unto the eyes of him with whom we have to do. Heb. iv. 13.

3. *Q.* Does he know things to come?
A. Yes: for he declareth the end from the beginning. Isa. xlvi. 10.

4. *Q.* Does he know our hearts?
A. Yes: for he understandeth our thoughts afar off. Ps. cxxxix. 2.

5. *Q.* Does he know all our actions?
A. Yes: for his eyes are upon the ways of man. Job. xxxiv 21.

§ VII.

1. *Q.* Is God infinitely wise?
A. Yes: for wisdom and might are his. Dan. ii. 20.

2. *Q.* Are all his works wisely done?

A. Yes: In wisdom he hath made them all. Ps. civ. 24.

3. *Q.* And particularly the work of redemption?

A. Yes: for it is the wisdom of God in a mystery. 1 Cor. ii. 7.

4. *Q.* Can the wisdom of God's counsels be fathomed?

A. No: O, the depth of the riches of the wisdom and knowledge of God! Rom. xi. 33.

§ VIII.

1. *Q.* Is he a God of power?

A. Yes: God hath spoken once, twice have I heard this, that power belongeth unto God. Ps. lxii. 11.

2. *Q.* Is he Almighty?

A. Yes: he is the Lord God Almighty. Rev. xv. 3.

3. *Q.* Is his power irresistible?

A. Yes: for none can stay his hand, Dan. iv. 35.

4. *Q.* Is his sovereignty incontestable?

A. Yes: for he giveth not account of any of his matters. Job xxxiii. 13.

5. *Q.* Is any thing too hard for him?

A. No: for, with God, all things are possible. Matt. xix. 26.

§ IX.

1. *Q.* Is he a God of perfect holiness?

A. Yes: for holy, holy, holy, is the Lord of Hosts. Isa. vi. 3.

2. *Q.* Is there iniquity with God?

A. No: he is of purer eyes than to behold iniquity. Heb. i. 13.

3. *Q.* Is this his glory?

A. Yes: for he is glorious in holiness. Exod. xv. 11.

4. *Q.* And must we give him the glory of it?

A. Yes: give thanks at the remembrance of his holiness. Ps. xxx. 4.

5. *Q.* And must we study herein to resemble him?

A. Yes: be ye holy, for I am holy. 1 Pet. i. 16.

§ X.

1. *Q.* Is he a just and righteous Governor?

A. Yes: the Lord is righteous in all his ways. Ps. cxlv. 17

2. *Q.* Did he ever do wrong to any of his creatures?

A. No: there is no unrighteousness in him. Ps. xcii. 15.

3. *Q.* And does justice please him?

A. Yes: the righteous Lord loveth righteousness. Ps. xi. 7

§ XI.

1. *Q.* Is he a merciful God?

A. Yes: He is the Lord, the Lord God, merciful and gracious. Exod. xxxiv. 6.

2. *Q.* And a good God?
A. Yes: thou art good, and dost good. Ps. cxix. 68.

3. *Q.* Is he universally good?
A. Yes: for He is good to all, and his tender mercies are over all his works. Ps. cxlv. 9.

4. *Q.* Is he, in a special manner, good to his own people?
A. Yes: for truly God is good to Israel. Ps. lxxiii. 1.

5. *Q.* And should we acquaint ourselves with his goodness?
A. Yes: O, taste, and see that the Lord is good. Ps. xxxiv. 8.

§ XII.

1. *Q.* Is he a God of truth?
A. Yes: the truth of the Lord endureth forever. Ps. cxvii. 2.

2. *Q.* Will he perform all his promises?
A. Yes: for he is faithful that hath promised. Heb. x. 23.

3. *Q.* Is there any danger of his deceiving us?
A. No: it is impossible for God to lie. Heb. vi. 18.

§ XIII.

1. *Q.* Is this a complete description of God?
A. No: for, lo, these are but parts of his ways; and how little a portion is heard of him! Job xxvi. 14.

2. *Q.* Must we, therefore, always speak of God, with reverence?
A. Yes: for behold, God is great, and we know him not. Job xxxvi. 26.

3. *Q.* And must we pray to him to teach us what we shall say?
A. Yes: for we cannot order our speech, by reason of darkness. Job xxxvii. 19.

V. *Q.* Are there more gods than one?

A. There is but one only, the living and true God.

§ I.

1. *Q.* Are there many gods?
A. No: for though there be that are called gods, yet there is but one God. 1 Cor. viii. 5, 6.

2. *Q.* Can there be but one?
A. No: for he has said, I am God, and there is none else; I am God, and there is none like me. Isa. xlvi. 9.

3. *Q.* Are you sure there is but one?

SCRIPTURE CATECHISM. 13

A. Yes: for the Lord our God is one Lord; and there is none other but he. Mark xii. 29, 32.

§ II.

1. *Q.* Is the God whom we serve that one God?
A. Yes: for Jehovah He is God; Jehovah, He is God. 1 Kings xviii. 39.

2. *Q.* Is he infinitely above all pretenders?
A. Yes: for he is a great King above all gods. Ps. xcv. 3.

3. *Q.* Is he God alone?
A. Yes: O Lord of Hosts, God of Israel, thou art the God, even thou alone. Isa. xxxvii. 16.

4. *Q.* Are all other gods false gods?
A. Yes: for all the gods of the nations are idols; but the Lord made the Heavens. Ps. xcvi. 5.

§ III.

1. *Q.* Is our God the true God?
A. Yes: the Lord, he is the true God. Jer. x. 10.

2. *Q.* Is he the only true God?
A. Yes: this is life eternal, to know the only true God. John xvii. 3.

3. *Q.* Is he the living God?
A. Yes: the living God, and an everlasting King. Jer. x. 10.

4. *Q.* Is he the sovereign Lord?
A. Yes: for he is God over all, blessed forevermore. Rom. ix. 5.

5. *Q.* Is this one God enough?
A. Yes: for He is God all-sufficient. Gen. xvii. 1.

§ IV.

1. *Q.* Is the Lord Jehovah the maker of all things?
A. Yes: He is the everlasting God, even the Lord, the Creator of the ends of the earth. Isa. xl. 28.

2. *Q.* Is he your Maker?
A. Yes: He is the Lord, our Maker. Ps. xcv. 6.

3. *Q.* Is he the owner of all things?
A. Yes: for He is the most high God, possessor of Heaven and earth. Gen. xiv. 19.

4. *Q.* Is he your rightful owner?
A. Yes: we are the people of his pasture, and the sheep of his hand. Ps. xcv. 7.

5. *Q.* Is he the ruler of all things?
A. Yes: for his kingdom ruleth over all. Ps. ciii. 19.

6. *Q.* Is he your ruler?

A. Yes: O, Lord, truly I am thy servant, I am thy servant. Ps. cxvi. 16.

7. *Q.* Is he the benefactor of all creatures?

A. Yes: for he giveth to all life, and breath, and all things. Acts xvii. 25.

8. *Q.* Is he your benefactor?

A. Yes: for he daily loadeth us with his benefits. Ps. lxviii. 19.

9. *Q.* Shall he therefore be yours by your own consent?

A. Yes: O God, thou art my God. Ps. lxiii. 1.

VI. *Q.* How many persons are there in the Godhead?

A. There are three persons in the Godhead; the Father, the Son, and the Holy Ghost; and these three are one God; the same in substance, equal in power and glory.

§ I.

1. *Q.* Are there three gods?

A. No: for the Lord is one, and his name is one. Zech. xiv. 9.

2. *Q.* Is there more than one person in the Godhead?

A. Yes: for God said, let *us* make man. Gen. i. 26.

3. *Q.* Are there distinct persons in the Godhead?

A. Yes: for he who is the brightness of his Father's glory, is the express image of his person. Heb. i. 3.

4. *Q.* Are there three persons in the Godhead?

A. Yes: for there are three that bear record in Heaven, the Father, the Word, and the Holy Ghost. 1 John v. 7.

§ II.

1. *Q.* Is the Father God?

A. Yes: for there is one God and Father of all. Ephes. iv. 6.

2. *Q.* Is Jesus Christ the Word?

A. Yes: his name is called the Word of God. Rev. xix. 13.

3. *Q.* Is the Word God?

A. Yes: for in the beginning was the Word, and the Word was with God, and the Word was God. John i. 1.

4. *Q.* Is the Holy Ghost a divine person?

A. Yes: for the Spirit searcheth all things. 1 Cor. ii. 10.

§ III.

1. *Q.* Is it the personal property of the Father to beget the Son?

A. Yes: thou art my Son, this day have I begotten thee. Ps. ii. 7.

2. *Q.* Is it the personal property of the Son, to be begotten of the Father?

A. Yes: for he is the only begotten of the Father. John i. 14.

3. *Q.* Is it the personal property of the Holy Ghost to proceed from the Father and the Son?

A. Yes: for Christ says, I will send you the comforter, even the Spirit of truth, which proceedeth from the Father. John xv. 26.

§ IV.

1. *Q.* Are these three one God?

A. Yes: for it is said expressly, these three are one. 1 John v. 7.

2. *Q.* Are they the same in substance, and equal in power and glory?

A. Yes: for Christ says, I and my Father are one. John x. 30.

3. *Q.* Can this doctrine be measured by reason?

A. No: for flesh and blood hath not revealed it to us. Matt. xvi. 17.

4. *Q.* But ought we to believe it?

A. Yes: for we are baptized in the name of the Father, and of the Son, and of the Holy Ghost. Matt. xxviii. 19; and we are blessed with the grace of the Lord Jesus Christ, the love of God, and the communion of the Holy Ghost. 2 Cor. xiii. 14.

5. *Q.* And ought we to improve it?

A. Yes: that we all may be one, as the Father is in Christ, and he in the Father, that we also may be one in them. John xvii. 21.

VII. *Q.* What are the decrees of God?

A. The decrees of God are his eternal purpose according to the counsel of his will, whereby for his own glory he hath ordained whatsoever comes to pass.

§ V.

1. *Q.* Does God dispose of all things that come to pass?

A. Yes: my times are in thy hand. Ps. xxxi. 15.

2. *Q.* Does he do it according to his own will?

A. Yes: for he hath done whatsoever he pleased. Ps. cxxxv. 6.

3. *Q.* Can any control his will?

A. No: for he doth according to his will, in the armies of Heaven, and among the inhabitants of the earth. Dan. iv. 35.

4. *Q.* Has he determined before, what he will do?

A. Yes: for known unto God are all his works, from the beginning of the world. Acts xv. 18.

§ II.

1. *Q.* Is there a counsel, then, in all the will of God?

A. Yes: for he worketh all things after the counsel of his own will. Ephes. i. 11.

2. *Q.* Is it an eternal counsel?

A. Yes: for it was ordained before the world. 1 Cor. ii. 7.

3. *Q.* Is it free?

A. Yes: even so, Father, for so it seemed good in thy sight. Matt. xi. 26.

4. *Q.* Is it unchangeable?

A. Yes: the counsel of the Lord standeth forever. Ps. xxxiii. 11.

5. *Q.* Is it for his own glory?

A. Yes: that we should be to the praise of his glory. Ephes. i. 12.

§ III.

1. *Q.* Were all the events of time ordained from eternity?

A. Yes: He performed the thing that is appointed for me. Job xxiii. 14.

2. *Q.* Does any thing come to pass by chance?

A. No: for the lot is cast into the lap; but the whole disposing thereof is of the Lord. Prov. xvi. 33.

3. *Q.* Does every thing come to pass as God has ordained it?

A. Yes: for there are many devices in a man's heart; nevertheless, the counsel of the Lord, that shall stand. Prov. xix. 21.

§ IV.

1. *Q.* Can we search out God's counsels?

A. No: for his judgments are a great deep. Ps. xxxvi. 6.

2. *Q.* Ought we not, therefore, to acquiesce in them?

A. Yes: here am I, let him do to me as seemeth good unto him. 2 Sam. xv. 26.

3. *Q.* May we question God's proceedings?

A. No: for his thoughts are above our thoughts. Is. lv. 9.

VIII. *Q.* How doth God execute his decrees?

A. God executeth his decrees, in the works of creation and providence.

§ I.

1. Q. Shall all God's decrees be executed?
A. Yes: for the Lord of hosts hath sworn, surely as I have thought, so shall it come to pass. Is. xiv. 24.
2. Q. Can any of them be defeated?
A. No: for the Lord of hosts hath proposed, and who shall disannul it? Is. xiv. 27.
3. Q. Did God execute his decree, in the work of creation?
A. Yes: he hath created all things, and for his pleasure, they are and were created. Rev. iv. 11.
4. Q. And does he execute his decrees in the works of Providence?
A. Yes: for out of the mouth of the Most High both evil and good proceed. Sam. iii. 38.

§ II.

1. Q. Did God begin to work in the creation of the world?
A. Yes: thou, Lord, in the beginning didst lay the foundations of the earth. Heb. i. 10.
2. Q. Is he still working?
A. Yes: for Christ says, My Father worketh hitherto, and I work. John v. 17.
3. Q. Are all his works copied out of his counsels?
A. Yes: for they are what his hand and his counsel determined before to be done. Acts iv. 28.

§ III.

1. Q. Are God's works many?
A. Yes: O Lord, how manifold are thy works! Ps. civ. 24.
2. Q. Are they great?
A. Yes: his work is honourable and glorious. Ps. cxi. 3.
3. Q. Are they perfect in their kind?
A. Yes: God is the Rock, his work is perfect. Deut. xxxii. 4.
4. Q. Can they be amended?
A. No: whatsoever God doth, nothing can be put to it, nor any thing taken from it. Eccl. iii. 14.
5. Q. Ought they to be studied?
A. Yes: they are sought out of all them that have pleasure therein. Ps. cxi. 2.
6. Q. Is it a great sin to neglect them?
A. Yes: because they regard not the work of the Lord, neither consider the operation of his hands, he shall destroy them, and not build them up. Ps. xxviii. 5.

§ IV.

1. Q. Can all God's works be thoroughly discovered?

A. No: for no man can find out the work that God makes from the beginning to the end. Eccl. iii. 11.

2. *Q.* Can his designs in them be accounted for?

A. No: for his way is in the sea, and his path in the great waters. Ps. lxxvii. 19.

3. *Q.* But is he glorified in them?

A. Yes: all his works do praise him. Ps. cxlv. 10.

IX. *Q.* What is the work of creation?

A. The work of creation is, God's making all things of nothing, by the word of his power, in the space of six days, and all very good.

§ I.

1. *Q.* Did God create the world?

A. Yes: In the beginning God created the heavens and the earth. Gen. i. 1.

2. *Q.* Did he create every thing in the world?

A. Yes: for, without him was not anything made that was made. John i. 3, and John xii. 7—9.

3. *Q.* Did he create the world by his word?

A. Yes: for through faith we understand that the worlds were framed by the word of God. Heb. xi. 3.

4. *Q.* Did all things come into being by that word?

A. Yes: for by the word of God the Heavens were of old. 2 Pet. iii. 5.

5. *Q.* And are they thereby preserved in being?

A. Yes: by the same word they are kept in store. v. 7.

6. *Q.* Did God find any difficulty in making the world?

A. No: for he spake and it was done; he said, let there be light, and there was light. Ps. xxxiii. 9. Gen. i. 3.

7. *Q.* Did he need assistance in it?

A. No: for he stretcheth forth the heavens alone, and spreadeth abroad the earth by himself. Is. xliv. 24.

§ II.

1. *Q.* Did he make all out of nothing?

A. Yes: for the things which are seen were not made of the things which do appear. Heb. xi. 3.

2. *Q.* Did he bring light out of darkness?

A. Yes: for God commanded the light to shine out of darkness. 2 Cor. iv. 6.

3. *Q.* And order out of confusion?

A. Yes: for the earth was without form and void. Gen. i. 2.

4. *Q.* Did he make all in six days?

A. Yes: for, in six days, the Lord made heaven and earth. Exod. xx. 11.

5. *Q.* Did God make all well?

A. Yes: God saw every thing that he had made, and behold it was very good. Gen. i. 31.

6. *Q.* Did he make all firm?

A. Yes: he hath made a decree which shall not pass. Ps. cxlviii. 6.

7. *Q.* And all for himself?

A. Yes: the Lord hath made all things for himself. Prov. xvi. 4.

§ III.

1 *Q.* Did God make all things by Jesus Christ?

A. Yes: for by him also he made the worlds. Heb. i. 2., and created all things by Jesus Christ. Ephes. iii. 9; Col. i. 16, and John i. 3.

2. *Q.* Did God manifest his own perfections in the work of creation?

A. Yes: for the heavens declare the glory of God. Ps. xix. 1.

3. *Q.* Must we give him the glory of this work?

A. Yes: we must worship him that made the heavens and the earth. Rev. xiv. 7.

4. *Q.* Must we give him thanks for his creatures?

A. Yes: every creature of God is good, and to be received with thanksgiving. 1 Tim. iv. 4.

5. *Q.* May we be encouraged, by the work of creation, to trust in God?

A. Yes: My help cometh from the Lord which made Heaven and earth. Ps. cxxi. 2.

§ IV.

1. *Q.* Did God create the angels?

A. Yes: he maketh his angels spirits. Heb. i. 7.

2. *Q.* Are they attendants upon him?

A. Yes: thousand thousands minister unto him, and ten thousand times ten thousand stand before him. Dan. vii. 10.

3. *Q.* Are they employed for the good of the saints?

A. Yes: they are sent forth to minister for them which shall be heirs of salvation. Heb. i. 14.

4. *Q.* Have true believers communion with them in faith, hope, and love?

A. Yes: for we are come to an innumerable company of angels. Heb. xii. 22.

§ V.

1. *Q.* Did all the angels continue in their integrity?
A. No: there were angels that left their first state. Jude 6.
2. *Q.* Is it probable that they who fell, fell by pride?
A. Yes: for they that are lifted up with pride, fall into the condemnation of the devil. 1 Tim. iii. 6.
3. *Q.* Were they punished for their sin?
A. Yes: God spared not the angels that sinned, but cast them down to hell. 2 Pet. ii. 4.

X. *Q.* How did God create man?

A. God created man, male and female, after his own image, in knowledge, righteousness, and holiness, with dominion over the creatures.

§ I.

1. *Q.* Is man God's creature?
A. Yes: for we are also his offspring. Acts xvii. 28.
2. *Q.* Were our first parents the work of his hands?
A. Yes: male and female created he them, and called their name Adam. Gen. v. 2.
3. *Q.* Was man made with a consultation?
A. Yes: for God said, Let us make man. Gen. i. 26.
4. *Q.* Do all the children of men descend from Adam and Eve?
A. Yes: for God has made of one blood all nations of men. Acts xvii. 26.

§ II.

1. *Q.* Was man's body at first made out of the earth?
A. Yes: God made man of the dust of the ground. Gen. ii. 7.
2. *Q.* Are our bodies of the earth earthy?
A. Yes: for I also am formed out of the clay. Job xxxiii. 6.
3. *Q.* But are they not curiously wrought?
A. Yes: for I am fearfully and wonderfully made. Ps. cxxxix. 14.
4. *Q.* Is God the former of our bodies?
A. Yes: thou hast clothed me with skin and flesh, and fenced me with bones and sinews. Job x. 11.
5. *Q.* Is he the author of our senses?
A. Yes: the hearing ear, and seeing eye, the Lord has made even both of them. Prov. xx. 12.

§ III.

1. *Q.* Is God the Father of our spirits?
A. Yes: for he breathed into man's nostrils the breath of life. Gen. ii. 7.

2. *Q.* Has God given each of us a soul?
A. Yes: the Lord liveth and made us this soul. Jer. xxxviii. 16.

3. *Q.* Is it a rational soul?
A. Yes: for the spirit of a man is the candle of the Lord. Prov. xx. 27.

4. *Q.* Is it immortal?
A. Yes: for the spirit of a man goes upward. Eccl. iii. 21.

5. *Q.* Does it die with the body?
A. No: for when the dust returns to the earth as it was, the spirit returns to God who gave it. Eccl. xii. 7.

6. *Q.* Is God, then, the sovereign of the heart?
A. Yes: for he has said, behold, all souls are mine. Ezek. xviii. 4.

7. *Q.* Must we, therefore, commit our souls to him?
A. Yes: into thine hands I commit my spirit. Ps. xxxi. 5.

§ IV.

1. *Q.* Was man made after God's image?
A. Yes: God created man, in his own image. Gen i. 27.

2. *Q.* Did that image consist in knowledge?
A. Yes: for we are renewed in knowledge after the image of him that created us. Col. iii. 10.

3. *Q.* Did it consist in righteousness and true holiness?
A. Yes: for the new man after God is created in righteousness and true holiness. Ephes. iv. 24.

4. *Q.* Was there in man, at first, a perfect purity and freedom from sin?
A. Yes: thou wast perfect in thy ways from the day that thou wast created. Ezek. xxviii. 15. Compare xvi. 13.

5. *Q.* Was there in him a perfect rectitude and disposition to do good?
A. Yes: for God made man upright. Eccl. vii. 29.

6. *Q.* Are there some remains of God's image still upon man?
A. Yes: for men are made after the similitude of God. James iii. 9.

7. *Q.* Was man made with a dominion over the creatures?
A. Yes: for thou hast put all things under his feet. Ps. viii. 6.

8. *Q.* Have we not reason to admire God's favour to man?

A. Yes: Lord, what is man, that thou art mindful of him? Ps. cxliv. 3.

XI. *Q.* What are God's works of Providence?

A. God's works of Providence are, his most holy, wise, and powerful preserving and governing all his creatures, and all their actions.

§ I.

1. *Q.* When God had made the world, did he leave it to itself?

A. No: for he upholdeth all things by the word of his power. Heb. i. 3.

2. *Q.* Does he see to the whole creation?

A. Yes: for the eyes of the Lord are in every place. Prov. xv. 3.

3. *Q.* Does he condescend to take notice of his creatures?

A. Yes: he humbleth himself to behold the things that are in heaven and in the earth. Ps. cxiii. 6.

4. *Q.* Is any thing at a distance from him?

A. No: for he is not far from every one of us. Acts xvii. 27.

5. *Q.* Does he look on, as one unconcerned?

A. No: for his eyes behold, and his eye-lids try the children of men. Ps. xi. 4.

§ II.

1. *Q.* Does God look after the world of angels?

A. Yes: for he maketh peace in his high places. Job xxv. 2.

2. *Q.* Does he look after this lower world?

A. Yes: for the eyes of all wait upon him. Ps. cxlv. 15.

3. *Q.* Does he take care of the fowls?

A. Yes: our Heavenly Father feedeth them. Matt. vi. 26.

4. *Q.* What! even the sparrows?

A. Yes: not one of them shall fall to the ground without our Father. Matt. x. 29.

5. *Q.* What! and the ravens?

A. Yes: He feeds the young ravens which cry. Ps. cxlvii. 9.

6. *Q.* Is he the Protector and Benefactor of all creatures?

A. Yes: thou preservest them all. Neh. ix. 6.

7. *Q.* Is he man's Protector and Benefactor?

A. Yes: for in him we live, and move and have our being. Acts xvii. 28.

8. *Q.* Do we depend upon God for the support of our life?

SCRIPTURE CATECHISM.

A. Yes: for he holdeth our soul in life. Ps. lxvi. 9.

9. *Q.* And for the comforts of life?

A. Yes: for he giveth us rain from Heaven, and fruitful seasons, filling our hearts with food and gladness. Acts xiv. 17.

10. *Q.* And do we depend upon him for the safety of our life?

A. Yes: He keepeth all our bones. Ps. xxxiv. 20.

11. *Q.* And for the continuance of life?

A. Yes: for he is thy life, and the length of thy days. Deut. xxx. 20.

§ III.

1. *Q.* Does God govern all things?
A. Yes: His kingdom ruleth over all. Ps. ciii. 19.

2. *Q.* Does he govern the holy angels?
A. Yes: for they do his commandments. Ps. ciii. 20.

3. *Q.* Does he govern the Heavenly bodies?
A. Yes: the stars in their courses fought against Sisera. Judg. v. 20.

4. *Q.* Does he govern the power of the air?
A. Yes: stormy winds fulfil his work. Ps. cxlviii. 8.

5. *Q.* Does he order what weather it shall be?
A. Yes: for he saith to the snow, be thou upon the earth. Job xxxvii. 6.

6. *Q.* And does he govern the inferior creatures?
A. Yes: He spake and locusts came. Ps. cv. 34.

7. *Q.* Can he command them?
A. Yes: I have commanded the ravens to feed thee. 1 Kings xviii 4.

8. *Q.* Can he control them?
A. Yes: He shut the lions' mouths. Dan. vi. 22.

9. *Q.* Has he a sovereign dominion over the whole creation?
A. Yes: for the Lord of Hosts is his name. Isa. xlvii. 4.

§ IV.

1. *Q.* Does God govern the children of men?
A. Yes: the Most High ruleth in the kingdom of men. Dan. iv. 32.

2. *Q.* Does he govern kings?
A. Yes: for the king's heart is in the hand of the Lord. Prov. xxi. 1.

3. *Q.* And does he govern kingdoms?
A. Yes: for he is the governor among the nations. Ps. xxii. 28.

4. *Q.* And families, too?

A. Yes: for, except the Lord build the house they labour in vain that build it. Ps. cxxvii. 1.

5. *Q.* Does he govern great men?

A. Yes: for God is the Judge; He puts down one, and sets up another. Ps. lxxv. 7.

6. *Q.* And mean men too?

A. Yes: for every man's judgment proceedeth from the Lord. Prov. xxix. 26.

7. *Q.* Can man make his own fortune?

A. No: for the way of man is not in himself, neither is it in man that walketh to direct his steps. Jer. x. 23.

8. *Q.* When man purposes, does God dispose?

A. Yes: a man's heart deviseth his way, but the Lord directeth his steps. Prov. xvi. 9.

9. *Q.* Do all comforts and crosses come from God's hand?

A. Yes: for he has said, I make peace, and create evil; I the Lord do all these things. Isa. xlv. 7.

10. *Q.* Does God's providence extend itself to the smallest things?

A. Yes: the very hairs of your head are all numbered. Matt. x. 30.

§ v.

1. *Q.* Is God's government holy?

A. Yes: He is holy in all his works. Ps. cxlv. 17.

2. *Q.* Is it wise?

A. Yes: He is wonderful in counsel, and excellent in working. Isa. xxviii. 29.

3. *Q.* Is it powerful?

A. Yes: for when he giveth quietness, who, then, can make trouble? Job xxxiv. 29.

4. *Q.* Is it rightful?

A. Yes: God is greater than man. Job xxxiii. 12.

5. *Q.* Is it just?

A. Yes: for shall not the Judge of all the earth do right? Gen. xviii. 25.

6. *Q.* Does God sometimes reward and punish in this life?

A. Yes: the righteous shall be recompensed in the earth, much more the wicked and the sinner. Prov. xi. 31.

7. *Q.* But does he always?

A. No: for all things come alike to all. Eccl. ix. 2.

§ vi.

1. *Q.* Does God govern the world for the good of his church?

A. Yes: for Jacob my servant's sake, and Israel mine elect, I have called thee by thy name. Isa. xlv. 4.

2. *Q.* Is the government of the world committed to the Lord Jesus?

A. Yes: for he is head over all things unto the church. Ephes. i. 22.

3. *Q.* And is all ordered for God's glory?

A. Yes: for the Lord alone shall be exalted. Isa. ii. 11.

4. *Q.* Is it a comfort to good men that God governs the world?

A. Yes: the Lord reigns, let the earth rejoice. Ps. xcvii. 1.

5. *Q.* Is it a terror to the wicked?

A. Yes: the Lord reigns, let the people tremble. Ps. xcix. 1

6. *Q.* Ought we to give him the praise of it?

A. Yes: Hallelujah, the Lord God omnipotent reigns. Rev. xix. 6.

XII. *Q.* What special act of Providence did God exercise toward man in the estate wherein he was created?

A. When God had created man, he entered into a covenant of life with him, upon condition of perfect obedience; forbidding him to eat of the tree of knowledge of good and evil, upon the pain of death.

§ I.

1. *Q.* Did God make man happy as well as holy?

A. Yes: for he put him into the garden of Eden. Gen. ii. 15.

2. *Q.* Did he provide comfortably for him?

A. Yes: for he said, I will make him a help meet for him Gen. ii. 18.

3. *Q.* Did he admit him into communion with himself?

A. Yes: for he then blessed the seventh day and sanctified it. Gen. ii. 3.

4. *Q.* Was God well pleased in him?

A. Yes: for his delights were with the sons of men. Prov. viii. 31.

§ II.

1. *Q.* Did God give him a law?

A. Yes: the Lord God commanded the man. Gen. ii. 16.

2. *Q.* Did he give him a command of trial?

A. Yes: of the tree of knowledge of good and evil, thou shalt not eat of it. Gen. ii. 17.

3. Q. Did he assure him of happiness, if he obeyed?
A. Yes: for of every tree in the garden (even the tree of life) thou mayest freely eat. Gen. ii. 16.
4. Q. Did he threaten death upon his disobedience?
A. Yes: for in the day thou eatest thereof thou shalt surely die. Gen. ii. 17.

§ III.

1. Q. Was this God's covenant with Adam?
Q. Yes: for we read of those who, like Adam, transgressed the covenant. Hos. vi. 7. Marg.
2. Q. Was, do this and live, one branch of that covenant?
A. Yes: for the man that doeth them, shall live in them. Gal. iii. 12.
3. Q. Was, fail and die, the other branch of the covenant?
A. Yes: the soul that sinneth, it shall die. Ezek. xviii. 4.
4. Q. Was this the covenant of innocency?
A. Yes: for the law was not of faith. Gal. iii. 12.
5. Q. Was there a mediator of this covenant?
A. No: for it is the better covenant that is established in the hands of a Mediator. Heb. viii. 6.

XIII. Q. Did our first parents continue in the estate wherein they were created?

A. Our first parents, being left to the freedom of their own will, fell from the estate wherein they were created, by sinning against God.

§ I.

1. Q. Is man now in the state wherein he was created?
A. No: for God made man upright, but they have sought out many inventions. Eccl. vii. 29.
2. Q. Can we now say we are perfectly holy?
A. No: if I say I am perfect, that shall prove me perverse. Job ix. 20.
3. Q. Can we say we are perfectly happy?
A. No: for man is born to trouble. Job v. 7.
4. Q. Are we as we were then?
A. No: man was planted a noble vine, but is turned into the degenerate plant of a strange vine. Jer. ii. 21.
5. Q. Did man continue long in his state of innocence?
A. No: for man being in honour abideth not. Ps. xlix. 12.

§ II.

1. Q. Did God leave man to the freedom of his own will?

A. Yes: for if thou scornest, thou alone shalt bear it. Prov. ix. 12.

2. *Q.* Did God draw Adam to sin?
A. No: for God tempteth no man. James i. 13.

3. *Q.* Is he any way the author of sin?
A. No: far be it from God that he should do wickedness. Job xxxiv. 10.

4. *Q.* Did he do what was fit to be done to prevent it?
A. Yes: what could have been done more to my vineyard? Isa. v. 4.

5. *Q.* Was he obliged to do more?
A. No: for may he not do what he will with his own? Matt. xx. 15.

6. *Q.* Does all the blame of man's sin lie upon himself, then?
A. Yes: O Israel, thou hast destroyed thyself. Hos. xiii. 9.

§ III.

1. *Q.* Did man fall by sinning against God?
A. Yes: thou hast fallen by thine iniquity. Hos. xiv. 1.

2. *Q.* Was that the beginning of sin, in this world?
A. Yes: for by one man sin entered into the world. Rom. v. 12.

XIV. *Q.* What is sin?
A. Sin is any want of conformity unto, or transgression of the law of God.

§ I.

1. *Q.* Is there a moral difference of good and evil?
A. Yes: for we must cease to do evil, and learn to do well. Isa. i. 16, 17.

2. *Q.* Is it all alike then what we do?
A. No: for God shall bring every work into judgment, whether it be good, or whether it be evil. Eccl. xii. 14.

3. *Q.* Is there such a thing as sin in thought?
A. Yes: for the thought of foolishness is sin. Prov. xxiv. 9.

4. *Q.* May sin be committed in word too?
A. Yes: for in the multitude of words there wanteth not sin. Prov. x. 19.

§ II.

1. *Q.* Does sin suppose a law?
A. Yes: for where there is no law, there is no transgression. Rom. iv. 15. and v. 13.

2. *Q.* Is sin the breach of a law?
A. Yes: for sin is the transgression of the law. 1 John iii. 4.
3. *Q.* Is it God's law only that can make a thing to be sin?
A. Yes: for against thee, thee only have I sinned. Ps. li. 4.
4. *Q.* Is every breach of God's law sin?
A. Yes: for all unrighteousness is sin. 1 John v. 17.
5. *Q.* Are we to judge of sin by the law?
A. Yes: for by the law is the knowledge of sin. Rom. iii. 20.
6. *Q.* Could we discover sin without some law?
A. No: for I had not known sin but by the law. Rom. vii. 7.
7. *Q.* Is the transgression of the law of nature sin?
A. Yes: for they that have not the written law, shew the work of the law written in their hearts. Rom. ii. 14, 15.
8. *Q.* But does the written law discover the root of sin?
A. Yes: I had not known lust, except the law had said, thou shalt not covet. Rom. vii. 7.

§ III.

1. *Q.* Is ignorance of God sin?
A. Yes: He shall take vengeance on them that know not God. 2 Thess. i. 8.
2. *Q.* Is disaffection to God's government sin?
A. Yes: my people would not hearken to my voice, and Israel would none of me. Ps. lxxxi. 11.
3. *Q.* Is all disobedience to God's law sin?
A. Yes: for the wrath of God comes upon the children of disobedience. Col. iii. 6.
4. *Q.* Is it a sin to omit the good which God has commanded?
A. Yes: for to him that knows to do good, and doth it not, to him it is sin. James iv. 17.
5. *Q.* Is it a sin to do it negligently?
A. Yes: for if thou doest not well, sin lies at the door. Gen. iv. 7.
6. *Q.* Is it a sin to do the evil which God has forbidden?
A. Yes: for he has said, O, do not this abominable thing which I hate. Jer. xliv. 4.
7. *Q.* Is the inclination to evil sin?
A. Yes: for St. Paul speaks of the sin that dwells in us. Rom. vii. 17.

§ IV.

1. *Q.* Is sin the worst of evils?
A. Yes: it is an evil thing, and a bitter, to forsake the Lord. Jer. ii. 19.
2. *Q.* Is the sinfulness of it the worst thing in it?

A. Yes: for sin by the commandment becomes exceeding sinful. Rom. vii. 13.

3. *Q.* Is sin worse than affliction?
A. Yes: for Moses, by faith chose rather to suffer affliction than to enjoy the pleasures of sin. Heb. xi. 25.

4. *Q.* Is it displeasing to God?
A. Yes: God is angry with the wicked every day. Ps. vii. 11.

5. *Q.* Is it destructive to ourselves?
A. Yes: be sure your sin will find you out. Numb. xxxii. 23.

§ v.

1. *Q.* Ought we not, therefore, to take heed of sin?
A. Yes: stand in awe, and sin not. Ps. iv. 4.

2. *Q.* And of all appearances of it?
A. Yes: abstain from all appearance of evil. 1 Thess. v. 22.

3. *Q.* And all approaches towards it?
A. Yes: touch not the unclean thing. 2 Cor. vi. 17.

4. *Q.* And must we hate it?
A. Yes: ye that love the Lord, hate evil. Ps. xcvii. 10.

5. *Q.* Must little children take heed of sin?
A. Yes: my little children, these things write I unto you, that ye sin not. 1 John ii. 1.

6. *Q.* Is it folly to make light of sin?
A. Yes: fools make a mock at sin. Prov. xiv. 9.

7. *Q.* Will our observing the law of God be the best preservative against sin?
A. Yes: thy word have I hid in my heart, that I might not sin against thee. Ps. cxix. 11.

8. *Q.* Will an eye to God be the best argument against sin?
A. Yes: how shall I do this great wickedness, and sin against God. Gen. xxxix. 9.

XV. *Q.* What was the sin whereby our first parents fell from the estate wherein they were created?

A. The sin whereby our first parents fell from the estate wherein they were created, was their eating the forbidden fruit.

§ I.

1. *Q.* Did our first parents eat the forbidden fruit?
A. Yes: thou hast eaten of the tree of which I commanded thee saying, thou shalt not eat of it. Gen. iii. 17.

2. *Q.* Was their doing so disobedience?

A. Yes: for it was by one man's disobedience that many were made sinners. Rom. v. 19.

3. *Q.* Did the woman eat forbidden fruit first?

A. Yes: the woman being deceived was in the transgression. 1 Tim. ii. 14.

4. *Q.* Did the serpent tempt her to it?

A. Yes: the serpent beguiled Eve through his subtilty. 2 Cor. xi. 3.

5. *Q.* Was that serpent the devil?

A. Yes: the Old Serpent is the devil and Satan. Rev. xx. 2.

6. *Q.* Did he aim to make man as miserable as himself?

A. Yes: he was a murderer from the beginning. John viii. 44.

§ II.

1. *Q.* Did the tempter teach them to question the command?

A. Yes: he said to the woman, hath God said ye shall not eat? Gen. iii. 1.

2. *Q.* Did he promise them safety in sin?

A. Yes: he said, ye shall not surely die. Gen. iii. 4.

3. *Q.* Did he promise them advantage by the sin?

A. Yes: in the day ye eat thereof, your eyes shall be opened. Gen. iii. 5.

4. *Q.* Did he feed them with high thoughts of themselves?

A. Yes: ye shall be as gods. Gen. iii. 5.

5. *Q.* Did he suggest to them hard thoughts of God?

A. Yes: for he said, God doth know this. Gen. iii. 5.

6. *Q.* Did Eve do well to parley with him?

A. No: for we should cease to hear the instruction that causeth to err from the words of knowledge. Prov. xix. 27.

§ III.

1. *Q.* Did the devil prevail in this temptation?

A. Yes: for she took of the fruit, and did eat, and gave also to her husband with her, and he did eat. Gen. iii. 6.

2. *Q.* Was there in this sin the lust of the flesh?

A. Yes: for she saw that the tree was good for food. Gen. iii. 6.

3. *Q.* Was there in it the lust of the eye?

A. Yes: for she saw that it was pleasant to the eyes. Gen. iii. 6.

4. *Q.* And the pride of life?

A. Yes: for she saw that it was a tree to be desired to make one wise. Gen. iii. 6.

5. *Q.* Was unbelief of the word of God at the bottom of it?
A. Yes: it is the evil heart of unbelief that departs from the living God. Heb. iii. 12.

6. *Q.* Was there in it an opposition to the divine law?
A. Yes: for sin took occasion by the commandment. Rom. vii. 8.

7. *Q.* Was disobedience in a small matter a great provocation?
A. Yes: for rebellion is as the sin of witchcraft, and stubbornness is iniquity and idolatry. 1 Sam. xv. 23.

8. *Q.* If Adam fell thus, have we any reason to be secure?
A. No: wherefore let him that thinketh he standeth, take heed lest he fall. 1 Cor. x. 12.

XVI. *Q.* Did all mankind fall in Adam's first transgression?

A. The covenant being made with Adam, not only for himself, but for his posterity; all mankind, descending from him by ordinary generation, sinned in him, and fell with him, in his first transgression.

§ I.

1. *Q.* Are we concerned in our first parents' disobedience?
A. Yes: for by the offence of one, judgment came upon all men to condemnation. Rom. v. 18.

2. *Q.* Were we in their loins when they ate the forbidden fruit?
A. Yes: for Adam called his wife's name Eve, because she was the mother of all living. Gen. iii. 20.

3. *Q.* Was Adam a common father?
A. Yes: for he was to be fruitful, and multiply, and replenish the earth. Gen. i. 28.

4. *Q.* Was he a public person?
A. Yes: for he was the figure of him that was to come. Rom. v. 14.

5. *Q.* Was the covenant made with him, and his posterity?
A. Yes: for God always established his covenant with men, and with their seed after them. Gen. ix. 9.

§ II.

1. *Q.* Was Adam's sin our ruin, then?
A. Yes: for through the offence of one many were dead. Rom. v. 15.

2. *Q.* Was the honour of human nature thereby stained?

A. Yes: for Adam begat a son in his own likeness. Gen. v. 3.

3. *Q.* Was the power of the human nature thereby weakened?

A. Yes: for when we were without strength, Christ died for us. Rom. v. 6.

4. *Q, Q.* Was the purity of it thereby corrupted?

A. Yes: for in us, that is, in our flesh, there dwells no good thing. Rom. vii. 18.

5. *Q.* Was Adam himself degenerated?

A. Yes: for God said to him, dust thou art. Gen. iii. 19.

6. *Q.* And are we, in like manner, degenerated?

A. Yes: for we have all borne the image of the earth. 1 Cor. xv. 49.

§ III.

1. *Q.* Is this degeneracy universal?

A. Yes: for all flesh hath corrupted his way. Gen. vi. 12.

2. *Q.* Did our Lord Jesus descend from Adam by ordinary generation?

A. No: for He is the Lord from Heaven. 1 Cor. xv. 47.

3. *Q.* Did He, then, sin in Adam?

A. No: for He is undefiled, separate from sinners. Heb. vii. 26.

4. *Q.* Did all the rest of mankind sin in Adam?

A. Yes: for how can he be clean that is born of a woman? Job xxv. 4.

5. *Q.* Are the ways of the Lord herein equal?

A. Yes: but our ways are unequal. Ezek. xviii. 29.

XVII. *Q.* Into what estate did the fall bring mankind?

A. The fall brought mankind into an estate of sin and misery.

§ I.

1. *Q.* Is mankind in a state of sin?

A. Yes: for both Jews and Gentiles are all under sin. Rom. iii. 9.

2. *Q.* Is a state of sin a sad state?

A. Yes: for they that are in the flesh cannot please God. Rom. viii. 8.

3. *Q.* Did the fall bring us into a state of sin?

A. Yes: for by it many were made sinners. Rom. v. 19.

4. *Q.* Does the world continue in that state?

A. Yes: for the whole world lies in wickedness. 1 John v. 19.

5. *Q.* And are you by nature in that state?

A. Yes: if I justify myself, my own mouth shall condemn me. Job ix. 20.

§ II.

1. *Q.* Is mankind in a state of misery?

A. Yes: the misery of man is great upon him. Eccl. viii. 6.

2. *Q.* Is sin the cause of all that misery?

A. Yes: for death entered by sin, and so death passed upon all men. Rom. v. 12.

3. *Q.* Is misery the consequence of sin?

A. Yes: for evil pursues sinners. Prov. xiii. 21.

4. *Q.* Do all the creatures share in the sad effects of sin?

A. Yes: cursed is the ground for thy sake. Gen. iii. 17.

5. *Q.* And could all this mischief come from that one sin?

A. Yes: for how great a matter does a little fire kindle! James iii. 5, 6.

§ III.

1. *Q.* Did the fall bring mankind into a state of apostacy from God?

A. Yes: for they are all gone aside. Ps. xiv. 3.

2. *Q.* Is that a sinful state?

A. Yes: for it is great whoredom to depart from the Lord. Hos. i. 2.

3. *Q.* And is it a miserable state?

A. Yes: woe unto them, for they have fled from me. Hos. vii. 13.

§ IV.

1. *Q.* Did the fall bring mankind into a state of slavery to Satan?

A. Yes: for they are taken captive by him at his will. 2 Tim. ii. 26.

2. *Q.* Is that a sinful state?

A. Yes: for the prince of the power of the air works in the children of disobedience. Ephes. ii. 2.

3. *Q.* Is it a miserable state?

A. Yes: for the god of this world hath blinded their minds. 2 Cor iv. 4.

4. *Q.* Is it like the condition of the prodigal son?

A. Yes: for he went into a far country; wasted his substance; began to be in want; and was sent into the fields to feed swine. Luke xv. 13—15.

XVIII. *Q.* Wherein consists the sinfulness of that estate whereinto man fell?

A. The sinfulness of that estate whereinto man fell, consists in the guilt of Adam's first sin, the want of original righteousness, and the corruption of his whole nature, which is commonly called Original Sin; together with all actual transgressions which proceed from it.

§ I.

1. *Q.* Are we all born under guilt?
A. Yes: For all the world is guilty before God. Rom. iii. 19.
2. *Q.* Does the whole race of mankind stand attainted at God's bar?
A. Yes: for the scripture hath concluded all under sin. Gal. iii. 22.
3. *Q.* Is this according to God's rule of judgment?
A. Yes: for he visiteth the iniquity of the fathers upon the children. Exod. xx. 5.
4. *Q.* Is not God unrighteous who thus takes vengeance?
A. No: God forbid, for then how shall God judge the world? Rom. iii. 6.

§ II.

1. *Q.* Are we all born in sin?
A. Yes: behold, I was shapen in iniquity, and in sin did my mother conceive me. Ps. li. 5.
2. *Q.* Are we of a sinful brood?
A. Yes: for we are a seed of evil doers. Isa. i. 4.
3. *Q.* May we be truly called sinners by nature?
A. Yes: thou wast called a transgressor from the womb. Isa. xlviii. 8.

§ III.

1. *Q.* Is there, in every one of us, by nature, the want of original righteousness?
A. Yes: there is none righteous, no not one. Rom. iii. 10.
2. *Q.* Is there in us, an aversion to that which is good?
A. Yes: for the carnal mind is enmity against God. Rom. viii. 7.

3. *Q.* Is there in us a moral impotence to that which is good?

A. Yes: for the carnal mind is not in subjection to the law of God, neither indeed can be. Rom. viii. 7.

4. *Q.* Can we, of ourselves, do any thing that is good?

A. No: for we are not sufficient of ourselves to think any thing as of ourselves. 2 Cor. iii. 5.

§ IV.

1. *Q.* Is there in us a proneness to that which is evil?

A. Yes: My people are bent to back-sliding from me. Hos. xi. 7.

2. *Q.* Are there the snares of sin in our bodies?

A. Yes: for there is a law in the members warring against the law of the mind. Rom. vii. 23.

3. *Q.* And are there the seeds of sin in our souls?

A. Yes: for when I would do good, evil is present with me. Rom. vii. 21.

4. *Q.* And is the stain of sin upon both?

A. Yes: for all have sinned, and come short of the glory of God. Rom. iii. 23.

§ V.

1. *Q.* Did we all bring sin into the world with us?

A. Yes: for man is born like the wild ass's colt. Job. xi. 12.

2. *Q.* Is it in little children?

A. Yes: for foolishness is in the heart of a child. Prov. xxii. 15.

3. *Q.* As reason improves does sin grow up with it?

A. Yes: for when the blade is sprung up, then appear the tares also. Matt. xiii. 26.

4. *Q.* Is it not a wonder of mercy, then, that we are any of us alive?

A. Yes: it is of the Lord's mercies that we are not consumed. Lam. iii. 22.

§ VI.

1. *Q.* Is the whole nature of man corrupted by the fall?

A. Yes: the whole head is sick, and the whole heart is faint. Isa. i. 5.

2. *Q.* Is the understanding corrupted?

A. Yes: the understanding is darkened, being alienated from the life of God. Ephes. iv. 18.

3. *Q.* Is that unapt to admit the rays of divine light?

A. Yes: for they are spiritually discerned. 1 Cor. ii. 14.

4. *Q.* Is the will corrupted?

A. Yes: the neck is an iron sinew. Isa. xlviii. 4.

5. *Q.* And is that unapt to submit to the rule of the divine law?

A. Yes: for what is the Almighty (say they) that we should serve him? Job. xxi. 15.

6. *Q.* Are the thoughts corrupted?

A. Yes: for the imagination of man's heart is evil from his youth. Gen. viii. 21.

7. *Q.* Is the fancy full of vanity?

A. Yes: vain thoughts lodge within us. Jer. iv. 14.

8. *Q.* Are the affections corrupted?

A. Yes: it is a carnal mind. Rom. viii. 7.

9. *Q.* Is conscience itself corrupted?

A. Yes: even the mind and conscience is defiled. Tit. i. 15.

10. *Q.* Is the whole soul corrupted?

A. Yes: the heart is deceitful above all things. Jer. xvii. 9.

§ VII.

1. *Q.* Is this corruption of the mind sin?

A. Yes: for it is enmity against God. Rom. viii. 7.

2. *Q.* Have we it from our original?

A. Yes: for that which is born of the flesh is flesh. John iii. 6.

3. *Q.* Do we derive it through our parents?

A. Yes: for who can bring a clean thing out of an unclean? Job. xiv. 4.

4. *Q.* Does it render us odious to God's holiness?

A. Yes: for the foolish shall not stand in his sight. Ps. v. 5.

5. *Q.* Does it render us obnoxious to his justice?

A. Yes: for death reigns over them that have not sinned after the similitude of Adam's transgressions. Rom. v. 14.

§ VIII.

1. *Q.* Does this original corruption produce actual transgression?

A. Yes: for a corrupt tree cannot bring forth good fruit. Matt. vii. 18.

2. *Q.* Does it produce it betimes?

A. Yes: for the wicked are estranged from the womb. They go astray, as soon they are born, speaking lies. Ps. lviii. 3.

3. *Q.* Does it produce it naturally?

A. Yes: as a fountain casteth out her waters. Jer. vi. 7.

4. *Q.* Does all sin begin in the heart?

A. Yes: for when lust hath conceived, it bringeth forth sin. James i. 15.

5. *Q.* Is it not necessary, therefore, we should have a new nature?
A. Yes: marvel not that I said unto you, ye must be born again. John iii. 7.
6. *Q.* Can we get to heaven without it?
A. No: for flesh and blood cannot inherit the kingdom of God. 1 Cor. xv. 50.

XIX. *Q.* What is the misery of that estate whereinto man fell?

A. All mankind, by their fall, lost communion with God, are under his wrath and curse, and so made liable to all the miseries of this life, to death itself, and to the pains of hell forever.

§ I.

1. *Q.* When our first parents had eaten the forbidden fruit, did they become as gods?
A. No: they were like the beasts that perish. Ps. xlix. 12.
2. *Q.* Did the devil make his words good then?
A. No: for he is a liar, and the father of it. John viii. 44.
3. *Q.* Did not he put a cheat upon them?
A. Yes: for the woman said, the serpent beguiled me. Gen. iii. 13.
4. *Q.* Did shame come in with sin?
A. Yes: for they knew that they were naked. Gen. iii. 7.
5. *Q.* Did fear come in with sin?
A. Yes: for they hid themselves from the presence of the Lord God, among the trees of the garden. Gen. iii. 8.
6. *Q.* Was not that their misery?
A. Yes: for fear hath torment. 1 John iv. 18.

§ II.

1. *Q.* Did they lose communion with God?
A. Yes: for he drove out the man. Gen. iii. 24.
2. *Q.* Is fallen man unworthy of communion with God?
A. Yes: for what communion hath light with darkness? 2 Cor. vi. 14.
3. *Q.* Is he unfit for communion with God?
A. Yes: for can two walk together except they be agreed? Amos iii. 3.
4. *Q.* Could fallen man ever get to heaven by virtue of the covenant of innocency?

A. No: for cherubims and a flaming sword were set to keep that way to the tree of life. Gen iii. 24.

§ III.

1. *Q.* Is fallen man under God's wrath?
A. Yes: for the wrath of God is revealed from heaven, against all ungodliness and unrighteousness of men. Rom. i. 18.
2. *Q.* Are we all so by nature?
A. Yes: we are, by nature, children of wrath, even as others. Ephes. ii. 3.
3. *Q.* Are we so by reason of sin?
A. Yes: for because of these things cometh the wrath of God upon the children of disobedience. Ephes. v. 6.
4. *Q.* Is there a distance between God and man, by reason of sin?
A. Yes: your iniquities have separated between you and your God. Isa lix. 2.
5. *Q.* Is there a quarrel between God and man, by reason of sin?
A. Yes: my soul loathed them, and their soul also it abhorred me. Zech. xi. 8.
6. *Q.* Is it not sad to lie under God's wrath?
A. Yes: for who knows the power of his anger? Ps. xc. 2.

§ IV.

1. *Q.* Is fallen man under God's curse?
A. Yes: for cursed is every one that continues not in all things which are written in the book of the law to do them. Gal. iii. 10.
2. *Q.* Is this curse in force against all wicked people?
A. Yes: the curse of the Lord is in the house of the wicked. Prov. iii. 33.
3. *Q.* Has sin brought a curse upon the world?
A, Yes: cursed is the ground for thy sake. Gen. iii. 17.

§ V.

1. *Q.* Is mankind, by the fall, become liable to the miseries of this life?
A. Yes: in sorrow shalt thou eat of it all the days of thy life. Gen. iii. 17.
2. *Q.* Are we all, by nature, liable to these miseries?
A. Yes: for man is born to trouble. Job. v. 7.
3. *Q.* Is all the hurtfulness of the creatures the effect of sin?
A. Yes: thorns and thistles shall it bring forth. Gen. iii. 18.
4. *Q.* Is the toil of business the effect of sin?

A. Yes: in the sweat of thy face, shalt thou eat bread. Gen. iii. 19.

5. *Q.* Is pain and sickness the effect of sin?
A. Yes: there is not any rest in my bones, because of my sin. Ps. xxxviii. 3.

6. *Q.* Are all our crosses the effect of sin?
A. Yes: our sins have withholden good things from us. Jer. v. 25.

7. *Q.* Should we not, therefore, bear them patiently?
A. Yes: wherefore doth a living man complain, a man for the punishment of his sin? Lam. iii. 39.

§ VI.

1. *Q.* Is all mankind, by the fall, become liable to death itself?
A. Yes: for so death passed upon all men, for that all have sinned. Rom. v. 12.

2. *Q.* Was a sentence of death immediately passed upon fallen man?
A. Yes: dust thou art, and to dust shalt thou return. Gen. iii. 19.

3. *Q.* Do we all deserve death?
A. Yes: the wages of sin is death. Rom. vi. 23.

4. *Q.* Is it the natural consequence of sin?
A. Yes: for sin, when it is finished brings forth death. James i. 15.

5. *Q.* Can any avoid it?
A. No: what man is he that liveth and shall not see death? Ps. lxxxix. 48.

6. *Q.* Is it determined?
A. Yes: it is appointed to men once to die. Heb. ix. 27.

7. *Q.* Do you expect it?
A. Yes: I know that thou wilt bring me to death. Job. xxx. 23.

8. *Q.* Is sin the sting of death?
A. Yes: The sting of death is sin. 1 Cor. xv. 56.

9. *Q.* Is the amazing fear of death, the effect of sin?
A. Yes: there are those who, through fear of death, are all their lifetime subject to bondage. Heb. ii. 15.

10. *Q.* Is the body's rotting in the grave, the effect of sin?
A. Yes: As drought and heat consume the snow-waters, so doth the grave those which have sinned. Job. xxiv. 19.

§ VII.

1. *Q.* Is mankind, by the fall, become liable to the pains of hell for ever?

A. Yes: for he that wanders out of the way of understanding shall remain in the congregation of the dead. Prov. xxi. 16. Ps. ix. 17.

2. *Q.* Can God make a soul for ever miserable?

A. Yes: for after he hath killed, he hath power to cast into hell. Luke xii. 5.

3. *Q.* Is there a state of punishment in the other life?

A. Yes: for we are warned to flee from the wrath to come. Matt. iii. 7.

4. *Q.* Is it the desert of sin?

A. Yes: for when God renders to every man according to his work, he will render indignation and wrath, tribulation and anguish, upon every soul of man that doeth evil. Rom. ii. 8, 9.

5. *Q.* Will it be the portion of impenitent sinners?

A. Yes: ye generation of vipers how can ye escape the damnation of hell. Matt. xxiii. 33.

§ VIII.

1. *Q.* Is Hell the wrath of an everlasting God?

A. Yes: for the breath of the Lord, like a stream of brimstone doth kindle it. Isa. xxx. 33.

2. *Q.* Is it the anguish of an immortal soul?

A. Yes: for their worm dieth not. Mark. ix. 44.

3. *Q.* Is any way of relief open to them?

A. No: Betwixt us and you there is a gulf fixed. Luke xvi. 26.

4. *Q.* Is their punishment therefore everlasting?

A. Yes: they shall go away into everlasting punishment. Matt. xxv. 46.

5. *Q.* Should we not, every one of us, dread it?

A. Yes: for it is a fearful thing to fall into the hands of the living God. Heb. x. 31. Isa. xxxiii. 14.

XX. *Q.* Did God leave all mankind to perish in the estate of sin and misery?

A. God having out of his mere good pleasure, from all eternity, elected some to everlasting life, did enter into a covenant of grace, to deliver them out of the estate of sin and misery, and to bring them into an estate of salvation, by a Redeemer.

§ I.

1. Q. Might not God justly have left all mankind to perish in their fallen estate?
A. Yes: for in his sight shall no man living be justified. Ps. cxliii. 2.

2. Q. Would God have been a loser by it, if they had been left to perish?
A. No: for can a man be profitable to God? Job. xxii. 2.

3. Q. But did he leave them to perish?
A. No: for the kindness and love of God our Saviour towards man appears. Tit. iii. 4.

4. Q. Was the case of fallen angels helpless and desperate?
A. Yes: for God spared not them. 2 Pet. ii. 4.

5. Q. But is the case of fallen man so?
A. No: for he is long-suffering to us-ward, not willing that any should perish. 2 Pet. iii. 9.

6. Q. Is God's patience a token for good?
A. Yes: the long-suffering of our God is salvation. 2 Pet. iii. 15.

7. Q. Does it appear that God has a good will to man's salvation?
A. Yes: as I live, saith the Lord God, I have no pleasure in the death of the wicked, but that he turn and live. Ezek. xxxiii. 11.

8. Q. Is this an encouragement to us all to hope in his mercy?
A. Yes: for if the Lord had been pleased to kill us, he would not have shewed us such things as these. Judg. xiii. 23.

§ II.

1. Q. Could man help himself out of his state of sin and misery?
A. No: for when we were without strength, Christ died for the ungodly. Rom. v. 6.

2. Q. Could any creature help us?
A. No: for none of them can, by any means redeem his brother. Ps. xlix. 7.

3. Q. Could God himself only help us?
A. Yes: O Israel! thou hast destroyed thyself, but in me is thy help. Hos. xiii. 9.

4. Q. Did God contrive a way for man's recovery?

A. Yes: he hath devised means that his banished may not be expelled from him. 2 Sam. xiv. 14.

5. *Q.* Was it the contrivance of infinite wisdom?

A. Yes: it is the wisdom of God in a mystery, ordained before the world for our glory. 1 Cor. ii. 7.

6. *Q.* Has he provided a way for our recovery?

A. Yes: I have found a ransom. Job. xxxiii.

§ III.

1. *Q.* Did God particularly design the salvation of a remnant of mankind?

A. Yes: there is a remnant according to the election of grace. Rom. xi. 5.

2. *Q.* Are there some whom God has chosen?

A. Yes: God hath from the beginning, chosen you to salvation, through sanctification of the spirit. 2 Thess. ii. 13.

3. *Q.* Is there a certain number of such?

A. Yes: for their names are in the book of life. Philipp. iv. 3. Rev. xiii. 8.

4. *Q.* Were they chosen from eternity?

A. Yes: he hath chosen us in him before the foundation of the world. Ephes. i. 4

5. *Q.* Were they chosen for the sake of any thing in themselves?

A. No: ye have not chosen me, but I have chosen you. John xv. 16.

6. *Q.* But of his mere good pleasure?

A. Yes: he hath predestinated us according to the good pleasure of his will. Ephes. i. 5.

7. *Q.* Were they chosen to salvation, as the end?

A. Yes: God had appointed us to obtain salvation. 1 Thess. v. 9.

8. *Q.* And to sanctification as the means?

A. Yes: he has chosen us, that we should be holy. Ephes. i. 4.

9. *Q.* Was it for the glory of God?

A. Yes: that he might make known the riches of his glory on the vessels of mercy. Rom. ix. 23.

§ IV.

1. *Q.* Shall the election obtain?

A. Yes: The purpose of God according to election, shall stand. Rom. ix. 11.

2. *Q.* Does our salvation begin there?

A. Yes: we love him, because he first loved us. 1 John iv. 19.

3. *Q.* Are others passed by?

A. Yes: when the election hath obtained, the rest are blinded. Rom. xi. 7.

4. *Q.* Does God know certainly whom he has chosen?

A. Yes: the Lord knows them that are his. 2 Tim. ii. 19.

5. *Q.* Do we know it?

A. No: for secret things belong not to us. Deut. xxix. 29.

6. *Q.* Can we know our own election otherwise than by our being sanctified?

A. No: we must make our calling and so make our election sure. 2 Pet. i. 10.

§ v.

1. *Q.* Were the elect given to Christ?

A. Yes: thine they were, and thou gavest them me. John xvii. 6.

2. *Q.* Did he undertake their salvation?

A. Yes: for this is the father's will, that of all which he hath given me, I should lose nothing. John vi. 39.

3. *Q.* Was it promised him that he should effect it?

A. Yes: he shall see his seed, and the pleasure of the Lord shall prosper in his hand. Isa. liii. 10.

4. *Q.* And was he himself assured of it?

A. Yes: all that the Father giveth me, shall come to me. John vi. 37.

5. *Q.* And does it always prove so?

A. Yes: as many as were ordained to eternal life believed. Acts xiii. 48.

6. *Q.* And shall any of them miscarry?

A. No: for it is said of seducers, they shall deceive, *if it were possible,* the very elect. Matt. xxiv. 24.

§ vi.

1. *Q.* Has God entered into a new covenant, pursuant hereto?

A. Yes: for we are not under the law but under grace. Rom. vi. 14.

2. *Q.* Does he insist upon the terms of the first covenant?

A. No: he hath not dealt with us after our sins. Ps. ciii. 10.

3. *Q.* Is he willing to deal with us upon new terms?

A. Yes: I will make a new covenant with them. Jer. xxxi. 31.

4. *Q.* Is he willing to be ours in covenant?

A. Yes: I will be to them a God. Heb. viii. 10.

5. *Q.* Will he accept us as his?

A. Yes: they shall be to me a people. Heb. viii. 10.

6. *Q.* And will he be at peace with us?

A. Yes: God was in Christ, reconciling the world unto himself. 2 Cor. v. 19.

§ VII.

1. *Q.* Is this wrought out by a Redeemer?

A. Yes: for there is not salvation in any other. Acts. iv. 12.

2. *Q.* Was that Redeemer of God's own providing?

A. Yes: God so loved the world, that he gave his only begotten Son. John iii. 16.

3. *Q.* Is the new covenant made with us in Christ?

A. Yes: for he is the mediator of the better covenant. Heb. viii. 6.

4. *Q.* Is it a covenant much for our advantage?

A. Yes: for it is well ordered in all things and sure. 2 Sam. xxiii. 5.

5. *Q.* Is perfect obedience the condition of it?

A. No: for if by grace, then it is no more of works. Rom. xi. 6.

6. *Q.* Is faith the condition of it?

A. Yes: for by grace ye are saved, through faith. Ephes. ii. 8.

7. *Q.* Is sincerity accepted as our gospel perfection?

A. Yes: walk before me, and be thou perfect. Gen. xvii.

8. *Q.* Is that which is required in the covenant, promised in the covenant?

A. Yes: I will cause you to walk in my statutes. Ezek. xxxvi. 27.

9. *Q.* Does every transgression in the covenant cast us out of the covenant?

A. No: I will visit their transgression with a rod, but my loving kindness will I not utterly take away. Ps. lxxxix. 32, 33.

§ VIII.

1. *Q.* Will this covenant deliver us out of a state of sin and misery?

A. Yes: whosoever believes in Christ shall not perish. John iii. 16.

2. *Q.* Will it bring us into a state of salvation?

A. Yes: he that believeth on the Son hath everlasting life. John iii. 36.

3. *Q.* And can we desire any more?

A. No: It is all my salvation, and all my desire. 2 Sam. xxiii. 5.

§ IX.

1. *Q.* Was there intimation given to Adam, of this way of salvation by a Redeemer?
A. Yes: for it was said to him, that the seed of the woman should break the serpent's head. Gen. iii. 15.

2. *Q.* Was it made known to the Old Testament saints?
A. Yes: for of this salvation have the prophets inquired, and searched diligently. 1 Pet i. 10.

3. *Q.* But is it brought to a clearer light in the New Testament?
A. Yes: go preach the gospel to every creature. He that believeth shall be saved, and he that believeth not shall be damned. Mark xvi. 15, 16.

4. *Q.* Is this good news to fallen man?
A. Yes: glory be to God in the highest, on earth peace, good will towards men. Luke ii. 14.

5. *Q.* Does this covenant exclude any that do not exclude themselves?
A. No: whosoever will, let him come, and take of the water of life freely. Rev. xxii. 17.

XXI. *Q.* Who is the Redeemer of God's elect?

A. The only Redeemer of God's elect is the Lord Jesus Christ, who, being the Eternal Son of God, became man, and so was, and continueth to be, God and man in two distinct natures, and one person, forever.

§1.

1. Q. Did mankind need a Redeemer?
A. Yes: for by our iniquities we had sold ourselves. Isa. l. 1.

2. Q. Did the elect, themselves, need a Redeemer?
A. Yes: for we ourselves also were sometimes disobedient. Tit. iii. 3.

3. Q. Would there have been a Redeemer, if Adam had not sinned?
A. No: for they that be whole need not a physician. Mat. ix. 12.

4. Q. Could an angel have been our Redeemer?

A. No: for his angels he charged with folly. Job iv. 18.

§ II.

1. Q. Is Jesus Christ the Redeemer?
A. Yes: there is one mediator between God and man, the man Christ Jesus. 1 Tim. ii. 5.
2. Q. Is he the only Redeemer?
A. Yes: for there is no other name under Heaven given among men whereby we must be saved. Acts, iv. 12.

* * * * * *

3. Q. Did he die, to purchase a general offer?
A. Yes: the Son of man was lifted up, that whosoever believeth in him should not perish. John iii. 14, 15.
4. Q. Is all the world the better for Christ's mediation?
A. Yes: for, by him, all things consist. Col. i. 17.
5. Q. Is it the fault† of Christ, then, that so many perish?
A. No: I would have gathered you, and you would not. Matt. xxiii. 37.

§ III.

1. Q. Is Christ, in a special manner, the Redeemer of God's elect?
A. Yes: I lay down my life for the sheep. John x. 15.
2. Q. Was their salvation particularly designed in Christ's undertaking?
A. Yes: thou hast given him power over all flesh, that he should give eternal life to as many as thou hast given him. John xvii. 2.
3. Q. Was their sanctification particularly designed?
A. Yes: for their sakes, I sanctify myself, that they also might be sanctified. John xvii. 19.
4. Q. Is all mankind redeemed from among devils?
A. Yes: for none must say as they did, "What have we to do with thee, Jesus, thou Son of God?" Matt. viii. 29.
5. Q. But, are the elect redeemed from among men?

---

* Here, one of the questions, found in the London Edition is omitted. See Editor's Preface.   Editor.

† The expression here used in Henry's miscellaneous works, is " *Is it long of Christ, then,*" &c. Believing this to be either a misprint, or an antiquated phrase, I have taken the liberty of changing it, so as to be better understood.   Ed.

A. Yes: these were redeemed from among men. Rev. xiv. 4.

§ IV.

1. Q. Is the Redeemer, LORD?
A. Yes: every tongue shall confess, that Jesus Christ is Lord. Phillipp ii. 11.
2. Q. Is he, Jesus, a Saviour?
A. Yes: thou shalt call his name Jesus, for he shall save his people from their sins. Matt. i. 21.
3. Is he Christ anointed?
A. Yes: for, God, even thy God, hath anointed thee. Heb. i. 9.
4. Q. Is he Emmanuel?
A. Yes: They shall call his name Emmanuel, which, being interpreted, is God with us. Matt. i. 23.

§ V.

1. Q. Is he the Son of God?
A. Yes: thou art Christ, the Son of the living God. Matt. xvi. 16.
2. Q. Is he the eternal Son of God?
A: Yes: for he is before all things. Col. i. 17.
3. Q. Is he God?
A. Yes. unto the Son, he says, Thy throne, O God, is for ever and ever. Heb. i. 8.
4. Q. Is he true God?
A. Yes: his Son, Jesus Christ, is the true God, and eternal life. 1 John v. 20.
5. Q. Is he the most high God?
A. Yes: for, Christ is over all, God, blessed, for ever. Rom. ix. 5.
6. Q. Is he equal with the Father?
A. Yes: for he thought it not robbery to be equal with God. Philipp, ii. 6.
7. Q. Is he one with the Father?
A. Yes: I and my Father are one. John x. 30.
8. Q. Is he to be worshipped, as God?
A. Yes: for all men should honor the Son even as they honor the Father. John v. 23.
9. Q. Is he worshipped by the angels?
A. Yes: let all the angels of God worship him. Heb. i. 6.
10. Q. And is there good reason for it?
A. Yes: for he is the brightness of his Father's glory. Heb. i. 3.

11. Q. Is he the only begotten Son of God?

A. Yes: We beheld his glory, the glory as of the only begotten of the Father. John i. 14.

12. Q. Was he begotten of his Father before all worlds?

A. Yes: Thou art my son, this day have I begotten thee. Ps. ii. 7.

§ VI.

1. Q. Did the Son of God become man?

A. Yes: The word was made flesh and dwelt among us. John i. 14.

2. Q. Did he come into this world?

A. Yes: he came forth from the Father, and came into the world. John xvi. 28.

3. Q. Did he come in the fittest time?

A. Yes: when the fulness of time was come, God sent forth his son. Gal. iv. 4.

4. Q. Did he come, with a full commission?

A. Yes: for the father sanctified him, and sent him into the world. John x. 36.

5. Q. Did he come, to save us?

A. Yes: the Son of man is come to seek and to save that which was lost. Luke, xix. 10.

6. Q. Did he come to conquer Satan?

A. Yes: for this purpose was the Son of God manifested that he might destroy the works of the devil. 1 John iii. 8.

§ VII.

1. Q. Did the Redeemer take our nature upon him?

A. Yes: he was found in fashion as a man. Philipp. ii. 8.

2. Q. Had he a being before his incarnation?

A. Yes: before Abraham was, I am. John viii. 58.

3. Q. Had he a being before the world?

A. Yes: for the same was, in the beginning, with God. John, i. 2.

4. Q. Is not his incarnation a great mystery?

A. Yes: without controversy, great is the mystery of godliness, God manifest in the flesh. 1 Tim. iii. 16.

5. Q. Is it necessary that we believe it?

A. Yes: for he that confesseth not that Jesus Christ is come in the flesh, is not of God. 1 John iv. 3.

6. Q. Was Jesus Christ God, even when he was upon earth?

A. Yes: I am in the Father, and the Father in me. John xiv. 11.

7. Q. Is he man, now he is in Heaven?

A. Yes: for he that descended is the same also that ascended. Ephes. iv. 10.

§ VIII.

1. *Q.* Is the Redeemer both God and man?

A. Yes: for, to us, a child is born, to us a son is given, and he shall be called the mighty God, the everlasting Father. Isa. ix. 6.

2. *Q.* Is he both the Son of God and the son of man?

A. Yes: he was the son of Adam, he was the Son of God. Luke iii. 38.

3. *Q.* Does he continue to be so?

A. Yes: for Jesus Christ is the same, yesterday, to-day, and forever. Heb. xiii. 8.

4. *Q.* Was he man, that he might suffer?

A. Yes: for without shedding of blood, is no remission. Heb. ix. 22.

5. *Q.* Was he God that he might satisfy?

A. Yes: for God has purchased the church with his own blood. Acts xx. 28.

6. *Q.* Is he God and man in two distinct natures?

A. Yes: for he is both the root and offspring of David. Rev. xxii. 16, compared with Matt. xxii. 45.

7. *Q.* Is he so in one person?

A. Yes: for to us there is but one Lord Jesus Christ, by whom are all things, and we by him. 1 Cor. viii. 6.

8. *Q.* Is he so, forever?

A. Yes: he is Alpha and Omega, the beginning and the ending, the first and the last. Rev. xxii. 13.

§ IX.

1. *Q.* Is this Jesus the true Messiah promised to the Fathers?

A. Yes: we know that this is, indeed, the Christ, the Saviour of the world. John iv. 42.

2. *Q.* Were the scriptures fulfilled in him?

A. Yes: to him give all the prophets witness. Acts x. 43.

3. *Q.* Did his miracles prove his doctrine?

A. Yes: the works that I do bear witness of me, that the Father hath sent me. John v. 36.

4. *Q.* Did the Father himself bear witness of him?

A. Yes: by a voice from heaven saying, This is my beloved Son, in whom I am well pleased; hear ye him. Matt. xvii. 5.

5. *Q.* May we venture our souls upon this foundation?

A. Yes: for this is the record that God hath given to us eternal life, and this life is in his Son. 1 John v. 11.

XXII. Q. How did Christ, being the Son of God become man?

A. Christ the Son of God, became man, by taking to himself a true body, and a reasonable soul, being conceived by the power of the Holy Ghost, in the womb of the Virgin Mary and born of her, yet without sin.

§ I.

1. *Q.* Did Christ the Son of God, become man?
A. Yes: for as much as the children are partakers of flesh and blood, he also himself likewise took part of the same. Heb. ii. 14.

2. *Q.* Was it requisite he should become man?
A. Yes: for in all things, it behoved him to be made like unto his brethren. Heb. ii. 17.

3. *Q.* Has the Son of man the fulness of the Godhead?
A. Yes: for in him dwells all the fulness of the Godhead bodily. Col. ii. 9.

4. *Q.* Has the Son of God the tenderness of a man?
A. Yes: for he was touched with the feeling of our infirmities. Heb. iv. 15.

§ II.

1. *Q.* Did Christ take unto himself a true body?
A. Yes: a body hast thou prepared me. Heb. x. 5.

2. *Q.* Was it a body like unto ours?
A. Yes: for he was in the likeness of sinful flesh. Rom. viii. 3.

3. *Q.* Did he take to himself a human soul?
A. Yes: for he said, my soul is exceedingly sorrowful. Matt. xxvi. 38.

§ III.

1. *Q.* Was he conceived by ordinary generation?
A. No: for he said, ye are from beneath, I am from above. John viii. 23.

2. *Q.* Was he conceived by the power of the Holy Ghost?
A. Yes: the Holy Ghost shall come upon thee, and the power of the highest shall overshadow thee. Luke i. 35.

3. *Q.* Was he born of the Virgin Mary?
A. Yes: the scripture was fulfilled, behold a virgin shall be with child, and bring forth a son, Matt. i. 23.

4. *Q.* Was his conception and birth supernatural?

A. Yes: that which was conceived in the Virgin Mary was of the Holy Ghost. Matt. i. 20.

5. *Q.* Yet, was he really and truly man?
A. Yes: for he is not ashamed to call us brethren. Heb. ii. 11.

§ IV.

1. *Q.* Was Christ the seed of the woman?
A. Yes: for he was made of a woman. Gal. iv. 4.
2. *Q.* Was the scripture therein fulfilled?
A. Yes: for the seed of the woman must break the serpent's head. Gen. iii. 15.
3. *Q.* Was he the son of Abraham?
A. Yes: for he took on him the seed of Abraham. Heb. ii. 16.
4. *Q.* Was the scripture therein fulfilled?
A. Yes: for it was said to Abraham, in thy seed shall all families of the earth be blessed. Gen. xii. 3.
5. *Q.* Was he the son of David?
A. Yes: hosanna to the son of David. Matt. xxi. 9.
6. *Q.* Was the scripture therein fulfilled?
A. Yes: he hath raised up a horn of salvation for us in the house of his servant David, as he spake by the mouth of all his holy prophets. Luke i. 69, 70.

§ V.

1. *Q.* Was Christ born in Bethlehem?
A. Yes: to you is born this day, in the city of David, a saviour. Luke. ii. 11.
2. *Q.* Was he born among the Jews?
A. Yes: of them as concerning the flesh, Christ came. Rom. ix. 5.
3. *Q.* And was it the honour of that nation?
A. Yes: he was the glory of his people Israel. Luke ii. 32.
4. *Q.* Did he come when the Messiah was expected?
A. Yes: they then looked for redemption in Jerusalem. Luke ii. 38.
5. *Q.* Did he come when the sceptre was departed from Judah?
A. Yes: for there then went out a decree that all the world should be taxed. Luke ii. 1.
6. *Q.* Did the angels attend him at his birth?
A. Yes: there was a multitude of the heavenly host, praising God. Luke ii. 13.

§ VI.

1. *Q.* Was the Redeemer born in sin, as we are?
A. No: he was without sin. Heb. iv. 15.
2. *Q.* Was he perfectly pure and holy?
A. Yes: that holy thing which shall be born of thee, shall be called the Son of God. Luke i. 35.
3. *Q.* Was he pure and holy in his whole life?
A. Yes: he did no sin neither was guile found in his mouth. 1 Pet. ii. 22.
4. *Q.* Was it requisite he should be so?
A. Yes: such a High Priest became us, that was holy, harmless, and undefiled. Heb. vii. 26.
5. *Q.* Could he have satisfied for our sin, if he had had any sin of his own?
A. No: for he must through the eternal Spirit, offer himself without spot. Heb. ix. 14.

§ VII.

1. *Q.* Was he subject to the sinless infirmities of our natures?
A. Yes: he was in all points, tempted like as we are. Heb. iv. 15.
2. *Q.* Was he hungry?
A. Yes: when he had fasted forty days, and forty nights, he was afterwards an hungered. Matt. iv. 2.
3. *Q.* Was he weary?
A. Yes: being weary with his journey he sat on the well. John iv. 6.
4. *Q.* Did he sleep?
A. Yes: when the ship was covered with waves, he was asleep. Matt. viii. 24.
5. *Q.* Did he pass through the ages of human life?
A. Yes: for Jesus increased in wisdom and stature. Luke ii. 52.

§ VIII.

1. *Q.* Was the Redeemer willing to be incarnate for us?
A. Yes: for when he cometh into the world, he saith, Lo, I come to do thy will, O God. Heb. x. 5. 7.
2. *Q.* Is it well for us, that he was so?
A. Yes: for, by this will, we are sanctified. Heb. x. 10.
3. *Q.* Was Christ's incarnation great condescension in him?
A. Yes: for hereby he was made a little lower than the angels. Heb. ii. 9.
4. *Q.* Was it a great honour to our nature?

A. Yes: what is man, that thou art mindful of him? Heb. ii. 6.

5. *Q.* Is it good news to mankind?
A. Yes: this is a faithful saying, and worthy of all acceptation, that Christ Jesus came into the world, to save sinners. 1 Tim. i. 15.

XXIII. *Q.* What offices doth Christ execute, as our Redeemer?

A. Christ as our Redeemer executeth the offices of a prophet, of a priest, and of a king, both in his estate of humiliation and exaltation.

§ I.

1. *Q.* Is Christ a complete Redeemer?
A. Yes: for it pleased the Father, that in him should all fulness dwell. Col. i. 19.

2. *Q.* Is he completely qualified for the undertaking?
A. Yes: for God giveth not the spirit by measure, unto him. John iii. 34.

3. *Q.* Is he authorized for it?
A. Yes: for all things are delivered to him, of the Father. Matt. xi. 27.

4. *Q.* Has he a full commission?
A. Yes: for the Father judgeth no man; but has committed all judgment to the Son. John v. 22.

5. *Q.* And has he an ability equal to his authority?
A. Yes: for as the Father hath life in himself, so hath he given to the Son, to have life in himself. John v. 26.

§ II.

1. *Q.* Is there all that in Christ, which fallen man stands in need of?
A. Yes: for Christ is all, and in all. Col. iii. 11.

2. *Q.* Is he light?
A. Yes: I am the light of the world. John viii. 12.

3. *Q.* Is he life?
A. Yes: in him was life; and the life was the light of men. John i. 4.

4. *Q.* Is he our peace?
A. Yes: he is our peace. Eph. ii. 14.

5. *Q.* Is he our head?
A. Yes: he is the head of the body, the church. Col. i. 18.

6. *Q.* Is he the door?

A. Yes: I am the door of the sheep. John x. 7.

7. *Q.* Is he the way?

A. Yes: I am the way, the truth, and the life. John xiv. 6.

8. *Q.* Can we come to God, as a Father, otherwise than by Jesus Christ, as Mediator?

A. No: for no man cometh to the Father but by me. John xiv. 6.

9. *Q.* Is he our food?

A. Yes: I am that bread of life. John vi. 48.

10. *Q.* Is he our friend?

A. This is my beloved, and this is my friend. Song of Solomon v. 16.

§ III.

1. *Q.* Is Jesus Christ a Redeemer in office?

A. Yes: for God hath exalted him with his own right hand, to be a Prince and a Saviour. Acts v. 31.

2. *Q.* Is he duly put in office?

A. Yes: for him hath God the Father sealed. John vi. 27.

3. *Q.* Does he duly execute his office?

A. Yes: for he was faithful to him that appointed him. Heb. iii. 2.

4. *Q.* Is he a prophet?

A. Yes: This is, of a truth, that prophet that should come into the world. John vi. 14.

5. *Q.* Is he a Priest?

A. Yes: he is the Apostle, and High Priest of our profession. Heb. iii. 1.

6. *Q.* Is he a King?

A. Yes: he is the King of kings, and Lord of lords. Rev. xix. 16.

§ IV.

1. *Q.* Did Christ execute these offices in his state of humiliation?

A. Yes: I have glorified thee on the earth. John xvii. 4.

2. *Q.* Does he execute them in his state of exaltation?

A. Yes: for in Heaven itself, he now appears, in the presence of God, for us. Heb. ix. 24.

3. *Q.* Is he then, an all-sufficient Saviour?

A. Yes: He is able to save to the uttermost, all those that come to God by him. Heb. vii. 25.

4. *Q.* And is he as willing to save, as he is able?

A. Yes: him that cometh unto me, I will in no wise cast out. John vi. 37.

XXIV. Q. How doth Christ execute the office of a Prophet?

A. Christ executeth the office of a Prophet, in revealing to us, by his Word and Spirit, the will of God for our salvation.

§ I.

1. *Q.* Does Christ execute the office of a Prophet?
A. Yes: we know that thou art a teacher come from God. John iii. 2.

2. *Q.* Does God speak to us, by him?
A. Yes: he hath, in these last days, spoken to us, by his Son. Heb. i. 2.

3. *Q.* Were there Prophets under the Old Testament?
A. Yes: God sent his servants, the Prophets. Jer. xxv. 4.

4. *Q.* But, was Christ above them all?
A. Yes: for He is the Lord God of the holy Prophets. Rev. xxii. 6.

5. *Q.* And were they his agents?
A. Yes: it was the Spirit of Christ, in them, that testified. 1 Pet. i. 11.

§ II.

1. *Q.* Was Moses the great type of Christ, as a Prophet?
A. Yes: a prophet shall the Lord your God raise up unto you, of your brethren, like unto me. Acts iii. 22.

2. *Q.* But was Christ greater than Moses?
A. Yes: for Moses was faithful as a servant; but Christ, as a Son. Heb. iii. 5, 6.

3. *Q.* And is the doctrine of Christ better than that of Moses?
A. Yes: for the law was given by Moses; but grace and truth came by Jesus Christ. John i. 17.

4. *Q.* Was Christ completely qualified to be a Prophet?
A. Yes: for in Him are hid all the treasures of wisdom and knowledge. Col. ii. 3.

5. *Q.* Was ever any other so well qualified?
A. No: for no man knows the Father, but the Son. Matt. xi. 27.

§ III.

1. *Q.* Has Christ, as a Prophet, revealed God's will to us?
A. Yes: for He said, my doctrine is not mine, but his that sent me. John vii. 16, and xii. 49, 50.

2. *Q.* Has he revealed God's will, concerning our duty?
A. Yes: for He did not come to destroy the law, but to fulfil. Matt. v. 17.

3. *Q.* And concerning our happiness?

A. Yes: for he was anointed to preach the acceptable year of the Lord. Luke iv. 19.

§ IV.

1. *Q.* Did Christ execute this office, when he was on earth?

A. Yes: for He taught them as one having authority. Matt. vii. 29.

2. *Q.* Did he introduce his doctrine with "Thus saith the Lord," like the Old Testament Prophets?

A. No: but "Verily, verily, I say unto you." John iii. 3.

3. *Q.* Did he confirm his doctrine, by miracles?

A. Yes: believe me, (said he,) for the very works' sake. John xiv. 11.

4. *Q.* Were his miracles many?

A. Yes: many signs did Jesus, in the presence of his disciples. John xx. 30.

5. *Q.* Were they profitable?

A. Yes: He went about, doing good. Acts x. 38.

6. *Q.* Did Christ teach by the example of his life?

A. Yes: that we might follow his steps. 1 Pet. ii. 21.

§ V.

1. *Q.* Does he still execute this office?

A. Yes: for He said, I have declared thy name unto them, and will declare it. John xvii. 26.

2. *Q.* Does he reveal God's will to us, by his Word?

A. Yes: for these things are written, that we may believe. John xx. 31.

3. *Q.* And by his Spirit?

A. Yes: the comforter, which is the Holy Ghost, He shall teach you all things. John xiv. 26.

4. *Q.* Does Jesus Christ teach his people?

A. Yes: all thy children shall be taught of the Lord. Isa. liv. 13.

5. *Q.* And does he teach effectually?

A. Yes: for the Son of God is come, and hath given us an understanding. 1 John v. 20.

6. *Q.* And does he teach compassionately?

A. Yes: for He can have compassion on the ignorant. Heb. v. 2.

§ VI.

1. *Q.* Must we learn of this teacher?

A. Yes: learn of me; for I am meek and lowly in heart. Matt. xi. 29.

2. *Q.* Are we to receive his doctrine?
A. Yes: let the word of Christ dwell in you richly. Col. iii. 16.
3. *Q.* And must we abide in it?
A. Yes: if ye continue in my word, then are ye my disciples indeed. John viii. 31.

XXV. *Q.* How doth Christ execute the office of a Priest?
A. Christ executeth the office of a Priest, in his once offering up of himself a sacrifice to satisfy divine justice, and reconcile us to God; and in making continual intercession for us.

§ I.

1. *Q.* Did fallen man need a Priest?
A. Yes: for every high priest is ordained for man, in things pertaining to God. Heb. v. 1.
2. *Q.* Did Christ execute the office of a Priest?
A. Yes: we have a great High Priest, Jesus the Son of God. Heb. iv. 14.
3. *Q.* Was he appointed to this office?
A. Yes: for Christ glorified not himself to be made a high-priest. Heb. v. 5.
4. *Q.* Was he confirmed in this office?
A. Yes: for the Lord sware, and will not repent, thou art a Priest forever. Heb. vii. 21.

§ II.

1. *Q.* Did Christ, as a Priest, make atonement for sin?
A. Yes: He is a merciful and faithful High Priest, to make reconciliation for the sins of the people. Heb. ii. 17.
2. *Q.* Did he do this by the sacrifice of himself?
A. Yes: He appeared, to put away sin, by the sacrifice of himself. Heb. ix. 26.
3. *Q.* Was he himself the Priest?
A. Yes: for, through the Eternal Spirit, he offered himself. Heb. ix. 14.
4. *Q.* Was he himself the sacrifice?
A. Yes: He made his soul an offering for sin. Isa. liii. 10.
5. *Q.* Was he himself the altar?
A. Yes: for we have an altar. Heb. xiii. 10.
6. *Q.* Would not the legal sacrifices serve?

A. No: for it was not possible that the blood of bulls and goats should take away sin. Heb. x. 4.

7. *Q.* Did God declare them insufficient?

A. Yes: sacrifice and offering thou wouldst not. Heb. x. 5.

8. *Q.* Was this sacrifice necessary, then?

A. Yes: what the law could not do, in that it was weak, that Christ did. Rom. viii. 3.

§ III.

1. *Q.* Did Christ, as a sacrifice, bear our sins?

A. Yes: His own self bare our sins in his own body on the tree. 1 Pet. ii. 24.

2. *Q.* Did he bear them by the Father's appointment?

A. Yes: the Lord laid on him the iniquities of us all. Isa. liii. 6.

3. *Q.* Did he suffer for them?

A. Yes: He was wounded for our transgressions, and bruised for our iniquities. Isa. liii. 5.

4. *Q.* And not for any sin of his own?

A. No: Messiah shall be cut off, but not for himself. Dan. ix. 26.

5. *Q.* Did he suffer, to satisfy for sin?

A. Yes: He was once offered, to bear the sins of many. Heb. ix. 28.

6. *Q.* And was the satisfaction accepted?

A. Yes: He gave himself for us, a sacrifice to God, of a sweet smelling savour. Ephes. v. 2.

§ IV.

1. *Q.* Did Christ offer himself voluntarily?

A. Yes: no man taketh my life from me, but I lay it down of myself. John x. 18.

2. *Q.* Was it his own act and deed, to make his soul an offering?

A. Yes: for he said, Father, into thy hands I commend my spirit. Luke xxiii. 46.

3. *Q.* Did this sacrifice need to be repeated?

A. No: for by one offering, he perfected forever them that are sanctified. Heb. x. 14.

4. *Q.* Did Christ do this for the purchase of our pardon?

A. Yes: for when he did it, he said, Father, forgive them. Luke xxiii. 34.

5. *Q.* Was it designed to save us from ruin?

A. Yes: He gave his life a ransom for many. Matt. xx. 28.

6. *Q.* And to reconcile us to God?

A. Yes: for he made peace through the blood of his cross. Col. i. 20.

7. *Q.* Is this our plea for peace and pardon?

A. Yes: who is he that condemns? It is Christ that died. Rom. viii. 34.

8. *Q.* Is Christ, then, the great propitiation?

A. Yes: He is the propitiation for our sins, and not for ours only, but for the sins of the whole world. 1 John ii. 2.

9. *Q.* And have we hereby access to God?

A. Yes: He suffered, the just for the unjust, that he might bring us to God. 1 Pet. iii. 18.

10. *Q.* And had the Old Testament saints the benefit of this sacrifice?

A. Yes: for he was the lamb slain from the foundation of the world. Rev. xiii. 8.

§ v.

1. *Q.* Does Christ, as a Priest, make intercession?

A. Yes: for he bare the sin of many, and made intercession for the transgressors. Isa. liii. 12.

2. *Q.* Is he always doing this?

A. Yes: He ever lives making intercession. Heb. vii. 25.

3. *Q.* Does he do this as an advocate?

A. Yes: If any man sin we have an advocate with the Father, Jesus Christ the righteous. 1 John ii. 1.

4. *Q.* And as a High Priest?

A. Yes: Aaron shall bear their names before the Lord. Exod. xxviii. 12.

5. *Q.* Does he make intercession in the virtue of his satisfaction?

A. Yes: for, by his own blood, he entered into the holy place. Heb. ix. 12.

§ vi.

1. *Q.* Is Christ a Priest, after the order of Aaron?

A. No: but after the order of Melchisedec. Ps. cx. 4.

2. *Q.* Is he a Royal Priest?

A. Yes: for, he is a Priest, upon his throne, and the counsel of peace shall be between them both. Zech. vi. 13.

3. *Q.* Is he a Priest, that needs a successor?

A. No: for this man, because he continueth for ever, hath an unchangeable Priesthood. Heb. vii. 24.

4. *Q.* Is he a Priest, that needs a sacrifice for himself?

A. No: for the law makes men High Priests which have

infirmity; but the word of the oath makes the Son, who is consecrated forever more. Heb. vii. 28.

5. *Q.* Have all believers an interest in Christ's Priesthood?

A. Yes: for we have a High Priest over the house of God. Heb. x. 21.

6. *Q.* Is this an encouragement, in our approaches to God?

A. Yes: let us, therefore, come boldly to the throne of grace. Heb. iv. 16.

7. *Q.* And is it this we must depend upon for our acceptance with God?

A. Yes: for spiritual sacrifices are acceptable to God only through Jesus Christ. 1 Pet. ii. 5.

XXVI. *Q.* How doth Christ execute the office of a King?

A. Christ executeth the office of a King in subduing us to himself, in ruling and defending us, and in restraining and conquering all his and our enemies.

§ I.

1. *Q.* Is Christ put into the office of a King?

A. Yes: I have set my King upon my holy hill of Zion. Ps. ii. 6.

2. *Q.* Does he execute that office?

A. Yes: He shall reign over the house of Jacob forever. Luke i. 33.

3. *Q.* Is he King, as Mediator?

A. Yes: He hath authority to execute judgment, because he is the Son of man. John v. 27.

4. *Q.* Is his kingdom a spiritual kingdom?

A. Yes: my kingdom is not of this world. John xviii. 36.

§ II.

1. *Q.* Is Christ universal monarch?

A. Yes: for all power is given to him, both in heaven and on earth. Matt. xxviii. 18.

2. *Q.* Has he a right to rule all?

A. Yes: He is Lord of all. Acts x. 36.

3. *Q.* Does he rule all?

A. Yes: He is the Governor among the nations. Ps. xxii. 28.

4. *Q.* Does he rule all, for the good of his church?

A. Yes: He is Head over all things to the church. Ephes. i. 22.

5. *Q.* Is he, in a special manner, the church's King?
A. Yes: O daughter of Zion, thy King cometh. Zech. ix. 9.

§ III.

1. *Q.* Does Christ, as King, subdue his people to himself?
A. Yes: thy people shall be willing in the day of thy power. Ps. cx. 3.

2. *Q.* Does he do it, by the word of his grace?
A. Yes: He draws with the cords of a man, and with the bands of love. Hos. xi. 4.

3. *Q.* Does he do it, effectually?
A. Yes: he makes ready a people prepared for the Lord. Luke i. 17.

4. *Q.* Does he conquer the opposition of the carnal mind?
A. Yes: for the weapons of our warfare are mighty through God, to the pulling down of strong-holds. 2 Cor. x. 4.

5. *Q.* Does he set up his throne in the soul?
A. Yes: bringing into captivity every thought to the obedience of Christ. 2 Cor. x. 5.

6. *Q.* And does he rule there?
A. Yes: for he writes his law in their hearts. Heb. viii. 10.

§ IV.

1. *Q.* Does Christ, as a king, reign in his church?
A. Yes: the Lord is our judge, the Lord is our law-giver; the Lord is our King. Isa. xxxiii. 22.

2. *Q.* Does he enact laws?
A. Yes: He gave commandments to his apostles. Acts. i. 2.

3. Does he commission officers?
A. Yes: by me kings reign. Prov. viii. 15.

4. *Q.* Does he give judgment?
A. Yes: we must all appear before the judgment-seat of Christ. 2 Cor. v. 10.

5. Is homage and allegiance due to him?
A. Yes: for at the name of Jesus, every knee shall bow. Philip. ii. 10.

6. *Q.* Does he rule in righteousness?
A. Yes: the sceptre of his kingdom is a right sceptre. Ps. xlv. 6.

§ V.

1. 2. Does Christ, as a King, protect his subjects?
A. Yes: for he shall be as a hiding-place from the wind. Isa. xxxii. 2.

2. *Q.* And does he secure the peace of his kingdom?

A. Yes: for this man shall be the peace. Micah v. 5.

3. *Q.* Has he authority to pardon sin?

A. Yes: the Son of man hath power on earth, to forgive sin. Matt. ix. 6.

4. *Q.* Has he authority to reward services?

A. Yes: I will give thee a crown of life. Rev. ii. 10.

§ VI.

1. *Q.* Does Christ, as King, restrain his enemies?

A. Yes: on this rock will I build my church; and the gates of hell shall not prevail against it. Matt. xvi. 18.

2. *Q.* Will he conquer them at last?

A. Yes: for he must reign till he hath put all enemies under his feet. 1 Cor. xv. 25.

3. *Q.* Will he conquer death itself?

A. Yes: the last enemy that shall be destroyed, is death. 1 Cor. xv. 26.

4. *Q.* Does he count those his enemies, that will not have him to reign over them?

A. Yes: those mine enemies which would not that I should reign over them, bring them hither, and slay them before me. Luke xix. 27.

§ VII.

1. *Q.* Is Christ a merciful king?

A. Yes: He is lowly, and having salvation. Zech. ix. 9.

2. *Q.* Is he the poor man's king?

A. Yes: He shall deliver the needy, when he cries. Ps. lxxii. 12.

3. *Q.* Has he a large kingdom?

A. Yes: he shall have dominion from sea to sea. Ps. lxxii. 8.

4. *Q.* Have we reason to hope it shall be larger than now it is?

A. Yes: for the kingdoms of the world are become the kingdoms of the Lord, and of his Christ. Rev. xi. 15.

5. *Q.* Shall it be a lasting kingdom?

A. Yes: his throne shall be as the days of heaven. Psalms lxxxix. 29.

6. *Q.* And, when the mystery of God shall be finished, shall the kingdom of the Redeemer be resigned to the Creator?

A. Yes: then cometh the end, when he shall have delivered up the kingdom to God, even the Father. 1 Cor. xv. 24.

§ VIII.

1. *Q.* Ought we to rejoice in Christ's dominion?

A. Yes: let the children of Sion be joyful in their King. Ps. cxlix. 2.

2. Must we accept him for our king?
A. Yes: take my yoke upon you. Matt. xi. 29.

3. *Q.* Must we pay tribute to him?
A. Yes: send ye the lamb, to the ruler of the land. Isa. xvi. 1.

4. *Q.* Must we obey him?
A. Yes: for he is the author of eternal salvation to all them that obey him. Heb. v. 9.

XXVII. *Q.* Wherein did Christ's humiliation consist?

A. Christ's humiliation consisted in his being born, and that in a low condition, made under the law, undergoing the miseries of this life, the wrath of God, and the cursed death of the cross; in being buried, and continuing under the power of death for a time.

§ I.

1. *Q.* Did Jesus Christ humble himself?
A. Yes: for, being in the form of God, he made himself of no reputation. Philipp. ii. 6, 7.

2. *Q.* Was it a deep humiliation?
A. Yes: for, he said, I am a worm, and no man. Ps. xxii. 6.

3. *Q.* Was it requisite he should humble himself?
A. Yes: for thus it is written, and thus it behooved Christ to suffer. Luke xxiv. 46.

4. *Q.* And was that a proper expedient to atone for our sin?
A. Yes: for the sinner had said, I will be like the most high. Isa. xiv. 14.

§II.

1. *Q.* Did Christ humble himself, in his birth?
A. Yes: for, he who thought it not robbery to be equal with God, was made in the likeness of men. Philipp. ii. 6, 7.

2. *Q.* Was he born of that which was then a poor family?
A. Yes: he was a root out of a dry ground. Isa. liii. 2.

3. *Q.* Was he born of a poor woman?
A. Yes: for she offered for her cleansing, only a pair of turtle doves, or two young pigeons, Luke ii. 24, compared with Lev. xii. 8.

4. *Q.* Was his supposed father, a poor man?

A. Yes: they said, is not this the carpenter's son? Matt. xiii. 55.

5. *Q.* Was he born in a poor place?
A. Yes: Bethlehem was little among the thousands of Judah. Mic. v. 2.

6. *Q.* Was he born in poor circumstances?
A. Yes: in the stable of an inn, and laid in a manger. Luke ii. 7.

7. *Q.* Had he the respect paid him, that was due to an incarnate deity?
A. No: for he was in the world, and the world knew him not. John i. 10.

8. *Q.* Was he respected by his countrymen?
A. No: he came to his own, and his own received him not. John i. 11.

9. *Q.* Was he born honorably?
A. No: for he took upon him the form of a servant. Philipp. ii. 7.

10. *Q.* Was he born wealthy?
A. No: though he was rich, yet, for our sakes, he became poor. 2 Cor. viii. 9.

§ III.

1. *Q.* Was Christ made under the law?
A. Yes: God sent forth his Son, made of a woman, made under the law. Gal. iv. 4.

2. *Q.* Was he circumcised?
A. Yes: when eight days were accomplished. Luke ii. 21.

3. *Q.* Was he presented in the temple?
A. Yes: they brought him to Jerusalem, to present him to the Lord. Luke ii. 22.

4. *Q.* Did he keep the Passover?
A. Yes: when he was twelve years old, he went up to Jerusalem, after the custom of the feast. Luke ii. 42.

5. *Q.* Was he obedient to his parents?
A. Yes: he went down with them to Nazareth, and was subject to them. Luke ii. 51.

6. *Q.* Did he pay tribute?
A. Yes: that give, for me and thee. Matt. xvii. 24, 27.

7. *Q.* Did he fulfil all righteousness?
A. Yes: thus, it becometh us to fulfil all righteousness. Matt. iii. 15.

8. *Q.* Did he submit to the law of the mediatorship.

A. Yes: thy law is within my heart. Ps. xl. 8.

§ IV.

1. *Q.* Was his education mean?
A. Yes: for they said, "is not this the carpenter? Mark vi. 3.
2. *Q.* Was the place of his abode despicable?
A. Yes: can any good thing come out of Nazareth. John i. 46.
3. *Q.* Did he live in honour?
A. No: for he was despised and rejected of men. Isa. liii. 3.
4. *Q.* Was he attended by great folks?
A. No: have any of the rulers or of the Pharisees believed on him? John vii. 48.
5. *Q.* Were his followers mean?
A. Yes: for they were fishers. Matt. iv. 18.
6. *Q.* Did he live in mirth and pleasure?
A. No: for he was a man of sorrows and acquainted with grief. Isa. liii. 3.
7. *Q.* Was the sin of sinners a grief to him?
A. Yes: he was grieved for the hardness of their hearts. Mark iii. 5.
8. *Q.* Were the sorrows of his friends a grief to him?
A. Yes: Jesus wept. John xi. 35.
9. *Q.* Had he a house of his own?
A. No: the foxes have holes, and the birds of the air have nests; but the Son of man hath not where to lay his head. Luke ix. 58.
10. *Q.* Was he fed with the finest of the wheat?
A. No: he had barley loaves. John vi. 9.
11. *Q.* Did he live upon alms?
A. Yes: for certain women ministered to him of their substance. Luke viii. 3.
12. *Q.* Had he a stately place to preach in?
A. No: he taught the people out of the ship. Luke v. 3.

§ V.

1. *Q.* Was he tempted of Satan.
A. Yes: he was in the wilderness, forty days, tempted of Satan. Mark i. 13.
2. *Q.* Was that a part of his sufferings?
A. Yes: for he suffered, being tempted. Heb. ii. 18.
3. *Q.* Was he persecuted betimes?
A. Yes: Herod sought the young child, to destroy him. Matt. ii. 13.

4. *Q.* Was he slandered and reproached?

A. Yes: they said of him, behold a gluttonous man and a wine bibber, a friend of publicans and sinners. Luke vii. 34.

5. *Q.* Was he represented as a madman?

A. Yes: they said, he hath a devil, and is mad. John x. 20.

6. *Q.* And as one that is in league with the devil?

A. Yes: they said, he casteth out devils by Beelzebub, the prince of the devils. Matt. xii. 24.

7. *Q.* Did they cavil at his preaching?

A. Yes: he endured the contradiction of sinners against himself. Heb. xii. 3.

8. *Q.* Did he bear all this patiently?

A. Yes: when he was reviled, he reviled not again. 1 Pet. ii. 23.

§ VI.

1. *Q.* But notwithstanding this, had he honour done him in his humiliation?

A. Yes: for it was said of him, he shall be great. Luke i. 32.

2. *Q.* Did God put honour upon him?

A. Yes: he received from God the Father, honour and glory. 2 Pet. i. 17.

3. *Q.* Did angels do him honour?

A. Yes: Behold, angels came and ministered to him. Matt. iv. 11.

4. *Q.* Did foreigners do him honour?

A. Yes: wise men of the East came to worship him. Matt. ii. 2.

5. *Q.* Did the common report of the people do him honour.

A. Yes: for some said he was Elias, others Jeremiah, or one of the prophets. Matt. xvi. 14.

6. *Q.* Did those that saw his miracles do him honour?

A. Yes: for they said, it was never so seen in Israel. Matt. ix. 33.

7. *Q.* Did inferior creatures do him honour?

A. Yes: even the winds and the seas obeyed him. Matt. viii. 27.

8. *Q.* Were devils themselves compelled to acknowledge him?

A. Yes: for they said we know thee, who thou art, the Holy One of God. Mark i. 24.

§ VII.

1. *Q.* Did he humble himself unto death?

A. Yes: he humbled himself and became obedient to death. Philipp. ii. 8.

2. *Q.* Did he die for us?
A. Yes: he was delivered for our offences. Rom. iv. 25.

3. *Q.* Was this according to the counsels of God?
A. Yes: he was delivered by the determinate counsel and foreknowledge of God. Acts ii. 23.

4. *Q.* Did he suffer in his soul?
A. Yes: for he said, now is my soul troubled. John xii. 27.

5. *Q.* Did he suffer from his Father?
A. Yes: he was stricken, smitten of God, and afflicted. Isa. liii. 4.

6. Did he suffer in soul from his Father?
A. Yes: for he put him to grief. Isa. liii. 10.

7. *Q.* Did this put him into an agony?
A. Yes: he began to be sorrowful and very heavy. Matt. xxvi. 37.

8. *Q.* Did he suffer this for us?
A. Yes: for he made him sin for us who knew no sin. 2 Cor. v. 21.

9. *Q.* And yet did the Father love him, even when he bruised him?
A. Yes: therefore doth my Father love me, because I lay down my life. John. x. 17.

§ VIII.

1. *Q.* Did he suffer from Satan?
A. Yes: thou shalt bruise his heel. Gen. iii. 15.

2. *Q.* Did Satan set upon him?
A. Yes: the prince of this world cometh. John xiv. 30.

3. *Q.* But did Satan conquer him?
A. No: he hath nothing in me. John xiv. 30.

4. *Q.* Did he suffer from the Jews?
A. Yes: for they cried, crucify him, crucfy him. Luke xxiii. 21.

5. *Q.* Did he suffer from the chief of the Jews?
A. Yes: he was the stone which the builders refused. Ps. cxviii. 22.

6. *Q.* Did he suffer from the Romans?
A. Yes: the princes of this world crucified the Lord of glory. 1 Cor. ii. 8.

7. *Q.* Was he betrayed by Judas?
A. Yes: they put it into the heart of Judas Iscariot to betray him. John xiii. 2.

8. *Q.* Was he sold for thirty pieces of silver?
A. Yes: a goodly price that I was prized at. Zech. xi. 13.
9. *Q.* Was he forsaken by his own disciples?
A. Yes: all his disciples forsook him, and fled. Matt. xxvi. 56.

§ IX.

1. *Q.* Was he falsely accused?
A. Yes: they sought false witness against him, to put him to death. Matt. xxvi. 59.
2. *Q.* Was he basely abused?
A. Yes: He hid not his face from shame and spitting. Isa. l. 6.
3. *Q.* Was he condemned as a blasphemer?
A. Yes: they said, He hath spoken blasphemy. Matt. xxvi. 65.
4. *Q.* Was he condemned, as a traitor?
A. Yes: for they said he perverted the nation, forbidding to give tribute to Cæsar. Luke xxiii. 2.
5. *Q.* Was he scourged?
A. Yes: for by his stripes, we are healed. Isa. liii. 5.
6. *Q.* Was he exposed to contempt?
A. Yes: He was a reproach of men, and despised of the people. Ps. xxii. 6.
7. *Q.* Did they scoff at him, as a Prophet?
A. Yes: they said, Prophesy, who smote thee. Matt. xxvi. 68.
8. *Q.* Did they scoff at him, as a King?
A. Yes: they said, hail, King of the Jews. Matt. xxvii. 29.
9. *Q.* Did they scoff at him, as a Priest and Saviour?
A. Yes: they said, He saved others, himself he cannot save. Matt. xxvii. 42.

§ X.

1. *Q.* Was he sentenced to the cross?
A. Yes: Pilate delivered him to be crucified. Matt. xxvii. 26.
2. *Q.* Was he crucified between two thieves?
A. Yes: He was numbered with the transgressors. Isa. liii. 12.
3. *Q.* Did he die a bloody death?
A. Yes: for the life of the flesh is in the blood, and it is the blood, that makes atonement for the soul. Lev. xvii. 11.
4. *Q.* Did he die a painful death?
A. Yes: they pierced his hands and feet. Ps. xxii. 16.

5. *Q.* And a shameful death?

A. Yes: He endured the cross, despising the shame. Heb. xii. 2.

6. *Q.* And a cursed death?

A. Yes: for he that is hanged is accursed of God. Deut. xxi. 23; and Gal. iii. 13.

7. *Q.* Did God seem to withdraw from him, in his sufferings?

A. Yes: He cried, with a loud voice, My God, My God, why hast thou forsaken me? Matt. xxvii. 46.

§ XI.

1. *Q.* Did Christ die to glorify God?

A. Yes: for this cause came I to this hour. Father, glorify thy name. John xii. 27, 28.

2. *Q.* Did he die, to satisfy for our sins?

A. Yes: it was to finish transgression, and to make an end of sins, to make reconciliation for iniquity, and bring in an everlasting righteousness. Dan. ix. 24.

3. *Q.* Did he die to conquer Satan?

A. Yes: He spoiled principalities and powers, triumphing over them, in his cross. Col. ii. 15.

4. *Q.* Did he die, to save us from sin?

A. Yes: He gave himself for us, that he might redeem us from all iniquity. Tit. ii. 14.

5. *Q.* Did he die, to purchase Heaven for us?

A. Yes: for it is the purchased possession. Ephes. i. 14; Heb. ix. 15.

6. *Q.* Was he, in his death, made a curse for us?

A. Yes: for Christ hath redeemed us from the curse of the law, being made a curse for us. Gal. iii. 13.

7. *Q.* Did Christ sweat for us?

A. Yes: His sweat was, as it were, great drops of blood. Luke xxii. 44.

8. *Q.* And, thorns being also a fruit of the curse, did Christ wear them for us?

A. Yes: they platted a crown of thorns, and put it upon his head. Matt. xxvii. 29.

§ XII.

1. *Q.* Did Christ do all that was to be done, in his sufferings for us?

A. Yes: He said, it is finished. John xix. 30.

2. *Q.* Did the events answer the predictions?

A. Yes: for the Scriptures must be fulfilled. Mark xiv. 49.

3. *Q.* Are we sure that Christ was truly dead?

A. Yes: for one of the soldiers, with a spear, pierced his side, and forthwith came thereout blood and water; and he that saw it bare record. John xix. 34, 35.

4. *Q.* Did Christ die, as a Martyr?

A. Yes: for, before Pontius Pilate, he witnessed a good confession. 1 Tim. vi. 13.

5. *Q.* Did he die, as a Testator?

A. Yes: for, where a testament is, there must needs be, the death of the Testator. Heb. ix. 16.

6. *Q.* Did he die, as a sacrifice?

A. Yes: Christ, our passover, is sacrificed for us. 1 Cor. v. 7.

§ XIII.

1. *Q.* Was there honour done to Christ, even in his sufferings?

A. Yes: the earth did quake, and the rocks rent, and the graves were opened. Matt. xxvii. 51, 52.

2. *Q.* And were some thereby convinced?

A. Yes: they feared greatly, saying, truly, this was the Son of God. Matt. xxvii. 54.

3. *Q.* Is the cross of Christ, then, a reproach to us?

A. No: God forbid that I should glory save in the cross of our Lord Jesus Christ. Gal. vi. 14.

4. *Q.* Is it what we should all be acquainted with?

A. Yes: I determined to know nothing, but Jesus Christ and him crucified. 1 Cor. ii. 2.

5. *Q.* And ought we to celebrate the praises of our crucified Saviour?

A. Yes: worthy is the Lamb that was slain, to receive honour, and glory, and blessing. Rev. v. 12.

§ XIV.

1. *Q.* When Christ was dead, was he buried?

A. Yes: they took him down from the tree, and laid him in a sepulchre. Acts xiii. 29.

2. *Q.* Was he buried according to the custom?

A. Yes: as the manner of the Jews is to bury. John xix. 40.

3. *Q* Did he continue under the power of death for a time?

A. Yes: for, as Jonas was three days and three nights in the whale's belly, so shall the Son of man be three days and three nights in the heart of the earth. Matt. xii. 40.

4. *Q.* Was this his descent into Hell?

A. Yes: He descended into the lower parts of the earth. Eph. iv. 9.

5. *Q.* Did his separate soul go to Paradise?

A. Yes: this day shalt thou be with me, in Paradise? Luke xxiii. 43.

6. *Q.* Did his body see corruption?

A. No: thou wilt not leave my soul in hell; neither wilt thou suffer thine Holy One to see corruption. Acts ii. 27.

XXVIII. *Q.* Wherein consisteth Christ's exaltation?

A. Christ's exaltation consisteth in his rising again from the dead on the third day, in ascending up into Heaven, in sitting at the right hand of God the Father, and in coming to judge the world at the last day.

§ I.

1. *Q.* Is Jesus Christ exalted?

A. Yes: because he humbled himself, therefore, God also hath highly exalted him. Philipp. ii. 9.

2. *Q.* Was his humiliation the way to exaltation?

A. Yes: he suffered these things, and so entered into his glory. Luke xxiv. 26.

3. *Q.* Was his exaltation the reward of his humiliation?

A. Yes: I have glorified thee on the earth, and now, O Father, glorify thou me. John xvii. 4, 5.

4. *Q.* Had he it in his eye, in his sufferings?

A. Yes: for the joy that was set before him, he endured the cross. Heb. xii. 2.

§ II.

1. *Q.* Was his resurrection the first step of his exaltation?

A. Yes: He was buried, and rose again the third day, according to the scriptures. 1 Cor. xv. 4.

2. *Q.* Did he continue always in the bands of death?

A. No: for it was impossible he should be holden of them. Acts. ii. 24.

3. Did he rise to life?

A. Yes: he both rose and revived. Rom. xiv. 9.

4. *Q.* Did the same body rise?

A. Yes: behold my hands and my feet, that it is I myself. Luke xxiv. 39.

5. *Q.* Is he the same Jesus still?

A. Yes: I am he that liveth, and was dead. Rev. i. 18.

6. *Q.* Did he lie in the grave all the Jewish Sabbath?

A. Yes: for he rose in the end of the Sabbath. Matt. xxviii. 1.

7. *Q.* Did he rise the same day of the week?

A. Yes: as it began to dawn towards the first day of the week. Matt. xxviii. 1.

8. *Q.* Have we sufficient proof of his resurrection?

A. Yes: he shewed himself alive, by many infallible proofs. Acts i. 3.

9. *Q.* Did he rise to die no more?

A. Yes: death hath no more dominion over him. Rom. vi. 9.

§ III.

1. *Q.* Did Christ rise by his own power?

A. Yes: destroy this temple, and in three days I will raise it up. John ii. 19, and x. 18.

2. *Q.* Was that a divine power?

A. Yes: for he was crucified through weakness, but he lived by the power of God. 2 Cor. xiii. 4.

3. *Q.* Was it the great proof of his being the Son of God?

A. Yes: he was declared to be the Son of God with power, by the resurrection from the dead. Rom. i. 4.

4. *Q.* Was it the will of the Father he should rise?

A. Yes: for the angel of the Lord descended from Heaven and came and rolled back the stone. Matt. xxviii. 2.

5. *Q.* Did the Father raise him?

A. Yes: God raised him from the dead. Acts xiii. 30.

6. *Q.* Was this an evidence of the acceptance of his satisfaction?

A. Yes: for he was raised again for our justification. Rom. iv. 25.

7. *Q.* And may we plead it?

A. Yes: it is Christ that died, yea, rather that is risen again. Rom. viii. 34.

§ IV.

1. *Q.* Did Christ rise, as a public person?

A. Yes: for since by man came death, by man came also the resurrection of the dead. 1 Cor. xv. 21.

2. *Q.* Are true believers raised with him to a spiritual life?

A. Yes: He hath quickened us together with Christ.

3. *Q.* And shall they be shortly raised to eternal life?

A. Yes: Christ the first fruits, afterward they that are Christ's at his coming. 1 Cor. xv. 23.

4. *Q.* Is the resurrection of Christ one of the great foundations of Christianity?
A. Yes: if Christ be not risen, our faith is vain. 1 Cor. xv. 14.

§ v.

1. *Q.* Did Christ stay on earth, forty days, after his resurrection?
A. Yes: he was seen of them, forty days. Acts i. 3.
2. *Q.* Did he then ascend up into Heaven?
A. Yes: while he blessed them, he was parted from them, and carried up into heaven. Luke xxiv. 51.
3. *Q.* Did he ascend in a cloud?
A. Yes: a cloud received him out of their sight. Acts i. 9.
4. *Q.* Was he welcome in heaven?
A. Yes: when the Son of man came with the clouds of heaven, he came to the ancient of days, and they brought him near before him. Dan. vii. 13.

§ vi.

1. *Q.* Was it for our advantage that he ascended up into heaven?
A. Yes: it is expedient for you that I go away. John xvi. 7.
2. *Q.* Did he ascend as a conqueror?
A. Yes: when he ascended on high, he led captivity captive. Ephes. iv. 8.
3. *Q.* Did he ascend as our forerunner?
A. Yes: as the forerunner he is for us entered. Heb. vi. 20.
4. *Q.* Is he gone, to prepare a place for us?
A. Yes: I go to prepare a place for you. John xiv. 2.
5. *Q.* Did he enter as our High Priest, within the veil?
A. Yes: by his own blood he entered in, once, into the holy place. Heb. ix. 12.

§ vii.

1. *Q.* Did he sit at the right hand of God?
A. Yes: he is seated on the right hand of the throne of the Majesty in the heavens. Heb. viii. 1.
2. *Q.* Has he authority to sit there?
A. Yes: the Lord said unto my Lord, sit thou on my right hand. Ps. cx. 1.
3. *Q.* Is he there now?
A. Yes: he is even at the right hand of God. Rom. viii. 34.
4. *Q.* Has he been seen there?
A. Yes: Stephen said, I see the heavens opened, and the Son of man standing on the right hand of God. Acts vii. 56.

5. *Q.* Will he continue there?

A. Yes: the heavens must receive him till the restitution of all things. Acts iii. 21.

6. *Q.* Has he the highest honour there?

A. Yes: God hath given him a name above every name. Philipp. ii. 9.

7. *Q.* Has he the sovereign power there?

A. Yes: for angels, authorities and powers, are made subject to him. 1 Pet. iii. 22.

8. *Q.* Is he Lord of all there?

A. Yes: thou crownest him with glory and honour, and didst set him over the works of thy hands. Heb. ii. 7.

9. *Q.* Ought we, therefore, to have our hearts in heaven?

A. Yes: seek those things which are above, where Christ sitteth on the right hand of God. Col. iii. 1.

§ VIII.

1. *Q.* Will Christ come again?

A. Yes: if I go to prepare a place for you, I will come again. John xiv. 3.

2. *Q.* Are you sure he will come again?

A. Yes: for he said, surely, I come quickly. Rev. xxii. 20.

3. *Q.* Will he come in glory?

A. Yes: he shall come, in the clouds of heaven, with power and great glory. Matt. xxiv. 30.

4. *Q.* Will his angels attend him?

A. Yes: he shall come in his glory, and all the holy angels with him. Matt. xxv. 31.

5. *Q.* Will he come publicly?

A. Yes: behold he cometh, in the clouds, and every eye shall see him. Rev. i. 7.

§ IX.

1. *Q.* Will Christ come to judge the world?

A. Yes: God hath appointed a day in which he will judge the world in righteousness, by that man whom he hath ordained. Acts xvii. 31.

2. *Q.* Will he come to the terror of all his enemies?

A. Yes: They also which pierced him shall wail because of him. Rev. i. 7.

3. *Q.* Will he come to the comfort of all his faithful followers?

A. Yes: to them that look for him, he will appear the second time, unto salvation. Heb. ix. 28.

4. *Q.* Will this be at the last day?

A. Yes: I will raise him up, at the last day. John vi. 39.

5. *Q.* Ought we to wait for that day?

A. Yes: looking for the blessed hope, and the glorious appearance of the great God, and our Saviour Jesus Christ. Tit. ii. 13.

XXIX. *Q.* How are we made partakers of the redemption purchased by Christ?

A. We are made partakers of the redemption purchased by Christ, by the effectual application of it to us by his Holy Spirit.

§ I.

1. *Q.* Is redemption purchased by Christ?
A. Yes: he obtained eternal redemption for us. Heb. ix. 12.
2. *Q.* Is he, then, the author of it?
A. Yes: he became the author of salvation. Heb. v. 9.
3. *Q.* Is it redemption by price?
A. Yes: ye are bought with a price. 1 Cor. vi. 20.
4. *Q.* Is it a redemption by power?
A. Yes: for he hath led captivity captive. Ps. lxviii. 18.
5. *Q.* Is this redemption offered to all?
A. Yes: he hath proclaimed liberty to the captives. Isa. lxi. 1.
6. *Q.* May all that will take the benefit of it?
A. Yes: ho, every one that thirsteth, come ye to the waters. Isa. lv. 1.
7. *Q.* Have all the world, therefore, some benefit by it?
A. Yes: go into all the world, and preach the gospel to every creature. Mark xvi. 15.
8. *Q.* But have all the world a like benefit by it?
A. No: thou wilt manifest thyself to us, and not unto the world. John xiv. 22.

§ II.

1. *Q.* Is it enough for us, that there is a redemption purchased?
A. No: for there are those who deny the Lord who bought them. 2 Pet. ii. 1.
2. *Q.* Is it enough to hear of it?
A. No: for to some it is a savour of death unto death. 2 Cor. ii. 16.
3. *Q.* Is it enough to have a name among the redeemed?
A. No: thou hast a name that thou livest and art dead. Rev. iii. 1.

4. *Q.* Is it necessary, therefore, that we be partakers of the redemption?

A. Yes: that we may say, who loved me, and gave himself for me. Gal. ii. 20.

5. *Q.* Do all partake of it?

A. No: thou has neither part nor lot in this matter. Acts. viii. 21.

6. *Q.* Do all believers partake of it?

A. Yes: we are made partakers of Christ. Heb. iii. 14.

7. *Q.* Do they receive the Redeemer?

A. Yes: we have received Christ Jesus the Lord. Col. ii. 6.

8. *Q.* Do any receive this of themselves?

A. No: a man can receive nothing except it be given him from above. John iii. 27.

§ III.

1. *Q.* Must the redemption be applied to us?

A. Yes: it is Christ in you, the hope of glory. Col. i. 27.

2. *Q.* Is it the Spirit's work, to apply it?

A. Yes: for it is the Spirit that quickens. John vi. 63.

3. *Q.* Is he sent for that purpose?

A. Yes: he shall take of mine and shall shew it unto you. John xvi. 15.

4. *Q.* Is he sent, in Christ's name?

A. Yes: he is the Comforter, which is the Holy Ghost, whom the Father will send, in my name. John xiv. 26.

5. *Q.* Have we as much need of the Spirit, to apply the redemption to us, as of the Son, to purchase it for us?

A. Yes: for when Christ had purchased it, it was expedient for us he should go away, that he might send the Comforter. John xvi. 7.

§ IV.

1. *Q.* Is the Spirit given to the church, in general?

A. Yes: another Comforter shall abide with you forever. John xiv. 16.

2. *Q.* Is he promised to particular persons?

A. Yes: turn ye at my reproof; behold, I will pour out my Spirit unto you. Prov. i. 23.

3. *Q.* Are we to pray for the Spirit, then?

A. Yes: our heavenly Father will give the Holy Spirit to them that ask him. Luke xi. 13.

4. *Q.* Do all believers receive of the Spirit?

A. Yes: God hath sent forth the Spirit of his Son into your hearts. Gal. iv. 6.

5. *Q.* Is he their teacher?
A. Yes: he shall teach them all things. John xiv. 26.
6. *Q.* Is he their remembrancer?
A. Yes: he shall bring all things to their remembrance. John xiv. 26.
7. *Q.* Is he the earnest?
A. Yes: he has given the earnest of the Spirit in our hearts. 2 Cor. i. 22.
8. *Q.* Does he begin the good work of grace in the heart?
A. Yes: for when he is come, he shall convince. John xvi. 8.
9. *Q.* And does he perfect it?
A. Yes: for he hath wrought us for the self-same thing. 2 Cor. v. 5.

XXX. *Q.* How doth the Spirit apply to us the redemption purchased by Christ?

A. The Spirit applieth to us the redemption purchased by Christ, by working faith in us, and thereby uniting us to Christ, in our effectual calling.

§ I.

1. *Q.* Does the Spirit act freely in applying the redemption?
A. Yes: the wind bloweth where it listeth: so is every one that is born of the Spirit. John iii. 8.
2. *Q.* Does he act mysteriously?
A. Yes: thou knowest not what is the way of the Spirit. Eccl. xi. 5.
3. *Q.* Does he act effectually?
A. Yes: all that the Father giveth me shall come to me. John vi. 37.

§ II.

1. *Q.* Is faith necessary to our interest in the redemption?
A. Yes: for without faith, it is impossible to please God. Heb. xi. 6.
2. *Q.* Is it the great thing necessary?
A. Yes: only believe: all things are possible to him that can believe. Mark v. 36, and ix. 23.
3. *Q.* Can we have a saving interest in the redemption, without faith?
A. No: he that believeth not, is condemned already. John iii. 18.

4. *Q.* Is it that which is required on our part?
A. Yes: by grace ye are saved through faith. Ephes. ii. 8.
5. *Q.* And is it of ourselves?
A. No: not of ourselves, it is the gift of God. Ephes. ii. 8.
6. *Q.* Is it given for Christ's sake?
A. Yes: unto you it is given, on the behalf of Christ, to believe on him. Phil. i. 29.

§ III.

1. *Q.* Does the Spirit work faith in us?
A. Yes: it is the faith of the operation of God. Col. ii. 12.
2. *Q.* Is it a divine work then?
A. Yes: this is the work of God, that ye believe. John vi. 29.
3. *Q.* Is it a work of divine power?
A. Yes: we believe according to the working of his mighty power, which he wrought in Christ. Ephes. i. 19, 20.
4. *Q.* Is it wrought in all the saints?
A. Yes: for they have all obtained a like precious faith. 2 Pet. i. 1.
5. *Q.* Shall it be wrought in all the chosen?
A. Yes: for it is the faith of God's elect. Tit. i. 1.

§ IV.

1. *Q.* Are all true believers united to Christ?
A. Yes: he that is joined to the Lord is one spirit. 1 Cor. vi. 17.
2. *Q.* Are they interested in his death?
A. Yes: we are crucified with Christ. Gal. ii. 20.
3. *Q.* And in his burial?
A. Yes: we are buried with him in baptism. Rom. vi. 4.
4. *Q.* And in his resurrection?
A. Yes: he has quickened us together with Christ. Ephes. ii. 5.
5. *Q.* And in his ascension?
A. Yes: he hath made us sit together in heavenly places, in Christ Jesus. Ephes. ii. 6.

§ V.

1. *Q.* Is there a real union between Christ and believers?
A. Yes: for both he that sanctifieth, and they who are sanctified, are all of one. Heb. ii. 11.
2. *Q.* Is he the head?
A. Yes: he is the head of the body, the church. Col. i. 18.
3. *Q.* Are they his members?
A. Yes: who are members of his body, of his flesh, and of his bones. Ephes. v. 30.

4. *Q.* Is he the Root?
A. Yes: for of his fulness all have received. John i. 16.
5. *Q.* Are they the branches?
A. Yes: I am the vine; ye are the branches. John xv. 5.
6. *Q.* Is he the Foundation?
A. Yes: behold I lay in Zion for a foundation a stone, a tried stone. Isa. xxviii. 16.
7. *Q.* Are they built upon him?
A. Yes: ye also as lively stones, are built up a spiritual house. 1 Pet. ii. 5.

§ VI.

1. *Q.* Is there a relative union between Christ and believers?
A. Yes: I ascend to my Father and your Father. John xx. 17.
2. *Q.* Are they his children?
A. Yes: here am I and the children which thou hast given me. Heb. ii. 13.
3. *Q.* Are they his brethren?
A. Yes: he is not ashamed to call them brethren, Heb. ii. 11.
4. *Q.* Are they his spouse?
A. Yes: I have espoused you to one husband. 2 Cor. xi. 2.
5. *Q.* Are they his subjects?
A. Yes: they are translated into the kingdom of his dear Son. Col. i. 13.
6. *Q.* Are they his soldiers?
A. Yes: good soldiers of Jesus Christ. 2 Tim. ii. 3.
7. *Q.* Are they his servants?
A. Yes: ye call me Master and Lord. John xiii. 13.
8. *Q.* Are they his scholars?
A. Yes: they sit at Jesus' feet and hear his word. Luke x. 39.
9. *Q.* Are they his sheep?
A. Yes: for he is the great Shepherd of the sheep. Heb. xiii. 20.

§ VII.

1. *Q.* Is it by faith that we are united to Christ?
A. Yes: for Christ dwells in the heart by faith. Ephes. iii. 17.
2. *Q.* Is that owing to the Spirit?
A. Yes: we are a habitation of God through the Spirit. Ephes. ii. 22.
3. *Q.* Does communion result from this union?
A. Yes: for truly our fellowship is with the Father, and with his Son Jesus Christ. 1 John i. 3.
4. *Q.* And is that owing to the Spirit?

A. Yes: we have an access by one Spirit, unto the Father. Ephes. ii. 18.

5. *Q.* Can we be united to Christ, without the indwelling of the Spirit?

A. No: for if any man have not the Spirit of Christ, he is none of his. Rom. viii. 9.

6. *Q.* Have all that are united to Christ an interest in the benefits of redemption?

A. Yes: for of him are we in Christ Jesus, who of God is made unto us, wisdom, righteousness, sanctification, and redemption. 1 Cor. i 30.

§ VIII.

1. *Q.* Are we united to Christ in our effectual calling?

A. Yes: for we are called into the fellowship of his Son, Jesus Christ, our Lord. 1 Cor. i. 9.

2. *Q.* Will the common call unite us to Christ?

A. No: for many are called but few chosen. Matt. xxii. 14.

3. *Q.* Is it the effectual call then, that does it?

A. Yes: for whom he called, them he justified. Rom. viii. 30.

§ IX.

1. *Q.* Does the gospel call us from sin to God?

A. Yes: it turns from the power of satan unto God. Acts xxvi. 18.

2. *Q.* Does it call us from self to Christ?

A. Yes: if any man will be my disciple, let him deny himself and follow me. Matt. xvi. 24.

3. *Q.* Does it call us from darkness to light?

A. Yes: he hath called us, out of darkness unto his marvellous light. 1 Pet. ii. 9.

4. *Q.* And from uncleanness to holiness?

A. Yes: God hath not called us to uncleanness, but to holiness. 1 Thess. iv. 7.

5. *Q.* And from this world to another and better?*

A. Yes: if ye be risen with Christ, seek those things that are above. Col. iii. 1.

6. *Q.* Is this call effectual, when we come at the call?

A. Yes: follow me; and he arose, and followed him. Matt. ix. 9.

7. *Q.* Is it our great concern to make this sure?

A. Yes: make your calling and your election sure. 2 Pet. i. 10.

---

* In the original work, it is, "to the other?"—ED.

XXXI. *Q.* What is effectual calling?

A. Effectual calling is the work of God's Spirit, whereby, convincing us of our sin and misery, enlightening our minds in the knowledge of Christ, and renewing our wills, he doth persuade and enable us to embrace Jesus Christ, freely offered to us in the gospel.

§ I.

1. *Q.* Is the common call given to the world?
A. Yes: he sent forth his servants, to call them that were bidden. Matt. xxii. 3.
2. *Q.* Can ministers make that call effectual?
A. No: for who hath believed our report? Isa. liii. 1.
3. *Q.* Is it the work of God, to make it effectual?
A. Yes: for it is God that giveth the increase. 1 Cor. iii. 7.
4. *Q.* Does he do it, in a way, suitable to our nature?
A. Yes: I drew them with the cords of a man. Hos. xi. 4.
5. *Q.* Is it necessary to our salvation, that the call should be effectual?
A. Yes: who hath saved us and called us, with a holy calling. 2 Tim. i. 9.

§ II.

1. *Q.* Are all who are effectually called, convinced of sin?
A. Yes: I was alive without the law once; but, when the commandment came, sin revived. Rom. vii. 9.
2. *Q.* Is it the Spirit's work to convince?
A. Yes: when he is come, he will convince the world of sin. John xvi. 8.
3. *Q.* Is the word the ordinary means of conviction?
A. Yes: for by the law is the knowledge of sin. Rom. iii. 20.
4. *Q.* Is it necessary we should be convinced of sin?
A. Yes: for they that are whole need not a physician. Matt. ix. 12.
5. *Q.* Must we be convinced of the fact of sin.
A. Yes: these things, thou hast done. Ps. l. 21.
6. *Q.* And of the fault of sin?
A. Yes: know, therefore, and see, that it is an evil thing. Jer. ii. 19.
7. *Q.* And of the folly of sin?
A. Yes: Herein thou hast done foolishly. 2 Chron. xvi. 9.
8. *Q.* And of the filth of sin?

A. Yes: for how canst thou say I am not polluted. Jer. ii. 23.

9. *Q.* And of the fruit of sin?

A. Yes: your sins have separated between you and your God. Isa. lix. 2.

10. *Q.* And of the fountain of sin?

A. Yes: they shall know, every man, the plague of his own heart. 1 Kings viii. 38.

§ III.

1. *Q.* Must we also be convinced of our misery?

A. Yes: thou art wretched and miserable. Rev. iii. 17.

2. *Q.* And of our danger?

A. Yes: flee from the wrath to come. Matt. iii. 7.

3. *Q.* Must we be convinced of our helplessness in ourselves?

A. Yes: when sin revived, I died. Rom. vii. 9.

4. *Q.* And of the possibility of our being helped by the grace of God?

A. Yes: how many hired servants of my Father, have bread enough, and to spare? Luke xv. 17.

5. *Q.* Will these convictions put us in pain?

A. Yes: when they heard this they were pricked to the heart. ii. 37.

6. *Q.* And bring us to be at a loss within ourselves?

A. Yes: men and brethren, what shall we do? Acts ii. 37.

7. *Q.* And put us upon inquiry?

A. Yes: they shall ask the way to Sion, with their faces thitherward. Jer. l. 5.

8. *Q.* Are these convictions necessary, to prepare us for an invitation to Christ?

A. Yes: come unto me, all ye that labor, and are heavy laden. Matt. xi. 28.

§ IV.

1. *Q.* Does the Spirit, when he has convinced us of sin and misery, leave us so?

A. No: for he has torn, and he will heal us. Hos. vi. 1.

2. *Q.* When he has shewed us our wound, does he shew us our remedy?

A. Yes: O, Israel, thou hast destroyed thyself, but in me is thy help. Hos. xiii. 9.

3. *Q.* Does he enlighten our minds?

A. Yes: the Spirit of wisdom and revelation is given, that the eyes of our understanding may be enlightened. Ephes. i. 17, 18.

4. *Q.* Does he enlighten them, with the knowledge of Christ?
A. Yes: he gives the light of the knowledge of the glory of God in the face of Jesus Christ. 2 Cor. iv. 6.

5. *Q.* Does he discover, to the soul, Christ's ability to save?
A. Yes: I have laid help upon one that is mighty. Psalm lxxxix. 19.

6. *Q.* And his willingness to save?
A. Yes: I will, be thou clean. Matt. viii. 3.

7. *Q.* Should we be most ambitious of the knowledge of Christ?
A. Yes: counting all things but loss for the excellency of the knowledge of Christ Jesus our Lord. Philipp. iii. 8.

8. *Q.* Does the Spirit direct convinced sinners to Christ?
A. Yes: turn ye to the strong hold. ye prisoners of hope. Zech. ix. 12.

§ V.

1. *Q.* Is it enough to have the mind enlightened?
A. No: for we are called into a professed subjection to the gospel of Christ. 2 Cor. ix. 13.

2. *Q.* Must the will, therefore, be renewed?
A. Yes: For it is God that worketh in us, both to will and to do, of his own good pleasure. Philipp. ii. 13.

3. *Q.* Is it the work of the Spirit, to incline the will to do that which is good?
A. Yes: incline my heart unto thy testimonies. Ps. cxix. 36.

4. *Q.* And is that the renewing of the will?
A. Yes: a new heart, will I give you, and a new spirit will I put within you. Ezek. xxxvi. 26.

5. *Q.* Does that make the will pliable?
A. Yes: I will take the stony heart out of their flesh and I will give them an heart of flesh. Ezek. xi. 19.

6. *Q.* Does it bring it into subjection to the will of God?
A. Yes: Lord, what wilt thou have me to do? Acts ix. 6.

7. *Q.* And is that a cheerful subjection?
A. Yes: because the love of God is shed abroad in our hearts, by the Holy Ghost. Rom. v. 5.

§ VI.

1. *Q.* Is Christ offered to us in the gospel?
A. Yes: behold, I stand at the door, and knock. Rev. iii. 20.

2. *Q.* Is he freely offered?
A. Yes: Come, buy, without money, and without price. Isa. lv. 1.

3. *Q.* Are we concerned to embrace that offer?

A. Yes: come, eat of my bread, and drink of my wine that I have mingled. Prov. ix. 5.

4. *Q.* Are we, by nature, averse to it?

A. Yes: ye will not come to me, that ye might have life. John v. 40.

5. *Q.* Do sinners perish, then, through their own wilfulness?

A. Yes: I have called, and ye have refused. Prov. i. 24.

6. *Q.* Does the Spirit, in effectual calling, overcome this aversion?

A. Yes: with loving kindness have I drawn thee. Jer. xxxi. 3.

7. *Q.* Does he persuade us to embrace this offer?

A. Yes: for every man that hath heard, and learned of the the Father, cometh unto me. John vi, 45.

8. *Q.* Does he enable us?

A. Yes: for you hath he quickened, who were dead in trespasses and sins. Ephes. ii. 1.

§ VII.

1. *Q.* Can we turn to God, by any power of our own?

A. No: for we are not sufficient, of ourselves. 2 Cor. iii. 5.

2. *Q.* Is it the grace of God, that turns us to him?

A. Yes: turn thou me, and I shall be turned. Jer. xxxi. 18.

3. *Q.* Is it free grace?

A. Yes: he went on frowardly in the way of his heart; I have seen his ways, and will heal him. Isa. lvii. 17, 18.

4. *Q.* Does it turn us, by a work upon the will?

A. Yes: the Lord opened the heart of Lydia. Acts xvi. 14.

5. *Q.* Is it special grace?

A. Yes: it is not of him that willeth, nor of him that runneth, but of God, that sheweth mercy. Rom. ix. 16.

6. *Q.* Shall this grace be given to all the elect?

A. Yes: all that the Father hath given me, shall come unto me. John vi. 37.

7. *Q.* Shall it be effectual?

A. Yes: his grace, which was bestowed upon me, was not in vain. 1 Cor. xv. 10.

8. *Q.* May we, in faith, pray for this grace?

A. Yes: I will, for this, be inquired of, by the house of Israel. Ezek. xxxvi. 37.

9. *Q.* Can any turn to God without this special grace?

A. No: for no man can come to me, except the Father, which hath sent me, draw him. John vi. 44.

10. *Q.* Must that grace, therefore have all the glory?

A. Yes: we must shew forth the praises of him that hath called us. 1 Pet. ii. 9.

XXXII. *Q.* What benefits, do they that are effectually called, partake of in this life?

A. They that are effectually called, do, in this life, partake of justification, adoption, and sanctification, and the several benefits, which, in this life, do either accompany or flow from them.

§ I.

1. *Q.* Are all those happy which are effectually called?
A. Yes: for God hath called us to his kingdom and glory. 1 Thess. ii. 12.

2. *Q.* Are they partakers of the blessings of the new covenant?
A. Yes: for the promise is sure to all the seed. Rom. iv. 16.

3. *Q.* Are they happy, even in this life?
A. Yes: for after that ye believed, ye were sealed with that Holy Spirit of promise. Ephes. i. 13.

§ II.

1. *Q.* Are they dignified, and preferred?
A. Yes: ye are a chosen generation, a royal priesthood. 1 Pet. ii. 9.

2. *Q.* Are they brought near?
A. Yes: ye who, sometimes, were afar off, are made nigh. Ephes. ii. 13.

3. *Q.* Are they enriched?
A. Yes: God hath called the poor in this world rich in faith. James ii. 5.

4. *Q.* Are they taken into the communion of saints?
A. Yes: for we are come to the church of the first born which are written in heaven. Heb. xii. 23.

5. *Q.* And into communion with the holy angels?
A. Yes: for we are come to an innumerable company of angels. Heb. xii. 22.

6. *Q.* Are they entitled to the best possessions?
A. Yes: all things are yours, whether Paul, or Apollos, or Cephas, or the world, or life, or death, or things present, or things to come, all are yours. 1 Cor. iii. 21, 22.

7. *Q.* Are they happy in the best blessings?
A. Yes: the God and father of our Lord Jesus, hath blessed us, with spiritual blessings, in heavenly things. Ephes. i. 3.

§ III.

8. Q. Are they happy, both for soul and body?
A. Yes: He hath given us all things that pertain to life and godliness. 2 Pet. i. 3.

1. Q. Are they justified?
A. Yes: Whom he called, them he also justified. Rom. viii. 30.

2. Q. Is that an unspeakable benefit?
A. Yes: blessed is the man, whose iniquity is forgiven. Ps. xxxii. 1.

3. Q. Are they adopted?
A. Yes: for he hath predestinated us to the adoption of children. Ephes. i. 5.

4. Q. And is that an unspeakable benefit?
A. Yes: for, if children, then heirs. Rom. viii. 17.

5. Q. Are they sanctified?
A. Yes: they are sanctified in Christ Jesus. 1 Cor. i. 2.

6. Q. And is that an unspeakable benefit?
A. Yes: for we are partakers of his holiness. Heb. xii. 10.

§ IV.

1. 1. Q. Do they partake of other benefits?
A. Yes: the Lord will give grace and glory, and no good thing will be withheld from them that walk uprightly. Ps. lxxxiv. 11.

2. Q. Are all these benefits given to them that are effectually called?
A. Yes: for the promise of the remission of sins, and the gift of the Holy Ghost, is to as many as the Lord our God shall call. Acts ii. 39.

3. Q. And shall every thing turn to their advantage?
A. Yes: all things work together for good to them that are the called. Rom. viii. 28.

4. Q. Will you, therefore, make it sure, that you are effectually called, by coming at the call?
A. Yes: behold we come unto thee, for thou art the Lord our God. Jer. iii. 22.

XXXIII. Q. What is justification?
A. Justification is an act of God's free grace, wherein he pardoneth all our sins, and accepteth us as righteous in his sight, only for the righteousness of Christ imputed to us, and received by faith alone.

§ I.

1. *Q.* Have we all need to be justified?
A. Yes: for we are all guilty before God. Rom. iii. 19.
2. *Q.* Is it enough, if we justify ourselves?
A. No: if I justify myself, my own mouth shall condemn me. Job ix. 20.
3. *Q.* Is it enough, if our neighbours justify us?
A. No: for that which is highly esteemed among men, is abomination in the sight of God. Luke xvi. 15.
4. *Q.* Must it be God's act, then?
A. Yes: it is God that justifieth. Rom. viii. 33.
5. *Q.* And his only?
A. Yes: for, none can forgive sins, but God only. Mark ii. 7.
6. *Q.* And is it an act of free grace?
A. Yes: we are justified freely, by his grace. Rom. iii. 24.

§ II.

1. *Q.* Are all that are justified discharged from the sentence of the law?
A. Yes: for there is no condemnation to them that are in Christ Jesus. Rom. viii. 1.
2. *Q.* Have they their sins pardoned?
A. Yes: we have redemption, through his blood, the forgiveness of sins. Ephes. i. 7.
3. *Q.* Does God forgive them?
A. Yes: I, even I, am he that blotteth out thy transgressions. Isa. xliii. 25.

§ III.

1. *Q.* When God forgives sin, does he forgive all?
A. Yes: having forgiven all your trespasses. Col. ii. 13.
2. *Q.* Does he forgive even great sins?
A. Yes: though your sins be as scarlet, they shall be white as snow. Isa. i. 18.
3. *Q.* Does he forgive many sins?
A. Yes: He will abundantly pardon. Isa. lv. 7.
4. *Q.* Does he forgive freely?
A. Yes: I will be merciful to their unrighteousness. Heb. viii. 12.
5. *Q.* Does he forgive fully?
A. Yes: their sins, and their iniquities will I remember no more. Heb. viii. 12.
6. *Q.* Is he forward to forgive?
A. Yes: I said I will confess, and thou forgavest. Ps. xxxii. 5.

7. *Q.* Does he forgive and forget?

A. Yes: thou wilt cast all their sins into the depths of the sea. Mic. vii. 19.

§ IV.

1. *Q.* Is forgiveness of sins offered to all, upon gospel terms?

A. Yes: for repentance and remission of sins is preached to all nations. Luke xxiv. 47.

2. *Q.* Is it secured, to all the chosen remnant?

A. Yes: for Christ is exalted, to be a Prince, and a Saviour, to give repentance and remission of sins. Acts v. 31.

3. *Q.* Have all believers their sins pardoned?

A. Yes: through him, all that believe are justified. Acts xiii. 39.

4. *Q.* Are they accepted, in God's sight?

A. Yes: He hath made us accepted in the beloved. Ephes. i. 6.

5. *Q.* Are they accepted, as righteous?

A. Yes: for we are made the righteousness of God in him. 2 Cor. v. 21.

6. *Q.* May those that have been ungodly be thus justified?

A. Yes: He justifies the ungodly. Rom. iv. 5.

§ V.

1. *Q.* Can we be justified by the covenant of innocency?

A. No: for who can say, I have made my heart clean? Prov. xx. 9.

2. *Q.* Can we be justified by any thing in ourselves?

A. No: how can man be justified with God? Job xxv. 4.

3. *Q.* If we know no ill by ourselves, will that justify us?

A. No: though I know nothing by myself, yet am I not thereby justified. 1 Cor. iv. 4.

4. *Q.* Will the law of Moses justify us?

A. No: we are justified from all things from which we could not be justified by the law of Moses. Acts xiii. 39.

5. *Q.* Will our own works justify us?

A. No: by the deeds of the law shall no flesh be justified. Rom. iii. 20.

6. *Q.* Would the ceremonial sacrifices justify men?

A. No: they could not make the comers thereunto perfect. Heb. x. 1.

7. *Q.* Are we justified for the righteousness of Christ?

A. Yes: by the obedience of one shall many be made righteous. Rom. v. 19.

8. *Q.* And for that only?

A. Yes: not having my own righteousness which is of the law, but that which is through the faith of Christ. Philipp. iii. 9.

§ VI.

1. *Q.* Is the righteousness of Christ imputed to us for our justification?

A. Yes: for he is made of God unto us, righteousness. 1 Cor. i. 30.

2. *Q.* Did Christ die, that it might be imputed?

A. Yes: He shall justify many; for he shall bear their iniquities. Isa. liii. 11.

3. *Q.* Do we owe our justification, then, to the death of Christ?

A. Yes: the blood of Christ, his Son, cleanseth us from all sin. 1 John i. 7.

4. *Q.* And does that lay the foundation of our salvation?

A. Yes: being justified by his blood, we shall be saved from wrath. Rom. v. 9.

5. *Q.* Were we justified from eternity?

A. No: for, in due time, Christ died for the ungodly. Rom. v. 6.

6. *Q.* If Christ had died, and not risen again, could he have justified us?

A. No: for he was delivered for our offences, and raised again for our justification. Rom. iv. 25.

7. *Q.* Is that, then, our plea, for peace and pardon?

A. Yes: for who, then, is he that shall condemn? Rom. viii. 34.

8. *Q.* May we, then, depend upon Christ for righteousness?

A. Yes: in the Lord, I have righteousness and strength. Isa. xlv. 24.

9. *Q.* Is it become an act of justice in God, to pardon sin, upon the account of Christ's righteousness?

A. Yes: for he is just, and the justifier of him that believeth in Jesus. Rom. iii. 26; and 1 John i. 9.

§ VII.

1. *Q.* Are we to receive the righteousness of Christ?

A. Yes: We have now received the atonement. Rom. v. 11.

2. *Q.* Do we receive it, by faith?

A. Yes: through his name, whosoever believeth in him shall receive remission of sins. Acts x. 43.

3. *Q.* And by faith only?

A. Yes: for, being justified by faith, we have peace with God. Rom. v. 1.

4. *Q.* Did Christ's death satisfy the law?

A. Yes: for Christ hath redeemed us from the curse of the law. Gal. iii. 13.

5. *Q.* Is that, then, our only righteousness, in the law court?

A. Yes: for we are reconciled to God, by the death of his Son. Rom. v. 10.

6. *Q.* Do we, by true faith, come up to the terms of the gospel?

A. Yes: believe in the Lord Jesus Christ, and thou shalt be saved. Acts xvi. 31.

7. *Q.* Is that, then, our righteousness, in the gospel court?

A. Yes: for to him that believeth, his faith is counted for righteousness. Rom. iv. 5.

8. *Q.* Is it, therefore, our life?

A. Yes: for the just shall live by faith. Hab. ii. 4.

9. *Q.* Is it so, as it applies Christ's righteousness?

A. Yes: this is the name whereby he shall be called, THE LORD, OUR RIGHTEOUSNESS. Jer. xxiii. 6.

§ VIII.

1. *Q.* Is justifying faith, a working faith?

A. Yes: for, by works is faith made perfect. James ii. 22.

2. *Q.* And will that faith justify us, which does not produce good works?

A. No: for, by works, a man is justified, and not by faith only. James ii. 24.

3. *Q.* Is faith, then, dead, without good works?

A. Yes: for as the body without the spirit is dead, so faith without works, is dead also. James ii. 26.

4. *Q.* And, are good works dead, without faith?

A. Yes: for, without faith, it is impossible to please God. Heb. xi. 6.

5. *Q.* Must they both act together, then?

A. Yes: for that which avails is faith, which works by love. Gal. v. 6.

6. *Q.* Do we, then, make void the law, through faith?

A. No: God forbid, yea, we establish the law. Rom. iii. 31.

7. *Q.* Is our faith our own?

A. No: it is not of ourselves, it is the gift of God. Ephes. ii. 8.

8. *Q.* Are our good works our own?

A. No: for thou also hast wrought all our works in us. Isa. xxvi. 12.

9. *Q.* Is any room left for boasting then?

A. No: it is excluded, by the law of faith. Rom. iii. 27.

10. *Q.* Must God, therefore, have all the glory?

A. Yes: for, by the grace of God, I am what I am. 1 Cor. xv. 10.

XXXIV. *Q.* What is adoption?

A. Adoption is an act of God's free grace, whereby we are received into the number, and have a right to all the privileges of the sons of God.

§ I.

1. *Q.* Are all believers God's children?
A. Yes: ye are all the children of God, by faith in Christ Jesus. Gal. iii. 26.

2. *Q.* Are they so, by nature?
A. No: we are, by nature, children of wrath. Ephes. ii. 3.

3. *Q.* Are they so, by adoption?
A. Yes: we receive the adoption of sons. Gal. iv. 5.

4. *Q.* Do they deserve to be made God's children?
A. No: how shall I put thee among the children, and give thee a pleasant land? Jer. iii. 19.

5. *Q.* Are they altogether unworthy of such a favour?
A. Yes: I am no more worthy to be called thy son. Luke xv. 19.

6. *Q.* Is it bestowed upon them, notwithstanding their unworthiness?
A. Yes: I will be a Father to you, and ye shall be my sons and daughters, saith the Lord Almighty. 2 Cor. vi. 18.

§ II.

1. *Q.* Is adoption an act of God's free grace?
A. Yes: behold what manner of love the Father hath bestowed upon us, that we should be called the sons of God! 1 John iii. 1.

2. *Q.* Are we, by it, received into the number of God's children?
A. Yes: there shall they be called the children of the living God. Rom. ix. 26.

3. *Q.* Are we received into that number, upon our believing?
A. Yes: as many as received him, to them gave he power to become the sons of God, even to them that believe on his name. John i. 12.

§ III.

1. *Q.* Have we leave to call God Father?

A. Yes: ye have received the spirit of adoption, whereby we cry, Abba, Father. Rom. viii. 15.

2. *Q.* Does he encourage us to do so?
A. Yes: thou shalt call me, My Father, and shalt not turn away from me. Jer. iii. 19.

3. *Q.* May we call him so, though we have been prodigals?
A. Yes: I will go to my Father, and will say unto him, Father. Luke xv. 18.

4. *Q.* May we look upon all good christians as brethren?
A. Yes: for all ye are brethren. Matt. xxiii. 8.

5. *Q.* And do they all make one family?
A. Yes: of whom the whole family of heaven and earth is named. Ephes. iii. 15.

§ IV.

1. *Q.* Does God give the nature of his children to all whom he receives into the number?
A. Yes: because ye are sons, God hath sent forth the Spirit of his Son into your hearts. Gal. iv. 6.

2. *Q.* Do they partake of a divine nature?
A. Yes: they are made partakers of a divine nature. 2 Pet. i. 4.

3. *Q.* Are all God's children born again, then?
A. Yes: they are born, not of the will of man, but of God. John i. 13.

4. *Q.* Is our adoption, then, to be known by our disposition?
A. Yes: for, in this, the children of God are manifest, and the children of the devil: whosoever doth not righteousness, is not of God. 1 John iii. 10.

§ V.

1. *Q.* Have all God's adopted children a right to the privileges of children?
A. Yes: they are brought into the glorious liberty of the children of God. Rom. viii. 21.

2. *Q.* Does their Father pity them?
A. Yes: like as a Father pitieth his children, so the Lord pitieth them that fear him. Ps. ciii. 13.

3. *Q.* Does he spare them?
A. Yes: as a man spares his own son that serves him. Mal. iii. 17.

4. *Q.* Does he take care of them?
A. Yes: children, have ye any meat? John xxi. 5.

5. *Q.* Does he provide for them?

A. Yes: for they that seek the Lord shall want no good thing. Ps. xxxiv. 10.

6. *Q.* Does he correct them in love?
A. Yes: for what son is he whom the Father chasteneth not? Heb. xii. 7.

7. *Q.* Does he hear their prayers?
A. Yes: your Father in Heaven will give good things to them that ask him. Matt. vii. 11.

8. *Q.* Will he give them the inheritance of sons?
A. Yes: it is your Father's good pleasure to give you the kingdom. Luke xii. 32.

9. *Q.* Will he bring them all safe to it?
A. Yes: He will gather together the children of God that are scattered abroad. John xi. 52.

10. *Q.* Will Christ present them all to the Father?
A. Yes: behold I and the children which thou hast given me! Heb. ii. 13.

§ VI.

1. *Q.* Must all God's children reverence him?
A. Yes: if I be a Father, where is my honour? Mal. i. 6.

2. *Q.* Must they obey him?
A. Yes: as obedient children. 1 Pet. i. 14.

3. *Q.* Must they imitate him?
A. Yes: be ye followers of God, as dear children. Ephes. v. 1.

4. *Q.* Must they submit to him?
A. Yes: Father, thy will be done. Matt. xxvi. 42.

XXXV. *Q.* What is sanctification?
A. Sanctification is the work of God's free grace, whereby we are renewed in the whole man after the image of God, and are enabled, more and more, to die unto sin, and live unto righteousness.

§ I.

1. *Q.* Are all that are justified sanctified?
A. Yes: for Jesus Christ is made both righteousness and sanctification. 1 Cor. i. 30.

2. *Q.* Is it necessary they should be so?
A. Yes; for, without holiness, no man shall see the Lord. Heb. xii. 14.

3. *Q.* Did Christ die, that they might be sanctified?

A. Yes: for their sakes I sanctify myself, that they also might be sanctified. John xvii. 19.

4. *Q.* And was this the intention of their election?

A. Yes: He hath chosen you to salvation, through sanctification. 2 Thess. ii. 13.

§ II.

1. *Q.* Is sanctification the work of God?
A. Yes: we are sanctified by God the Father. Jude v. 1.
2. *Q.* Is it the work of the Spirit of God?
A. Yes: it is sanctification of the Spirit. 1 Pet. i. 2.
3. *Q.* Is it a work of free grace?
A. Yes: according to his mercy, he saved us, by the washing of regeneration. Tit. iii. 5.
4. *Q.* Is it a work wrought in us?
A. Yes: for we are his workmanship, created unto good works. Ephes. ii. 10.

§ III.

1. *Q.* Is sanctification something more than being civilized?
A. Yes: for he is not a Jew, that is one outwardly. Rom. ii. 28.
2. *Q.* Is it more than being baptized?
A. Yes: it is not the putting away the filth of the flesh, but the answer of a good conscience. 1 Pet. iii. 21.
2. *Q.* Is it an inward change of the heart?
A. Yes: we must be renewed in the spirit of our mind. Ephes. iv. 23.
4. *Q.* Is it the renovation of the whole man?
A. Yes: if any man be in Christ, he is a new creature. 2 Cor. v. 17.
5. *Q.* Will it suffice to have a new name?
A. No: for thou hast a name that thou livest, and art dead. Rev. iii. 1.
6. *Q.* Will it suffice to have a new face?
A. No: for there are those that have the form of godliness, but deny the power of it. 2 Tim. iii. 5.
7. *Q.* Must there be a new heart?
A. Yes: a new heart will I give you, and a new spirit will I put within you. Ezek. xxxvi. 26.
8. *Q.* And a new nature?
A. Yes: put on the new man. Ephes. iv. 24.
9. *Q.* And a new birth?
A. Yes: except a man be born again, he cannot see the kingdom of God. John iii. 3.

§ IV.

1. Q. Must we be cleansed from sin?
A. Yes: from all your filthiness, and from all your idols, will I cleanse you. Ezek. xxxvi. 25.

2. Q. Must we be consecrated to God?
A. Yes: for we are the temple of God. 1 Cor. iii. 16.

3. Q. Must the law be written in the heart?
A. Yes: I will put my law in their heart. Heb. viii. 10.

4. Q. Must the understanding be enlightened?
A. Yes: anoint thine eyes with eye-salve, that thou mayest see. Rev. iii. 18.

5. Q. Must the heart be softened?
A. Yes: I will take away the stony heart, and give a heart of flesh. Ezek. xi. 19.

6. Q. Must the will be bowed?
A. Yes: Lord, what wilt thou have me to do. Acts ix. 6.

7. Q. Must the affections be made spiritual?
A. Yes: set your affections on things above. Col. iii. 2.

8. Q. Must the body also be an instrument of holiness?
A. Yes: present your bodies a living sacrifice. Rom. xii. 1.

§ V.

1. Q. Must we be renewed after the image of God?
A. Yes: put on the new man which is renewed after the image of him that created him. Col. iii. 10.

2. Q. And after the pattern of Christ?
A. Yes: for Christ must be formed in us. Gal. iv. 19.

3. Q. Is sin mortified, in all that are sanctified?
A. Yes: they that are Christ's have crucified the flesh. Gal. v. 24.

4. Q. Is grace planted in them?
A. Yes: there is a well of water springing up to eternal life. John iv. 14.

5. Q. Is this work perfect, at first?
A. No: it is first the blade, then the ear, after that the full corn in the ear. Mark iv. 28.

§ IV.

1. Q. Do all that are sanctified die unto sin?
A. Yes: reckon ye yourselves dead unto sin. Rom. vi. 11.

2. Q. Do they live unto righteousness?
A. Yes: being dead to sin, we live unto righteousness. 1 Pet. ii. 24.

3. Q. Are they called to do so?
A. Yes: for it is through the Spirit that we mortify the deeds of the body. Rom. viii. 13.

4. *Q.* And is the course of their conversation accordingly?
A. Yes: they walk not after the flesh, but after the Spirit. Rom. viii. 1.

5. *Q.* Is it our duty to submit to the Spirit, as a sanctifier?
A. Yes: walk in the Spirit, and ye shall not fulfil the works of the flesh. Gal. v. 16.

6. *Q.* And is the grace of God promised us for this purpose?
A. Yes: sin shall not have dominion over you. Rom. vi. 14.

XXXVI. *Q.* What are the benefits which, in this life, do accompany or flow from justification, adoption, and sanctification?

A. The benefits which, in this life do accompany or flow from justification, adoption, and sanctification, are assurance of God's love, peace of conscience, joy in the Holy Ghost, increase of grace, and perseverance therein to the end.

§ I.

1. *Q.* Are they that are justified happy in this life?
A. Yes: for being justified by faith, we have peace with God. Rom. v. 1.

2. *Q.* And are they so that are adopted?
A. Yes: beloved now are we the sons of God. 1 John iii. 2.

3. *Q.* And are they so that are sanctified.
A. Yes: for to the pure, all things are pure. Tit. i. 15.

§ II.

1. *Q.* May they have an assurance of God's love.
A. Yes: ye know that ye have eternal life. 1 John v. 13.

2. *Q.* Is the Spirit the author of that assurance?
A. Yes: the Spirit itself bears witness with our spirits, that we are the children of God. Rom. viii. 16.

3. *Q.* Is it wrought by evidences?
A. Yes: hereby we know that we know him, if we keep his commandments. 1 John ii. 3.

4. *Q.* Do all believers attain this assurance?
A. No: some walk in darkness, and have no light. Isa. l. 10.

5. *Q.* But, should they labour after it?
A. Yes: shew the same diligence unto the full assurance of hope unto the end. Heb. vi. 11.

6. *Q.* And is it an unspeakable comfort?

A. Yes: for the love of God is shed abroad in our hearts, through the Holy Ghost. Rom. v. 5.

7. *Q.* And is it just cause for triumph?

A. Yes: I know whom I have believed. 2 Tim. i. 12.

§ III.

1. *Q.* Is peace of conscience a precious privilege?

A. Yes: for, if our hearts condemn us not, then have we confidence towards God. 1 John iii. 21.

2. *Q.* Is it the fruit of grace?

A. Yes: for the work of righteousness shall be peace, and the effect of righteousness quietness and assurance forever. Isa. xxxii. 17.

3. *Q.* Has Christ left it, as a legacy to his disciples?

A. Yes: peace I leave with you, My peace I give unto you. John xiv. 27.

4. *Q.* Can those who are unjustified have this peace?

A. No: there is no peace, saith my God, to the wicked. Isa. lvii. 21.

5. *Q.* Should those that are justified labour after it?

A. Yes: return to thy rest, O my soul. Ps. cxvi. 7.

6. *Q.* Should this peace govern us?

A. Yes: let the peace of God rule in your hearts. Col. iii. 15.

7. *Q.* And will it preserve us?

A. Yes: the peace of God shall keep your hearts and minds. Philipp. iv. 7.

8. *Q.* And will it be our comfort in the day of evil?

A. Yes: our rejoicing is this, the testimony of our conscience. 2 Cor. i. 12.

9. *Q.* Is it, therefore, our interest to secure it?

A. Yes: herein do I exercise myself, to have always a conscience void of offence. Acts xxiv. 16.

§ IV.

1. *Q.* May those who are justified have joy in the Holy Ghost?

A. Yes: for, believing, we rejoice, with joy unspeakable, and full of glory. 1 Pet. i. 8.

2. *Q.* Have they cause for joy?

A. Yes: for, gladness is sown for the upright in heart. Ps. xcvii. 11.

3. *Q.* Is it their duty to rejoice?

A. Yes: rejoice in the Lord always, and again I say rejoice. Phillipp. iv. 4.

4. *Q.* Is it their interest to rejoice?

A. Yes: for the joy of the Lord is their strength. Neh. viii. 10.

5. *Q.* May they rejoice, in all conditions?
A. Yes: for we glory in tribulations also. Rom. v. 3.

6. *Q.* And is this a superlative joy?
A. Yes: it is gladness in the heart more than in the time that their corn and wine increased. Ps. iv. 7.

§ v.

1. *Q.* Is grace growing?
A. Yes: he that hath clean hands shall be stronger and stronger. Job. xvii. 9.

2. *Q.* Is it so, in its nature?
A. Yes: for it is as the shining light, which shines more and more unto the perfect day. Prov. iv. 18.

3. *Q.* Is it our duty to grow in grace?
A. Yes: grow in grace, and in the knowledge of our Lord and Saviour Jesus Christ. 2 Pet. iii. 18.

4. *Q.* And may we rest in what we have attained?
A. No: but press forward towards the mark. Philipp. iii. 14.

5. *Q.* Is it promised to all believers that they shall grow?
A. Yes: for to him that hath shall be given. Matt. xxv. 29.

6. *Q.* Will the grace of God make them grow?
A. Yes: I will be as the dew unto Israel. He shall grow as the lily. Hos. xiv. 5.

§ vi.

1. *Q.* Shall true believers persevere to the end?
A. Yes: for He that hath begun a good work will perform it. Philipp. i. 6.

2. *Q.* Will hypocrites persevere?
A. No: these have no root, which for a while believe, and in time of temptation fall away. Luke viii. 13.

3. *Q.* Does it appear, by their apostacy, that they never were sincere?
A. Yes: they went out from us because they were not of us; for if they had been of us, they would, no doubt, have continued with us. 1 John ii. 19.

4. *Q.* But shall any that are justified finally fall away?
A. No: for, whom he justified, them he glorified. Rom. viii. 30.

5. *Q.* Is every fall a falling away?
A. No: for though he falls, he shall not be utterly cast down. Ps. xxxvii. 24.

6. *Q.* May the appearances of grace be lost?

A. Yes: from him shall be taken away, even that which he seemed to have. Luke viii. 18.

7. *Q.* But, can true grace be finally lost?
A. No: it is that good part which shall never be taken away. Luke x. 42.

8. *Q.* Will God recal his gifts?
A. No: the gifts and callings of God, are without repentance. Rom. xi. 29.

9. *Q.* Will he secure them?
A. Yes: we are kept by the power of God, through faith, unto salvation. 1 Pet. i. 5; and v. 7.

10. *Q.* Is the perseverance of the saints secured by the divine power?
A. Yes: no man is able to pluck them out of my Father's hands. John x. 29.

11. *Q.* And by the divine providence?
A. Yes: for he will not suffer you to be tempted above that ye are able. 1 Cor. x. 13.

12. *Q.* And by the divine grace?
A. Yes: I will put my fear in their hearts, that they shall not depart from me. Jer. xxxii. 40.

13. *Q.* And by the intercession of Christ?
A. Yes: I have prayed for thee, that thy faith fail not. Luke xxii. 32.

14. *Q.* And by the indwelling of the Spirit?
A. Yes: the anointing which you have received, abideth in you. 1 John ii. 27.

15. *Q.* And by the stability of the promise?
A. Yes: My covenant will I not break. Ps. lxxxix. 34.

16. *Q.* May they be secure, then?
A. No: be not high-minded, but fear. Rom. xi. 20.

17. *Q.* But may they be encouraged?
A. Yes: He will preserve me, to his Heavenly kingdom. 2 Tim. iv. 18.

XXXVII. *Q.* What benefits do believers receive from Christ, at death?

A. The souls of believers are, at their death, made perfect in holiness, and do immediately pass into glory; and their bodies, being still united to Christ, do rest in their graves, till the resurrection.

§ I.

1. *Q.* Is the happiness of believers confined to this present life?

A. No: if, in this life only, we have hope in Christ, we are, of all men most miserable. 1 Cor. xv. 19.

2. *Q.* Is the best of their happiness in this life?

A. No: for, in this world, ye shall have tribulation. John xvi. 33.

3. *Q.* Must they die, as well as others?

A. Yes: it is appointed unto men once to die. Heb. ix. 27.

4. *Q.* Must the best, and most useful die?

A. Yes: the righteous perisheth, and merciful men are taken away. Isa. lvii. 1.

5. *Q.* Ought they, then, to wait for it?

A. Yes: all the days of my appointed time will I wait, till my change come. Job xiv. 14.

6. *Q.* And to prepare for it?

A. Yes: therefore, be ye also ready. Matt. xxiv. 44.

§ II.

1. *Q.* Is death loss to a good christian?

A. No: for to me to live is Christ, and to die is gain. Philipp. i. 21.

2. *Q.* Should it, therefore, be a terror?

A. No: for the righteous hath hope in his death. Prov. xiv. 32.

3. *Q.* Does God take special care of the death of his people?

Q. Yes: for, precious, in the sight of the Lord, is the death of his saints. Ps. cxvi. 15.

4. *Q.* Is death in the covenant?

A. Yes: all is yours, whether life or death. 1 Cor. iii. 22.

5. *Q.* Can it separate them from the love of God?

A. No: neither death nor life can do that. Rom. viii. 38.

§ III.

1. *Q.* Are believers perfect in holiness, in this life?

A. No: I have not yet attained, neither am already perfect. Philipp. iii. 12.

2. *Q.* Are their souls made perfect, at death?

A. Yes: the spirits of just men are made perfect. Heb. xii. 23.

3. *Q.* Are they delivered from sin?

A. Yes: he that is dead is freed from sin. Rom. vi. 7.

4. *Q.* Are they made perfect in knowledge?

A. Yes: then shall I know, even as also I am known. 1 Cor. xiii. 12.

5. *Q.* And perfect in holiness?

A. Yes: for they are come to the perfect man, to the measure of the stature of the fulness of Christ. Ephes. iv. 13.

6. *Q.* Might they pass into glory without being made perfect in holiness?

A. No: for corruption cannot inherit incorruption. 1 Cor. xv. 50.

7. *Q.* Being made perfect in holiness, are they confirmed in it?

A. Yes: he that is holy, let him be holy still. Rev. xxii. 11.

§ IV.

1. *Q.* Do the souls of believers, at death, sleep with their bodies?

A. No: for when we are absent from the body we are present with the Lord. 2 Cor. v. 8.

2. *Q.* Do they go to Christ?

A. Yes: having a desire to depart, and to be with Christ. Philipp. i. 23.

3. *Q.* And will he receive them?

A. Yes: Lord Jesus, receive my spirit. Acts vii. 59.

4. *Q.* Shall they be where he is?

A. Yes: that where I am, there ye may be also. John xiv. 3.

5. *Q.* Will they be with him in Heaven?

A. Yes: we have a house, not made with hands, eternal in the Heavens. 2 Cor. v. 1.

6. *Q.* Do they pass into this glory, at death?

A. Yes: that, when ye fail, ye may be received into everlasting habitations. Luke xvi. 9.

7. *Q.* Do they immediately pass into it?

A. Yes: this day shalt thou be with me in Paradise. Luke xxiii. 43.

8. *Q.* Are they guarded by angels thither?

A. Yes: he was carried by angels into Abraham's bosom. Luke xvi. 22.

9. *Q.* Are they happy, then, in their death?

A. Yes: blessed are the dead which die in the Lord. Rev. xiv. 13.

10. *Q.* Happier than in life?

A. Yes: the day of their death is better than the day of their birth. Eccl. vii. 1.

11. *Q.* And is their end peace?

A. Yes: mark the perfect man and behold the upright, for the end of that man is peace. Ps. xxxvii. 37.

§ V.

1. Q. Is death gain to the wicked man?
A. No: for, when a wicked man dies, his expectation shall perish. Prov. xi. 7.
2. Q. Is it, therefore, a terror to the wicked?
A. Yes: this night, thy soul shall be required of thee. Luke xii. 20.
3. Q. Do the souls of the wicked, at death, go into torment?
A. Yes: the rich man died, and was buried, and in hell he lifted up his eyes, being in torment. Luke xvi. 22, 23.
4. Q. Do they go away, under the guilt of their sins?
A. Yes: if ye believe not that I am he, ye shall die in your sins. John viii. 24.
5. Q. Is it a fearful thing to fall into the hands of the living God?
A. Yes: for our God is a consuming fire. Heb. xii. 29.
6. Q. Are the souls of believers distinguished from them?
A. Yes: but God will redeem my soul from the power of the grave. Ps. xlix. 15.

§ VI.

1. Q. Are the bodies of believers well provided for at death?
A. Yes: for the Lord is for the body. 1 Cor. vi. 13.
2. Q. May they be cheerfully committed to the grave?
A. Yes: my flesh also shall rest in hope. Ps. xvi. 9.
3. Q. Do they still remain united to Christ?
A. Yes: for they sleep in Jesus. 1 Thess. iv. 14.
4. Q. Do they rest in their graves?
A. Yes: for there the weary be at rest. Job iii. 17.
5. Q. Is the grave a good christian's bed?
A. Yes: he shall enter into peace: they shall rest in their beds. Isa. lvii. 2.
6. Q. May the saints triumph over the grave, then?
A. Yes: O, grave, where is thy victory? 1 Cor. xv. 55.
7. Q. And need they to fear any evil in it?
A. No: for the sucking child shall play upon the hole of the asp. Isa. xi. 8.
8. Q. Are all who are regenerate delivered from the second death?
A. Yes: blessed and holy is he that hath part in the first resurrection. On such, the second death shall have no power. Rev. xx. 6.

§ VII.

1. Q. Shall the dead be raised again?

A. Yes: there shall be a resurrection of the dead, both of the just and of the unjust. Acts xxiv. 15.

2. *Q.* Shall the same body be raised again?
A. Yes: though after my skin worms destroy this body, yet in my flesh shall I see God. Job xix. 26.

3. *Q.* Shall it be done by the power of Christ?
A. Yes: for as, in Adam, all die, so in Christ shall all be made alive. 1 Cor. xv. 22.

4. *Q.* Shall there be a vast difference between the godly and the wicked, at the resurrection?
A, Yes: for some shall awake to everlasting life, and some to shame and everlasting contempt. Dan. xii. 2.

5. *Q.* Has Christ himself assured us of this?
A. Yes: the hour is coming when all that are in the graves shall hear his voice, and shall come forth, they that have done good unto the resurrection of life, and they that have done evil, to the resurrection of condemnation. John v. 28, 29.

6. *Q.* Is it certain, when this shall be?
A. Yes: for he hath appointed a day. Acts xvii. 31.

7. *Q.* But, is it known to us?
A. A. No: for of that day and hour knoweth no man. Mark xiii. 32.

XXXVIII. *Q.* What benefits do believers receive from Christ, at the resurrection?

A. At the resurrection, believers being raised up in glory, shall be openly acknowledged and acquitted in the day of judgment, and made perfectly blessed in the full enjoying of God, to all eternity.

§ I.

1. *Q.* Shall the dead bodies of believers be raised?
A. Yes: for the dead shall be raised. 1 Cor. xv. 52.

2. *Q.* Is it possible, that the same body, should return to life again?
A. Yes: why should it seem a thing incredible with you that God should raise the dead? Acts xxvi. 8.

3. *Q.* Is it certain that they shall be raised?
A. Yes: for, if there be no resurrection of the dead, then is Christ not risen. 1 Cor. xv. 13.

4. *Q.* Has Christ undertaken for the resurrection of believers?
A. Yes: I am the resurrection and the life. John xi. 25.

5. *Q.* Are they in error who deny it?

A. Yes: ye do err, not knowing the scriptures, nor the power of God. Matt. xxii. 29.

§ II.

1. *Q.* Shall the believer's body be raised up in glory?

A. Yes: it is sown in dishonour, it is raised in glory. 1 Cor. xv. 43.

2. *Q.* Shall it be the glory of Christ's glorified body?

A. Yes: He shall change our vile bodies, that they may be fashioned like unto his glorious body. Philipp. iii. 21.

3. *Q.* Shall they be raised, by virtue of their union with Christ?

A. Yes: together with my dead body shall they arise. Isa. xxvi. 19.

4. *Q.* Shall they be raised to such a life as we now live?

A. No: for, in the resurrection, they neither marry nor are given in marriage. Matt. xxii. 30.

5. *Q.* Shall they be raised to an immortal life?

A. Yes: for this mortal shall put on immortality. 1 Cor. xv. 53.

6. *Q.* Shall they that are found alive be changed?

A. Yes: behold I shew you a mystery. We shall not all sleep, but we shall all be changed. 1 Cor. xv. 51.

§ III.

1. *Q.* Shall all the saints, at that day, be brought to Jesus Christ?

A. Yes: at the coming of our Lord Jesus Christ, there shall be a gathering together unto him. 2 Thess. ii. 1.

2. *Q.* Shall they be separated from the wicked?

A. Yes: as the shepherd divideth the sheep from the goats. Matt. xxv. 32.

3. *Q.* Shall all the saints be there together?

A. Yes: for he shall gather his elect from the four winds. Matt. xxiv. 31.

4. *Q.* And none but saints?

A. Yes: for he shall gather out of his kingdom, all things that offend. Matt. xiii. 41.

5. *Q.* And saints made perfect?

A. Yes: for, then, that which is perfect is come. 1 Cor. xiii. 10.

6. *Q.* Shall they attend upon Christ, at his coming?

A. Yes: behold the Lord cometh, with ten thousands of his saints. Jude 14.

7. *Q.* Shall they be assessors with him, in his judgment?
A. Yes: for the saints shall judge the world. 1 Cor. vi. 2.

§ IV.

1. *Q.* Shall they be openly acknowledged, in the day of judgment?
A. Yes: him will I confess, before my Father which is in Heaven. Matt. x. 32.

2. *Q.* Will God own them, as his own?
A. Yes: they shall be mine, saith the Lord, in that day when I make up my jewels. Mal. iii. 17.

3. *Q.* And will that be their honour?
A. Yes: if any man serve me, him will my Father honour. John xii. 26.

4. *Q.* Shall they be openly acquitted?
A. Yes: for their sins shall be blotted out, when the times of refreshing come. Acts iii. 19.

§ V.

1. *Q.* Shall the wicked be condemned, then?
A. Yes: He shall say to them on his left hand, depart from me. Matt. xxv. 41.

2. *Q.* Shall they be sent away, with a blessing?
A. No: depart, ye cursed. Matt. xxv. 41.

3. *Q.* Shall they go into a place of ease?
A. No: into fire. Matt. xxv. 41.

4. *Q.* Into ordinary fire?
A. No: into fire prepared. Matt. xxv. 41.

5. *Q.* Shall it be for a short time?
A. No: but into everlasting fire. Matt. xxv. 41.

6. *Q.* Shall they have good company?
A. No: but the devil and his angels. Matt. xxv. 41.

7. *Q.* Will the salvation of the saints aggravate their condemnation?
A. Yes: for they shall see Abraham, and Isaac, and Jacob, in the kingdom of Heaven. Luke xiii. 28.

§ VI.

1. *Q.* Shall the saints, at the day of judgment, be put in possession of eternal life?
A. Yes: the righteous into life eternal. Matt. xxv. 46.

2. *Q.* Shall they be blest?
A. Yes: come ye blessed of my Father. Matt. xxv. 34.

3. *Q.* Shall they be perfectly blessed?
A. Yes: for in thy presence is fulness of joy. Ps. xvi. 11.

4. *Q.* Shall there be any sin in Heaven?

A. No: for they are as the angels of God in Heaven. Matt. xxii. 30.

5. *Q.* Shall there be any sorrow there?
A. No: for God shall wipe away all tears from their eyes. Rev. xxi. 4.

6. *Q.* Shall there be any dying there?
A. No: there shall be no more death. Rev. xxi. 4.

§ VII.

1. *Q.* Is Heaven a place of rest?
A. Yes: there remaineth a rest for the people of God. Heb. iv. 9.

2. *Q.* Is it light?
A. Yes: it is the inheritance of the saints in light. Col. i. 12.

3. *Q.* Is it honour?
A. Yes: it is a crown of glory that fadeth not away. 1 Pet. v. 4.

4. *Q.* Is it wealth?
A. Yes: it is an inheritance incorruptible. 1 Pet. i. 4.

5. *Q.* Is it joy?
A. Yes: enter thou into the joy of thy Lord. Matt. xxv. 21.

§ VIII.

1. *Q.* Shall we, in Heaven, see God?
A. Yes: when he shall appear, we shall be like him, for we shall see him as he is. 1 John iii. 2.

2. *Q.* Shall we see him clearly?
A. Yes: now we see through a glass darkly, but then face to face. 1 Cor. xiii. 12.

3. *Q.* Shall we enjoy him?
A. Yes: God himself shall be with them, and be their God. Rev. xxi. 3.

4. *Q.* Shall we be satisfied in the vision and fruition of God?
A. Yes: I shall be satisfied, when I awake with thy likeness. Ps. xvii. 15.

5. *Q.* Shall this be everlasting?
A. Yes: so shall we ever be with the Lord. 1 Thess. iv. 17.

§ IX.

1. *Q.* Is this happiness purchased?
A. Yes: it is the purchased possession. Ephes. i. 14.

2. *Q.* Is it promised?
A. Yes: it is eternal life, which God, that cannot lie, promised. Tit. i. 2.

3. *Q.* Is it sure to all good christians?

A. Yes: even the poor in the world, if rich in faith, are heirs of the kingdom. James ii. 5.

4. *Q.* Should we not be solicitous that it may be sure with us?

A. Yes: What shall I do, that I may inherit eternal life? Luke xviii. 18.

5. *Q.* Should we not, then, have it much in our eye?

A. Yes: for we look not at the things that are seen, but the things that are not seen. 2 Cor. iv. 18.

6. *Q.* And should we not be comforted, and encouraged with the prospect of it?

A. Yes: for the sufferings of this present time are not worthy to be compared with the glory which shall be revealed. Rom. viii. 18.

XXXIX. *Q.* What is the duty which God requireth of man?

A. The duty which God requireth of man, is obedience to his revealed will.

§ I.

1. *Q.* Does God require duty of men?

A. Yes: now, O Israel, what doth the Lord thy God require of thee? Deut. x. 12.

2. *Q.* Of every man?

A. Yes: he that hath ears to hear, let him hear. Matt. xiii. 9.

3. *Q.* Has he authority to require duty?

A. Yes: if I be a master, where is my fear? Mal. i. 6.

4. *Q.* Is it fit he should rule us?

A. Yes: for we are his people, and the sheep of his pasture. Ps. c. 3.

5. *Q.* Is it fit we should obey him?

A. Yes: for the borrower is servant to the lender and the fool is servant to the wise in heart. Prov. xxii. 7; xi. 29.

6. *Q.* Ought we, therefore, to inquire what our duty is?

A. Yes: teach me, O Lord, the way of thy statutes. Ps. cxix. 33.

§ II.

1. *Q.* Has God made known his will, concerning our duty?

A. Yes: he sheweth his word unto Jacob, his statutes and his judgments unto Israel. Ps. cxlvii. 19.

2. *Q.* Are we to obey it?

A. Yes: thou shalt obey the voice of the Lord thy God, and do his commandments. Deut. xxvii. 10.

3. *Q.* Is that obedience the condition of our acceptance?
A. Yes: obey my voice, and I will be your God. Jer. vii. 23.
4. *Q.* Is obedience to God reasonable?
A. Yes: it is our reasonable service. Rom. xii. 1.
5. *Q.* Is it easy?
A. Yes: for his commandments are not grievous. 1 John v. 3.
6. *Q.* And will it be acceptable?
A. Yes: for to obey is better than sacrifice. 1 Sam. xv. 22.

§ III.

1. *Q.* Must our obedience to God be sincere?
A. Yes: fear the Lord, and serve him, in sincerity, and in truth. Josh. xxiv. 14.
2. *Q.* Must it be universal?
A. Yes: then shall I not be ashamed, when I have respect unto all thy commandments. Ps. cxix. 6.
3. *Q.* Must it be with delight?
A. Yes: I delight in the law of God, after the inward man. Rom. vii. 22.
4. *Q.* Must it be constant?
A. Yes: be thou in the fear of the Lord all the day long. Prov. xxiii. 17.
5. *Q.* Must God's commands take place of men's?
A. Yes: we ought to obey God rather than man. Acts v. 29, and iv. 19.

§ IV.

1. *Q.* Should we, therefore, labour to know the will of God?
A. Yes: understand what the will of the Lord is. Ephes. v. 17.
2. *Q.* Are we to study his secret will?
A. No: for secret things belong not to us. Deut. xxix. 29.
3. *Q.* But his revealed will?
A. Yes: for things revealed belong to us, and to our children, that we may do all the words of this law. Deut. xxix. 29.
4. *Q.* Is obedience to God's revealed will, the whole duty of man?
A. Yes: let us hear the conclusion of the whole matter: Fear God and keep his commandments, for this is the whole duty of man. Eccl. xii. 13.

XL. *Q.* What did God at first, reveal to man, for the rule of his obedience?

A. The rule which God at first revealed to man, for his obedience, was, the moral law.

§ I.

1. Q. Was the moral law revealed to man in innocency?
A. Yes: for God created man in his own image. Gen. i. 27.
2. Q. Is it written in the heart of man?
A. Yes: they shew the work of the law written in their heart. Rom. ii. 15.
3. Q. Is there, then, a law of nature?
A. Yes: doth not even nature itself teach you? 1 Cor. xi. 14.
4. Q. Is that a law of God?
A. Yes: for he openeth the ears of men, and sealeth their instruction. Job. xxxiii. 16.
5. Q. Does natural conscience enforce that law?
A. Yes: for the Gentiles, which have not the law, do, by nature, the things contained in the law. Rom. ii. 14.
6. Q. Did the Gentiles sin, by the breach of that law?
A. Yes: what they know naturally, in these things they corrupt themselves. Jude 10.
7. Q. And will they be punished for the breach of it?
A. Yes: they that have sinned without law, shall perish without law. Rom. ii. 12.

§ II.

1. Q. Has God given us the moral law, more fully?
A. Yes: I have written unto him the great things of my law. Hos. viii. 12.
2. Q. Are we under that law, as a covenant?
A. No: for a man is not justified by the works of the law. Gal. ii. 16.
3. Q. Are we under it as a rule?
A. Yes: we are under the law to Christ. 1 Cor. ix. 21.

§ III.

1. Q. Is the law of God very extensive?
A. Yes: thy commandment is exceeding broad. Ps. cxix. 96.
2. Q. And very excellent?
A. Yes: the law is holy and the commandment is holy, and just, and good. Rom. vii. 12.
3. Q. Is it admirable?
A. Yes: thy testimonies are wonderful. Ps. cxix. 129.
4. Q. Is any thing unjust in it?
A. No: I esteem all thy precepts concerning all things to be right. Ps. cxix. 128.
5. Q. Is it beyond any other law?
A. Yes: what nation is there so great, that hath statutes and judgments so righteous. Deut. iv. 8.

§ IV.

1. *Q.* Does the law of God bind the inward man?
A. Yes: for the law is spiritual. Rom. vii. 14.
2. *Q.* Does it forbid heart-sins?
A. Yes: wash thy heart from wickedness. Jer. iv. 14.
3. *Q.* Does it require heart-service?
A. Yes: my son, give me thy heart. Prov. xxiii. 26.
4. *Q.* Does the law shew us our way?
A. Yes: it is a light to our feet. Ps. cxix. 105.
5. *Q.* Does it discover sin to us?
A. Yes: by the law is the knowledge of sin. Rom. iii. 20.
6. *Q.* Does it warn us concerning sin and duty?
A. Yes: by them is thy servant warned. Ps. xix. 11.
7. *Q.* Does it shew us the need of Christ?
A. Yes: the law was our school-master, to bring us to Christ. Gal. iii. 24.
8. *Q.* And does Christ do that for us which the law could not?
A. Yes: Christ is the end of the law for righteousness. Rom. x. 4.

§ V.

1. *Q.* Ought we to love the law of God?
A. Yes: I love thy commandments above gold. Ps. cxix. 127.
2. *Q.* And to consult it, upon all occasions?
A. Yes: thy testimonies are my delight and my counsellors. Ps. cxix. 24.
3. *Q.* And to confirm it?
A. Yes: we must walk in the law of the Lord. Ps. cxix. 1

XLI. *Q.* Wherein is the moral law summarily comprehended?

A. The moral law is summarily comprehended in the ten commandments.

§ I.

1. *Q.* Was the law in force before the ten commandments were given?
A. Yes: for Abraham commanded his children to keep the way of the Lord. Gen. xviii. 19.
2. *Q.* Was it at last summed up in these commandments?
A. Yes: for the law was given by Moses. John i. 17.
3. *Q.* Was the law of the ten commandments given first to Israel?

A. Yes: he made known his ways unto Moses, his acts to the children of Israel. Ps. ciii. 7.

4. *Q.* But are they binding to us now?

A. Yes: for Christ came not to destroy the law, but to fulfil. Matt. v. 17.

§ II.

1. *Q.* Did God himself give these commandments?

A. Yes: from his right hand went a fiery law for them. Deut. xxxiii. 2.

2. *Q.* Did God himself speak to them?

A. Yes: thou camest down upon Mount Sinai, and speakest with them from Heaven. Neh. ix. 13.

3. *Q.* Did he use the ministry of angels therein?

A. Yes: they received the law by the disposition of angels. Acts vii. 53.

4. *Q.* Did God himself write them?

A. Yes: He gave unto Moses two tables of testimony, tables of stone, written with the finger of God. Exod. xxxi. 18.

§ III.

1. *Q.* Was the law given with much terror?

A. Yes: for it was given upon a mount that burned with fire, and with blackness and darkness and tempest Heb. xii. 18.

2. *Q.* Was the sight terrible to Moses himself?

A. Yes: for he said, I exceedingly fear and quake. Heb. xii. 21.

3. *Q.* Did it strike an awe upon the people?

A. Yes: for they said, all that the Lord hath said will we do, and be obedient. Exod. xxiv. 7.

4. *Q.* And should not we be awed by the consideration of it?

A. Yes: knowing the terror of the Lord, we persuade men. 2 Cor. v. 11.

5. *Q.* Did the ten commandments include the whole moral law?

A. Yes: if thou wilt enter into life, keep these commandments. Matt. xix. 17.

XLII. *Q.* What is the sum of the ten commandments?

A. The sum of the ten commandments is, to love the Lord our God with all our heart, and all our soul, with all our strength, and with all our mind; and our neighbour as ourselves.

§ I.

1. *Q.* Is all the law summed up in a word?
A. Yes: all the law is fulfilled in one word. Gal. v. 14.
2. *Q.* Is that a short and sweet word?
A. Yes: for it is love; love is the fulfilling of all the law. Rom. xiii. 10.

§ II.

1. *Q.* Is it our duty to love God?
A. Yes: take good heed to yourselves, that ye love the Lord your God. Josh. xxiii. 11.
2. *Q.* Must we love him, with a sincere love?
A. Yes: grace be with them that love him in sincerity. Ephes. vi. 24.
3. *Q.* And with a strong love?
A. Yes: my soul thirsteth for God, for the living God. Ps. xlii. 2.
4. *Q.* And with a superlative love?
A. Yes: there is none upon earth that I desire besides thee. Ps. lxxiii. 25.
5. *Q.* And is all this included in the first and great commandment?
A. Yes: thou shalt love the Lord thy God with all thy heart, and with all thy soul, and with all thy mind. This is the first and great commandment. Matt. xxii. 37, 38.
6. *Q.* And is this the sum of our duty to God?
A. Yes: for if any man love God, the same is known of him. 1 Cor. viii. 3.
7. *Q.* Must those who love God be careful to please him?
A. Yes: for this is the love of God, that we keep his commandments. 1 John v. 3.
8. *Q.* And must they be afraid to offend him?
A. Yes: ye that love the Lord, hate evil. Ps. xcvii. 10.

§ III.

1. *Q.* Is there good reason why we should thus love God?
A. Yes: therefore, thou shalt love the Lord thy God. Deut. xi. 1.
2. *Q.* For is he most lovely in himself?
A. Yes: God is love, 1 John iv. 8.
3. *Q.* And most loving to us?
A. Yes: we love him, because he first loved us. 1 John iv. 19.
4. *Q.* Will he return our love?
A. Yes: I love those that love me. Prov. viii. 17.
5. *Q.* Will he reward it in this world?

A. Yes: all things shall work together for good to them that love God. Rom. viii. 28.

6. *Q.* And in another and better world?

A. Yes: for eye hath not seen what God hath prepared for them that love him. 1 Cor. ii. 9.

7. *Q.* Will you, then, love God above all?

A. Yes: I will love thee, O Lord, my strength. Ps. xviii. 1.

8. *Q.* And pray to God to give you grace to love him?

A. Yes: the Lord direct our hearts into his love. 2 Thess. iii. 5.

§ IV.

1. *Q.* Is it our duty to love our neighbour too?

A. Yes: he that loveth God, must love his brother also. 1 John iv. 21.

2. *Q.* Can we pretend to love God, if we do not love our neighbor?

A. No: He that loveth not his brother, whom he hath seen, how can he love God, whom he hath not seen? 1 John iv. 20.

3. *Q.* Is this the fulfilling of the law?

A. Yes: all is comprehended in this saying. Thou shalt love thy neighbor as thyself. Rom. xiii. 9, and James ii. 8, and Gal. v. 14.

4. *Q.* Is it the second great commandment?

A. Yes: the second is like unto it, thou shalt love thy neighbour as thyself. Matt. xxii. 39.

5. *Q.* Is it an old commandment?

A. Yes: thou shalt love thy neighbour as thyself. I am the Lord. Lev. xix. 18.

6. *Q.* Is it a new commandment?

A. Yes: a new commandment I give unto you, that ye love ne another. John xiii. 4.

§ V.

1. *Q.* Must we have a respect for all men?

A. Yes: honour all men. 1 Pet. ii. 17.

2. *Q.* Especially for all good men?

A. Yes: we must honour them that fear the Lord. Ps. xv. 4.

3. *Q.* Must we esteem one another?

A. Yes: let each esteem other better than themselves. Philipp. ii. 3.

4. *Q.* Must we sympathize with one another?

A. Yes: rejoice with them that do rejoice, and weep with them that weep. Rom. xii. 15.

5 *Q.* Must we please one another?

A. Yes: for even Christ pleased not himself. Rom. xv. 2, 3.

6. *Q.* Must we help one another?

A. Yes: Bear ye one another's burthens. Gal. vi. 2.

7. *Q.* Must we do good to one another?

A. Yes: as we have opportunity we must do good to all men! Gal. vi. 10.

8. *Q.* Must we pray for one another?

A. Yes: pray, one for another, that ye may be healed. James v. 16.

9. *Q.* Must we love, even our enemies?

A. Yes: love your enemies bless them that curse you. Matt. v. 44.

§ VI.

1. *Q.* Must you hurt nobody, in word or deed?

A. No: a citizen of Zion doth not evil to his neighbour, nor taketh up a reproach against his neighbour. Ps. xv. 3.

2. *Q.* Must you be true and just in all your dealings?

A. Yes: that which is altogether just shalt thou follow. Deut. xvi. 20.

3. *Q.* Must you bear no malice or hatred in your heart?

A. No: for whosoever hateth his brother, is a murderer. 1 John iii. 15.

§ VII.

1. *Q.* Are we to love our neighbors as ourselves?

A. Yes: for we are members one of another. Ephes. iv. 25.

2. *Q.* As truly as we love ourselves?

A. Yes: let love be without dissimulation. Rom. xii. 9.

3. *Q.* And as fruitfully?

A. Yes: not seeking my own profit, but the profit of many. 1 Cor. x. 33.

4. *Q.* And as constantly as we love ourselves?

A. Yes: let brotherly love continue. Heb. xiii. 1.

5. *Q.* Ought we, therefore, to do as we would be done by?

A. Yes: whatsoever ye would that men should do to you, do ye even so to them. Matt. vii. 12.

6. *Q.* Should we, in our places, promote christian love?

A. Yes: for every one that loveth is born of God. **1 John iv. 7.**

7. *Q.* And will this be our comfort?

A. Yes: live in peace, and the God of love and **peace shall** be with you. 2 Cor xiii. 11.

XLIII. *Q.* What is the preface to the **ten commandments?**

A. The preface to the ten commandments is in these words, *I am the Lord thy God, which have brought thee out of the land of Egypt, out of the house of bondage.*

§ I.

1. *Q.* Did God himself speak the ten commandments?
A. Yes: God spake all these words, saying. Exod. xx. 1.
2. *Q.* Was it fit they should be introduced with a solemn preface?
A. Yes: hear, O heavens, and give ear O earth, for the Lord hath spoken. Isa. i. 2.
3. *Q.* Did he therein assert his own authority?
A. Yes: I am the Lord thy God. Exod. xx. 1.
4. *Q.* Did he remind them of the great things he had lately done for them.
A. Yes: I am the Lord thy God, from the land of Egypt. Hos. xii. 9.

§ II.

1. *Q.* Was the condition of Israel in Egypt very miserable?
A. Yes: for the Egyptians made them to serve, with rigour. Exod. i. 13.
2. *Q.* Did God bring them out of Egypt?
A. Yes: he brought Israel from among them; for his mercy endureth forever. Ps. cxxxvi. 11.
3. *Q.* Did he do it miraculously?
A. Yes: With a strong hand, and a stretched out arm, for his mercy endureth forever. Ps. cxxxvi. 12.
4. *Q.* Did this oblige them to keep his commandments?
A. Yes: When I brought them out of the land of Egypt, I said, obey my voice. Jer. vii. 22, 23.
5. *Q.* But does this concern us?
A. Yes: for unto us was the gospel preached, as well as unto them. Heb. iv. 2.
6. *Q.* For is God the God of the Jews only? Is he not also of the Gentiles?
A. Yes: of the Gentiles also. Rom. iii. 29.

XLIV. *Q.* What doth the preface to the ten commandments teach us?

A. The preface to the ten commandments teacheth us, that because God is the Lord, and our God, and Redeemer, therefore, we are bound to keep all his commandments.

§ I.

1. *Q.* Is God the Lord Jehovah?
A. Yes:, I am the Lord, that is my name. Is. xlii. 8.
2. *Q.* Is that a reason why we should keep his commandments?
A. Yes: ye shall observe my statutes, and do them. I am the Lord. Lev. xix. 37.
3. *Q.* Is he our God?
A. Yes: he is thy praise, and he is thy God. Deut. x. 21.
4. *Q.* Is that a reason why we should keep his commandments?
A. Yes: for all people will walk every one in the name of their God. Mich. iv. 5. Ps. xcv. 7.

§ II.

1. *Q.* Is he our Redeemer?
A. Yes: thou, O Lord, art our father, our redeemer. Isa. lxiii. 16.
2. *Q.* Has he redeemed us from outward troubles?
A. Yes: behold, the Lord hath kept me alive. Josh. xiv. 10.
3. *Q.* And are we, therefore, bound to keep his commandments?
A. Yes: truly, I am thy servant, thou hast loosed my bonds. Ps. cxvi. 16.
4. And are we very ungrateful, if we do not?
A. Yes: now thou hast given us such deliverance as this, should we again break thy commandments? Ezra ix. 13, 14.

§ III.

1. *Q.* Has God brought us out of a spiritual Egypt?
A. Yes: for Christ proclaims liberty to the captives. Is. lxi. 1.
2. *Q.* Are we delivered from the bonds of sin?
A. Yes: he shall redeem Israel from all their iniquities. Ps. cxxx. 8.
3. *Q.* And is our deliverance by Christ greater than theirs out of Egypt?
A. Yes: for, if the son make you free, then you shall be free indeed. John viii. 36.
4. *Q.* And are we, therefore, bound to keep all his commandments?

A. Yes: for we are delivered out of the hands of our enemies, that we might serve him. Luke i. 74.

5. *Q.* And was this the design of our redemption?

A. Yes: he gave himself for us, that he might redeem us from all iniquity. Tit. ii. 14.

6. *Q.* Is there, then, all the reason in the world why we should be religious?

A. Yes: come, now, and let us reason together, saith the Lord. Is. i. 18.

XLV. *Q.* Which is the first commandment?

A. The first commandment is, *Thou shalt have no other gods before me.*

§I.

1. *Q.* Is it an essential duty of religion, to worship God?

A. Yes: for those have no hope, that are without God in the world. Ephes. ii. 12.

2. *Q.* Are we concerned to be right, in the object of our worship?

A. Yes: we must know what we worship. John iv. 32.

3. *Q.* Does the first commandment direct us in this?

A. Yes: for the first of all the commandments is this, Hear O Israel, the Lord our God is one Lord. Mark xii. 29.

§II.

1. *Q.* Does God lay a stress upon our having him for our God?

A. Yes: Hear, O, my people, and I will speak: I am God, even thy God. Ps. i. 7.

2. *Q.* And upon our having him only?

A. Yes: hear, O my people, and I will testify unto thee; there shall no strange god be in thee, neither shalt thou worship any strange god. Ps. lxxxi. 8, 9.

3. *Q.* Did Israel need this commandment?

A. Yes: for their fathers served other gods. Josh. xxiv. 2.

4. *Q.* And were they tempted to serve other gods?

A. Yes: the gods of the people that were round about them. Deut. xiii. 7.

XLVI. *Q.* What is required in the first commandment?

A. The first commandment requireth us to know and acknowledge God to be the only true

God, and our God, and to worship and glorify him accordingly.

§ I.

1. *Q.* Does that which forbids us to have any other gods, require us to have the true God?

A. Yes: Put away the strange gods, and serve the Lord only. 1 Sam. vii. 3, 4.

2. *Q.* Is it our duty to acknowledge God?

A. Yes: the Lord he is God; the Lord, he is God. 1 Kings xviii. 39.

3. *Q.* And must we acknowledge him to be the only true God?

A. Yes: thou art the God, even thou alone. 2 Kings, xix. 15.

§ II.

1. *Q.* Is it our duty to acquaint ourselves with him?

A. Yes: acquaint, now, thyself with him, and be at peace. Job. xxii. 21.

2. *Q.* Must we grow in that acquaintance?

A. Yes: increasing in the knowledge of God. Col. i. 10.

3. *Q.* And may we attain to it?

A. Yes: then shall we know, if we follow on to know the Lord. Hos. vi. 3.

§ III.

1. *Q.* Must we accept of God for our God?

A. Yes: Thou hast avouched the Lord this day, to be thy God. Deut. xxvi. 17.

2. *Q.* And must we join ourselves to him?

A. Yes: come and let us join ourselves to the Lord in an everlasting consent. Jer. l. 5.

3. *Q.* And covenant to be his?

A. Yes: O Lord, truly I am thy servant, I am thy servant. Ps. cxvi. 16.

4. *Q.* Must we take God the Father to be our chief good and highest end?

A. Yes: O God, thou art my God. Ps. lxiii. 1.

5. *Q.* And God the Son, to be our Prince and Saviour?

A. Yes: my Lord and my God. John xx. 28.

6. *Q.* And God the Holy Ghost to be our sanctifier, teacher, guide, and comforter?

A. Yes: for they that are led by the Spirit of God, are the sons of God. Rom. viii. 14.

7. *Q.* Must we renounce all others?
A. Yes: for by thee only will we make mention of thy name. Is. xxvi. 13.

8. *Q.* Must we do this deliberately?
A. Yes: choose ye, this day, whom ye will serve. Josh. xxiv. 15.

9. *Q.* Must we do it solemnly?
A. Yes: one shall say I am the Lord's and another shall subscribe with his hand unto the Lord. Is. xliv. 5.

10. *Q.* Must we do it resolutely?
A. Yes: nay, but we will serve the Lord. Josh. xxiv. 21.

11. *Q.* May we be at liberty to change our Master?
A. No: but with purpose of heart must cleave to the Lord. Acts xi. 23.

§ IV.

1. *Q.* When we have avouched the Lord for our God, must we apply ourselves to him?
A. Yes: if the Lord be God, then follow him. 1 Kings xviii. 21.

2. *Q.* Must we glorify him accordingly?
A. Yes: give unto the Lord the glory due unto his name. Ps. xxix. 2.

3. *Q.* Must we worship him?
A. Yes: thou shalt worship the Lord thy God, and him only shalt thou serve. Matt. iv. 10.

4. *Q.* Must we worship him with inward worship?
A. Yes: we must serve him with our spirits. Rom. i. 9.

5. *Q.* Is that the worship he requires?
A. Yes: for such the Father seeks to worship him. John iv. 23.

§ V.

1. *Q.* Must we remember God?
A. Yes: remember now thy Creator in the days of thy youth. Eccl. xii. 1.

2. *Q.* And think of him with delight?
A. Yes: my meditation of him shall be sweet. Ps. civ. 34.

3. *Q.* Must we adore and admire him?
A. Yes: who is like unto thee, O Lord, among the gods? Exod. xv. 11.

4. *Q.* Must we fear him above all?
A. Yes: let him be your fear, and let him be your dread. Isa. viii. 13.

5. *Q.* And reverence him?

A. Yes: he is to be had in reverence of all them that are about him. Ps. lxxxix. 7.

6. *Q.* Must we submit to his word?

A. Yes: speak, Lord, for thy servant heareth. 1 Sam. iii. 9.

7. *Q.* And submit to his will?

A. Yes: it is the Lord, let him do what seemeth him good. 1 Sam. iii. 18.

§ VI.

1. *Q.* Must we love God, above all?

A. Yes: O love the Lord, all ye his saints. Ps. xxxi. 23.

2. *Q.* Must our desire be towards him?

A. Yes: so panteth my soul after thee, O God. Ps. xlii. 1.

3. *Q.* Must our delight be in him?

A. Yes: delight thyself always in the Lord. Ps. xxxvii. 4.

4. *Q.* Must our dependence be upon him?

A. Yes: in thee, O Lord, do I put my trust. Ps. xxxi. 1.

§ VII.

1. *Q.* Must we live a life of communion with God?

A. Yes: mine eyes are ever towards the Lord. Ps. xxv. 15.

2. *Q.* And a life of complacency in him?

A. Yes: rejoice in the Lord always. Philipp. iv. 4.

3. *Q.* And a life of conformity to him?

A. Yes: be ye holy, for I am holy. 1 Pet. i. 16.

4. *Q.* And a life of confidence in him?

A. Yes: commit thy way unto the Lord. Ps. xxxvii. 5.

5. *Q.* And a life of regard to him?

A. Yes: in all thy ways acknowledge him. Prov. ii. 6.

6. *Q.* Must our hearts go out towards him?

A. Yes: unto thee, O Lord, do I lift up my soul. Ps. xxv. 1.

7. *Q.* And must we have him always in our eye?

A. Yes: I have set the Lord always before me. Ps. xvi. 8.

8. *Q.* And must we walk with him, in the whole course of our conversation?

A. Yes: as Enoch walked with God. Gen. v. 24.

9. *Q.* And is this inward worship, the life of religion?

A. Yes: it is better than all burnt-offerings and sacrifices. Mark xii. 33.

XI. VII. *Q.* What is forbidden in the first commandment?

A. The first commandment forbiddeth the denying, or not worshipping and glorifying the true God as God, and our God; and the giving of that worship and glory to any other, which is due to him alone.

§ I.

1. *Q.* Is it a great sin to deny the being of God?
A. Yes: the fool hath said in his heart, there is no God. Ps. xiv. 1.

2. *Q.* Or to deny his omniscience?
A. Yes: they say, the Lord shall not see. Ps. xciv. 7.

3. *Q.* Or to deny his justice?
A. Yes: He hath said in his heart, thou wilt not require it. Ps. x. 13.

4. *Q.* Or his holiness?
A. Yes: thou thoughtest that I was altogether such a one as thyself. Ps. l. 21.

5. *Q.* Or his goodness?
A. Yes: I knew thee to be a hard man. Matt. xxv. 24.

6. *Q.* Or his faithfulness?
A. Yes: where is the promise of his coming? 2 Pet. iii. 4.

7. *Q.* Is it a sin to question God's providence?
A. Yes: is the Lord among us? or is he not? Exod. xvii. 7.

8. *Q.* Or to question his power?
A. Yes: can God furnish a table in the wilderness? Ps. lxxviii. 19.

9. *Q.* And is there such a thing as practical Atheism?
A. Yes: they profess that they know God, but in works they deny him. Tit. i. 16.

§ II.

1. *Q.* Is it a great sin to be ignorant of God?
A. Yes: some have not the knowledge of God; I speak it to your shame. 1 Cor. xv. 35.

2. *Q.* Is it a damning sin?
A. Yes: He shall take vengeance on them that know not God. 2 Thess. i. 8.

3. *Q.* Is it the cause of all other sins?
A. Yes: there is neither truth nor mercy nor knowledge of God in the land. Hos. iv. 1.

4. *Q.* Is it a great sin to forget God?
A. Qes: thou hast forgotten the God that formed thee. Deut. xxxii. 18.

5. *Q.* And to cast off the fear of him?
A. Yes: there is no fear of God before his eyes. Ps. xxxvi. 1.

6. *Q.* And to live without prayer?

A. Yes: thou hast not called upon me, O Jacob. Is. xliii. 22.

7. *Q.* And not to glorify him?

A. Yes: the God in whose hand thy breath is, hast thou not glorified. Dan. v. 23.

§ III.

1. *Q.* Is all distrust of God a sin?

A. Yes: the evil heart of unbelief departs from the living God. Heb. iii. 12.

2. *Q.* And tempting God?

A. Yes: thou shalt not tempt the Lord thy God. Matt. iv. 7.

3. *Q.* And all the coldness of our love to him?

A. Yes: but their heart is far from me. Matt. xv. 8.

4. *Q.* Does this commandment forbid all ungodliness?

A. Yes: for the wrath of God is revealed against all ungodliness. Rom. i. 18.

5. *Q.* And all idolatry?

A. Yes: little children, keep yourselves from idols. 1 John v. 21.

§ IV.

1. *Q.* Had the Gentiles other gods besides the true God?

A. Yes: they had gods many, and lords many. 1 Cor. viii. 5.

2. *Q.* And were those gods devils?

A. Yes: they sacrificed to devils, and not to God. 1 Cor. x. 20.

3. *Q.* May we have communion with them?

A. No: I would not that ye should have fellowship with devils. 1 Cor. x. 20.

4. *Q.* Have those fellowship with them who consult with witches?

A. Yes: is it because there is not a God in Israel, that thou goest to inquire of Baal-zebub, the god of Ekron? 2 Kings i. 3.

5. *Q.* Did the gentiles multiply their Gods?

A. Yes: according to the number of thy cities are thy gods. Jer. ii. 28.

6. *Q.* Were they gods of their own making?

A. Yes: and they that made them are like unto them. Ps. cxv. 8.

7. *Q.* Was not that a great affront to the living God?

A. Yes: they changed the truth of God into a lie. Rom. i. 25.

§ V.

1. *Q.* Is there not such a thing as spiritual idolatry?

A. Yes: these men have set up their idols in their hearts. xiv. 4.

2. *Q.* Is it idolatry to make a god of our appetites?
A. Yes: whose god is their belly. Philipp. iii. 19.
3. *Q.* Or a god of our money?
A. Yes: for covetousness is idolatry. Col. iii. 5.
4. *Q.* May we give that respect to any creature, which is due to God alone?
A. No: for his glory, he will not give to another Is. xlii. 8.
5, *Q.* Is it, therefore, a sin, to love them more than God?
A. Yes: he that loveth father or mother more than me, is not worthy of me. Matt. x. 37.
6. *Q.* And to trust in them?
A. Yes: cursed is the man that trusteth in man. Jer. xvii. 5.
7. *Q.* Is this spiritual adultery?
A. Yes: she went after her lovers, and forgot me, saith the Lord. Hos. ii. 13.

XLVIII. *Q.* What are we specially taught by these words [BEFORE ME] in the first commandment?

A. These words [BEFORE ME] in the first commandment teach us, that God, who seeth all things, taketh notice of, and is much displeased with, the sin of having any other God.

§ I.
1. *Q.* Are we always in God's sight?
A. Yes: thou knowest my down-sitting, and my up-rising. Ps. cxxxix. 2.
2. *Q.* Are all our actions in his sight?
A. Yes: all my ways are before thee. Ps. cxix. 168.
3. *Q.* Does he take notice of them?
A. Yes: He pondereth all our goings. Prov. v. 21.

§ II.
1. *Q.* Are all our good works before him?
A. Yes: I know thy work, and thy labour, and thy patience. Rev. ii. 2.
2. *Q.* Does he know all our inward worship of him?
A. Yes: the Lord hearkened, and heard those that thought on his name. Mal. iii. 16.
3. *Q.* And should that encourage us to have him for our God?
A. Yes: for your Father sees in secret, and will reward openly. Matt. vi. 4.

§ III.

1. *Q.* Are all our evil works before him?

A. Yes: He sets our iniquities before him. Ps. xc. 8.

2. *Q.* Is the having of other Gods oftentimes a secret sin?

A. Yes: they do it in the dark, and say, the Lord sees us not. Ezek. viii. 12.

3. *Q.* But does God see?

A. Yes: He that formed the eye, shall he not see it? Ps. xciv. 9.

4. *Q.* Does he take notice of all our neglects of him?

A. Yes: if we have forgotten the name of our God, he knows it. Ps. xliv. 20, 21.

5. *Q.* And does he take notice of all our inclinations to other gods?

A. Yes: if we have stretched out our hands to a strange god, shall not God search this out? Ps. xliv. 20, 21.

6. *Q.* And is he much displeased with secret idolatry?

A. Yes: seest thou the great abominations that they commit? Ezek. viii. 6.

7. *Q.* And should this oblige us to be faithful to him?

A. Yes: for the Lord searcheth all hearts. 1 Chron. xxviii. 9.

XLIX. *Q.* Which is the second commandment?

A. The second commandment is, *Thou shalt not make unto thee any graven image, or any likeness of any thing that is in Heaven above, or that is in the earth beneath, or that is in the water under the earth. Thou shalt not bow down thyself to them, nor serve them: for I the Lord thy God am a jealous God, visiting the iniquity of the fathers upon the children unto the third and fourth generation of them that hate me; and shewing mercy unto thousands of them that love me, and keep my commandments.*

§ I.

1. *Q.* Does the second commandment concern the ordinances of God's worship, as the first object of it?

A. Yes: therefore, ye shall keep mine ordinance. Lev. xviii. 30.

2. *Q.* Was it requisite there should be a law concerning them?

A. Yes: lest ye say, how did these nations serve their gods? so will I do likewise. Deut. xii. 30.

3. *Q.* Is this binding to us now?

A. Yes: dearly beloved, flee from idolatry. 1 Cor. x. 14.

4. *Q.* Are we christians forbidden to worship images?

A. Yes: that they should not worship idols of gold, and silver, and brass, and stone. Rev. ix. 20.

§ II.

1. *Q.* Does this commandment forbid the making of images for a religious use?

A. Yes: cursed be the man that maketh any graven image. Deut. xxvii. 15.

2. *Q.* Does it forbid the making an image of what is in Heaven above?

A. Yes: lest thou lift up thine eyes unto Heaven, and when thou seest the sun, and the moon, and the stars, shouldst be driven to worship them. Deut. iv. 19.

3. *Q.* Or on earth beneath?

A. Yes: as they changed their glory into the similitude of an ox. Ps. cvi. 20.

4. *Q.* Or in the waters under the earth?

A. Yes: as they made the likeness of creeping things. Rom. i. 23.

§ III.

1. *Q.* Does it forbid us to bow down to them?

A. Yes: shall I bow down to the stock of a tree? Isa. xliv. 19.

2. *Q.* Or to worship them?

A. Yes: thou shalt worship no other God. Exod. xxxiv. 14.

3. *Q.* Or to shew any respect to them?

A. Yes: I will take away the names of Baalim out of their mouth. Hos. ii. 17.

4. *Q.* Was it requisite this commandment should be thus enlarged?

A. Yes: precept must be upon precept, and line upon line. Isa. xxviii. 10.

5. *Q.* And that it should be backed with many reasons?

A. Yes: for they are mad upon their idols. Jer. l. 38.

L. *Q.* What is required in the second commandment?

A. The second commandment requireth the receiving, observing, and keeping pure and entire, all such religious worship and ordinances as God hath appointed in his word.

§ I.

1. *Q.* Is it our duty solemnly to worship God?
A. Yes: thou shalt worship the Lord thy God. Matt. iv. 10.
2. *Q.* Do we thereby honour him?
A. Yes: we give unto him the glory due unto his name. Ps. xxix. 2.
3. *Q.* Does the light of nature teach us to worship God?
A. Yes: they cried, every man, unto his god. Jonah i. 5.
4. *Q.* But, does it teach us, sufficiently, how to worship him?
A. No: whom, therefore, ye ignorantly worship. Acts xvii. 23.
5. *Q.* Has God, in his word, appointed us, in what way to worship him?
A. Yes: for this was ordained in Joseph, for a testimony. Ps. lxxxi. 5.
6. *Q.* And must we worship him in the appointed way?
A. Yes: see thou make all things according to the pattern showed thee. Heb. viii. 5.

§ II.

1. *Q.* Are we to receive such ordinances as God has appointed?
A. Yes: the Lord our God will we serve, and his voice will we obey. Josh. xxiv. 24.
2. *Q.* Should we labour to understand them?
A. Yes: what mean ye by this service? Exod. xii. 26.
3. *Q.* And are we to observe them?
A. Yes: observe all things whatsoever I have commanded you. Matt. xxviii. 20.
4. *Q.* And to observe them duly?
A. Yes: as the duty of every day requires. Ezra iii. 4.

§ III.

1. *Q.* Are we to keep God's ordinances?
A. Yes: that good thing which was committed to thee, keep. 2 Tim. i. 14.
2. *Q.* Are we to keep them carefully?
A. Yes: keep them as the apple of thine eye. Prov. vii. 2.
3. *Q.* Must we keep them pure, without corruption?
A. Yes: add thou not to his words. Prov. xxx. 6.

4. *Q.* And entire, without diminution?

A. Yes: we must walk in all the ordinances of the Lord. Luke i. 6.

5. *Q.* May we neither add nor diminish?

A. No: thou shalt neither add thereto, nor diminish from it. Deut. xii. 32.

§ IV.

1. *Q.* Must we worship God in the spirit?

A. Yes: we are the circumcision that worship God in the spirit. Philipp. iii. 3.

2. *Q.* Must we be inward with God, in every service?

A. Yes: for bodily exercise profiteth little. 1 Tim. iv. 8.

3. *Q.* Is ignorance the mother of devotion?

A. No: for if ye offer the blind for sacrifice, is it not evil? Mal. i. 8.

4. *Q.* Is it the mother of destruction?

A. Yes: My people are destroyed for lack of knowledge. Hos. iv. 6.

§ V.

1. *Q.* Ought we to have an eye to the word of God, in our religious worship?

A. Yes: for, whatsoever is not of faith, is sin. Rom. xiv. 23.

2. *Q.* And to glorify God in it?

A. Yes: I will be sanctified in them that come nigh unto me. Lev. x. 3.

3. *Q.* And ought we to shun all idolatrous worships?

A. Yes: for I would not that ye should have fellowship with devils. 1 Cor. x. 20.

LI. *Q.* What is forbidden in the second commandment?

A. The second commandment forbiddeth the worshipping of God by images, or any other way not appointed in his word.

§ I.

1. *Q.* Is it a sin to worship the true God by images?

A. Yes: for it changes the truth of God into a lie. Rom. i. 25.

2. *Q.* Are not images laymen's books?

A. No: for an image is a teacher of lies. Hab. ii. 18.

3. *Q.* Is it possible to make an image of God?

A. No: we ought not to think that the God-head is like unto gold, or silver, or stone, graven by art and man's device. Acts xvii. 29.

4. *Q.* Do we know what to represent God by?

A. No: to whom, then, will ye liken God? Isa. xl. 18.

5. *Q.* Do they that pretend to it put a great affront upon him?

A. Yes: for they change the glory of the incorruptible God into an image made like to corruptible man. Rom. i. 23.

§ II.

1. *Q.* May we worship Christ by an image?

A. No: for though we have known Christ after the flesh, yet now henceforth know we him no more. 2 Cor. v. 16.

2. *Q.* Is it idolatry to worship the consecrated host?

A. Yes: for it is bread which we break. 1 Cor. x. 16.

3. *Q.* Is it idolatry to pray to saints and angels?

A. Yes: see thou do it not, but worship God. Rev. xix. 10, and xxii. 9.

§ III.

1. *Q.* Must we be careful to avoid all appearances of idolatry?

A. Yes: take ye, therefore, good heed to yourselves, lest ye corrupt yourselves. Deut. iv. 15, 16.

2. *Q.* Should we choose to die rather than worship images?

A. Yes: but if not, be it known unto thee, O King, we will not serve thy gods, nor worship the golden image which thou hast set up. Dan. iii. 18.

§ IV.

1. *Q.* Is it a sin to worship God in any way not appointed in his word?

A. Yes: in vain do they worship me, teaching for doctrines, the commandments of men. Matt. xv. 9.

2. *Q.* May we ourselves invent ordinances of worship?

A. No: they went a whoring with their own inventions. Ps. cvi. 39.

3. *Q.* Is it not enough if what we invent is not forbidden?

A. No: they offered a strange fire before the Lord, which he commanded them not. Lev. x. 1.

4. *Q.* Is it a sin to despise any of God's ordinances?

A. Yes: ye said also, behold what a weariness is it! Mal. i. 13.

5. *Q.* Or to be careless in our attendance upon them?

A. Yes: cursed be the deceiver that hath in his flock a male, and vows and sacrifices to the Lord a corrupt thing. Mal. i. 14.

6. *Q.* Are they spiritual idolaters who make images of God in their fancy?

A. Yes: they are vain in their imaginations, and their foolish heart is darkened. Rom. i. 21.

LII. *Q.* What are the reasons annexed to the second commandment?

A. The reasons annexed to the second commandment are, God's sovereignty over us, his propriety iu us, and the zeal he hath to his own worship.

§ I.

1. *Q.* Is there good reason why we should take heed of idolatry?

A. Yes: turn ye not to idols, neither make to yourselves molten gods, I am the Lord your God. Lev. xix. 4.

2. *Q.* Has God a sovereignty over us?

A. Yes: for he is a great God, and a great King above all gods. Ps. xcv. 3.

3. *Q.* Ought we, therefore, to worship him, as he has appointed us?

A. Yes: O come, let us worship, and bow down, and kneel before the Lord our Maker. Ps. xcv. 6.

4. *Q.* And not to worship idols?

A. Yes: for they can do neither good nor evil. Isa. xli. 23.

§ II.

1. *Q.* Has God a propriety in us?

A. Yes: for we are the people of his pasture. Ps. xcv. 7.

2. *Q.* Ought we, therefore, to worship him?

A. Yes: He is thy Lord, and worship thou him. Ps. xlv. 11.

3. *Q.* And not to worship other gods?

A. Yes: for hath a nation changed their gods? Jer. ii. 11.

§ III.

1. *Q.* Is God jealous in the matters of his worship?

A. Yes: the Lord, whose name is Jealous, is a jealous God. Exod. xxxiv. 14.

2. *Q.* Is he much displeased with those who corrupt it?

A. Yes: they provoked the Lord God of Israel to anger with their vanities. 1 Kings xvi. 13.

3. *Q.* Do those who do so hate him?

A. Yes: idolaters are haters of God. Rom. i. 25, 30.

4. *Q.* Will he visit their iniquity?

A. Yes: in the day when I visit, I will visit their sin upon them. Exod. xxxii. 34.

5. *Q.* Will he visit it upon the children?

A. Yes: our Fathers sinned, and are not, and we have borne their iniquities. Lam. v. 7.

6. Q. And is it just with him to do so?
A. Yes: for they are the children of whoredoms. Hos. ii. 2.
7. Q. But will he visit it for ever?
A. No: but to the third and fourth generation. Exod. xxxiv. 7.

§ IV.

1. Q. Will those who love God keep his commandments?
A. Yes: if ye keep my commandments, ye shall abide in my love. John xv. 10.
2. Q Will he shew mercy to such?
A. Yes: for he hath said, I love them that love me. Prov. viii. 17.
3. Q. Will he shew mercy to thousands of such?
A. Yes: for the mercy of the Lord is from everlasting to everlasting. Ps. ciii. 17.

LIII. Q. Which is the third commandment?
A. The third commandment is, thou shalt not take the name of the Lord thy God in vain: for the Lord will not hold him guiltless that taketh his name in vain.

§ I.

1. Q. Does the third commandment concern the manner of our worshipping God?
A. Yes: that we serve the Lord with fear. Ps. ii. 11.
2. Q. Is it enough, that we seek God in a due ordinance?
A. No: but we must seek him after the due order. 1 Chron. xv. 13.

§ II.

1. Q. Is God's name all that whereby he makes himself known?
A. Yes: He proclaimed the name of the Lord. Exod. xxxiv 5.
2. Q. Ought we to make use of his name?
A. Yes: by thee only will we make mention of thy name. Isa. xxvi. 13.
3. Q. And to take heed of abusing it?
A. Yes: neither shalt thou profane the name of thy God. I am the Lord. Lev. xviii. 21.

LIV. Q. What is required in the third commandment?
A. The third commandment requireth the

holy and reverend use of God's names, titles, attributes, ordinances, word, and works.

§ I.

1. *Q.* Does this commandment require us to glorify the name of God?

A. Yes: they shall worship before thee, O Lord, and shall glorify thy name. Ps. lxxxvi. 9.

2. *Q.* Are we to think of God's name, with seriousness?

A. Yes: they feared the Lord, and thought upon his name. Mal. iii. 16.

3. *Q.* Are we to speak of it with reverence?

A. Yes: for God is in Heaven, and thou upon earth, therefore let thy words be few. Eccl. v. 2.

4. *Q.* Are we to call upon his name with a holy awe?

A. Yes: for we that are but dust and ashes speak to the Lord of glory. Gen. xviii. 27.

5. *Q.* Are we to worship God reverently, in every religious duty?

A. Yes: we must serve him acceptably, with reverence and godly fear. Heb. xii. 28.

6. *Q.* And is there good reason for it?

A. Yes: for our God is a consuming fire. Heb. xii. 29.

7. *Q.* Ought we to behave ourselves very reverently in public worship?

A. Yes: for God is greatly to be feared in the assembly of his saints, and to be had in reverence of all them that are about him. Ps. lxxxix. 7.

§ II.

1. *Q.* Must we be holy, in worshipping God?

A. Yes: worship the Lord in the beauty of holiness. Ps. xcvi. 9.

2. *Q.* Must we be holy, in prayer and praise?

A. Yes: lifting up holy hands. 1 Tim. ii. 8.

3. *Q.* Must our thoughts be fixed?

A. Yes: O God, my heart is fixed. Ps. cviii. 1.

4. *Q.* Must pious and devout affections be working in us?

A. Yes: we must be fervent in spirit, serving the Lord. Rom. xii. 11.

5. *Q.* Must we be very humble in our approaches to God?

A. Yes: as the publican that stood afar off, and would not so much as lift up his eyes to Heaven. Luke xviii. 13.

§ III.

1. *Q.* Must we give glory to God, in his word?

A. Yes: for thou hast magnified thy word above all thy name. Ps. cxxxviii. 2.

2. *Q.* Must we hear it with reverence?

A. Yes: we are all here present before God to hear all things that are commanded thee of God. Acts x. 33.

3. *Q.* Must we give glory to God, in swearing, when we are called to it?

A. Yes: thou shalt fear the Lord thy God, and shalt swear by his name. Deut. vi. 13.

4. *Q.* Must we be cautious in swearing?

A. Yes: we must fear an oath. Eccl. ix. 2.

5. *Q.* Must we be conscientious in swearing?

A. Yes: thou shalt swear in truth, in judgment, and in righteousness. Jer. iv. 2.

6. *Q.* Must we give glory to God in vowing?

A. Yes: vow and pay unto the Lord your God. Ps. lxxvi. 11.

§ IV.

1. *Q.* Must me glorify God, in his great works?

A. Yes: we must magnify his works which men behold. Job. xxxvi. 24.

2. *Q.* And must we glorify him, by our good works?

A. Yes: let every one that names the name of Christ depart from iniquity. 2 Tim. ii. 19.

LV. *Q.* What is forbidden in the third commandment?

A. The third commandment forbiddeth all profaning or abusing of any thing whereby God maketh himself known.

§ I.

1. *Q.* Do all hypocrites take God's name in vain?

A. Yes: for they make mention of the God of Israel, but not in truth and righteousness, Isa. xlviii. 1.

2. *Q.* Do they, therefore profane that name?

A. Yes: for the name of God is blasphemed through them. Rom. ii. 24.

3. *Q.* Do hypocritical worshippers take God's name in vain?

A. Yes: for with their mouth they shew much love, but their heart goeth after their covetousness. Ezek. xxxiii. 31.

4. *Q.* And is their seeming religion a vain religion?

A. Yes: that man's religion is vain. James. i. 26.

5. *Q.* Can it be pleasing to God?
A. No: bring no more vain oblations. Isa. i. 13.
6. *Q.* Can it be profitable to themselves?
A. No: for they receive the grace of God in vain. 2 Cor. vi. 1.
7. *Q.* Do covenant breakers take God's name in vain?
A, Yes: for they lie unto him with their tongues. Ps. lxxviii. 36.

§ II.

1. *Q.* Is it a sin against this commandment, to use the name of God lightly and carelessly?
A. Yes: for thou shalt fear this glorious and fearful name, the Lord thy God. Deut. xxviii. 58.
2. *Q.* Will God's friends thus affront him?
A. No: thine enemies take thy name in vain. Ps. cxxix. 20.
3. *Q.* Is it the character of the wicked?
A. Yes: thou art near in their mouth, and far from their reins. Jer. xii. 2.

§ III.

1. *Q.* Is it a sin against this comandment, to swear rashly?
A. Yes: above all things, my brethren, swear not. James v. 12.
2. *Q.* Is it a sin to swear by creatures?
A. Yes: whether by Heaven, or by earth, or by the head. Matt. v. 34—36.
3. *Q.* Must our communication be yea, yea, and nay, nay?
A. Yes: for whatsoever is more than these cometh of evil. Matt. v. 37.
4. *Q.* Is it a sin to swear falsely?
A. Yes: thou shalt not forswear thyself. Matt. v. 33.
5. *Q.* Is profane swearing a great sin?
A. Yes: for it blasphemes that worthy name by which we are called. James ii. 7.
6. *Q.* Is it an inexcusable sin?
A. Yes: for they transgress without cause. Ps. xxv. 3.
7. *Q.* Does it bring judgments upon families?
A. Yes: for the curse shall enter into the house of him that swears falsely, and shall consume it. Zech. v. 4,
8. *Q.* And upon nations?
A. Yes: because of swearing the land mourns. Jer. xxiii. 10.

§ IV.

1. *Q.* Is it a sin against this commandment, to jest with the word of God?

A. Yes: be ye not mockers, lest your hands be made strong. Isa. xxviii. 22.

2. *Q.* Or to use it as a charm?

A. Yes: as those exorcists which said, we adjure you by Jesus, whom Paul preacheth. Acts xix. 13.

3. *Q.* Is it a sin to put a slight upon sacred things?

A. Yes: ye have profaned my name, in that ye say, The table of the Lord is contemptible. Mal. i. 12.

LVI. *Q.* What is the reason annexed to the third commandment?

A. The reason annexed to the third commandment is, that however the breakers of this commandment may escape punishment from men, yet the Lord our God will not suffer them to escape his righteous judgment.

§ I.

1. *Q.* Do the breakers of the third commandment commonly escape punishment from men?

A. Yes: for men hear the voice of swearing and utter it not. Lev. v. 1.

2. *Q.* And do they fancy they shall escape God's judgments?

A. Yes: the wicked condemn God, and yet say in their heart, he will not require it. Ps. x. 13.

3. *Q.* But shall they escape God's judgments?

A. No: be not deceived, God is not mocked. Gal. vi. 7.

§ II.

1. *Q.* Shall those who profane God's holy name escape his righteous judgments?

A. No: the Lord will make their plagues wonderful. Deut. xxviii. 59.

2. *Q.* Shall hypocrites escape them?

A. No: woe unto you, scribes and pharisees, hypocrites. Matt. xxiii. 13.

3. *Q.* Shall scoffers escape them?

A. No: for they shall be broken, and snared and taken. Isa. xxviii. 13.

4. *Q.* Shall covenant-breakers escape them?

A. No: seeing he despised the oath, by breaking the covenant, he shall not escape. Ezek. xvii. 18.

§ III.

1. *Q.* Shall swearers go unpunished?
A. No: for he that sweareth shall be cut off. Zech. v. 3.
2. *Q.* Shall they who use God's name vainly go unpunished?
A. No: for every idle word that men speak, they must give account. Matt. xii. 36.
3. *Q.* And shall their words be witnesses against them?
A. Yes: God shall cause their own tongues to fall upon them. Ps. lxiv. 8.

LVII. *Q.* Which is the fourth commandment?

A. The fourth commandment is, *Remember the Sabbath day to keep it holy. Six days shalt thou labour, and do all thy work, but the seventh day is the Sabbath of the Lord thy God: in it thou shalt not do any work; thou, nor thy son, nor thy daughter, thy manservant, nor thy maid-servant, nor thy cattle, nor thy stranger that is within thy gates. For in six days the Lord made Heaven and Earth, the Sea, and all that in them is, and rested the seventh day: wherefore the Lord blessed the Sabbath day and hallowed it.*

§ I.

1. *Q.* Does the fourth commandment concern the time of worship?
A. Yes: for there is a time to every purpose. Eccl. iii. 1.
2. *Q.* Must our worship be confined to that time?
A. No: for we must pray always, Ephes. vi. 18.
3. *Q.* But is that appointed for the certain time?
A. Yes: blow up the trumpet in the time appointed. Ps. lxxxi. 3.
4. *Q.* Is it the will of God we should take special notice of this command?
A. Yes: for he has said remember it.
5. *Q.* Are we apt to forget it?
A. Yes: they have hid their eyes from my sabbaths. Ezek. xxii. 26.

§ II.

1. *Q.* Must we keep holy the Sabbath day?
A. Yes: keep the Sabbath day, to sanctify it. Deut. v. 12.
2. *Q.* Is a Sabbath a day of rest?
A. Yes: it shall be a Sabbath of rest unto you. Lev. xvi. 31.
3. *Q.* Must we labour the six days, and do all our work?
A. Yes: for in the sweat of thy face shalt thou eat bread. Gen. iii. 19.
4. *Q.* But is not work for God part of our work?
A. Yes: for we must work the works of God. John vi. 28.
5. *Q.* Must we not, then, do that on the six days?
A. Yes: every day will I bless thee. Ps. cxlv. 2.
6. *Q.* But must we especially do it on Sabbath days?
A. Yes: for it is the holy of the Lord. Isa. lviii. 13.
7. *Q.* Must we, therefore, rest, from other work, on that day?
A. Yes: that we may attend upon the Lord without distraction. 1 Cor. vii. 35.

§ III.

1. *Q.* Must children keep holy the Sabbath day?
A. Yes: thou, and thy son, and thy daughter.
2. *Q.* And servants?
A. Yes: that thy man servant and maid servant may rest as well as thou. Deut. v. 14.
3. *Q.* And is there good reason for the sanctification of the Sabbath?
A. Yes: ye shall keep my Sabbaths, I am the Lord your God. Lev. xix. 3.

LVIII. *Q.* What is required in the fourth commandment?

A. The fourth commandment requireth the keeping holy to God such set times as he hath appointed in his word; expressly one whole day in seven, to be a holy Sabbath to himself.

§ I.

1. *Q.* Must holy time be kept holy?
A. Yes: for every thing is beautiful in its season. Eccl. iii. 11.
2. *Q.* Can man make time holy?
A. No: for I am the Lord which sanctify you. Lev. xx. 8.

§ II.

1. *Q.* Has God appointed a Sabbath?

A. Yes: it is as the Lord thy God hath commanded thee. Deut. v. 12.

2. *Q.* Had he authority to do so?
A. Yes: for the day is thine, the night also is thine. Ps. lxxiv. 16.

3. *Q.* Did he appoint it for us?
A. Yes: for the Sabbath was made for man. Mark ii. 27.

4. *Q.* Did he appoint one day in seven?
A. Yes: for a seventh day is the Sabbath of the Lord thy God.

5. *Q.* One whole day?
A. Yes: for the evening and the morning were the first day. Gen. i. 5.

§ III.

1. *Q.* Must we keep it?
A. Yes: verily my Sabbaths ye shall keep. Exod. xxxi. 13.

2. *Q.* Must we keep it as a treasure?
A. Yes: we must call the Sabbath honourable. Isa. lviii. 13.

3. *Q.* And keep it as a talent?
A. Yes: for thou madest known unto them thy holy Sabbaths. Neh. ix. 14.

4. *Q.* Must we keep it with care?
A. Yes: we must lay hold on it to keep the Sabbath from polluting it. Isa. lvi. 2.

5. *Q.* Must we keep it holy to God?
A. Yes: for he that regardeth the day, regardeth it to the Lord. Rom. xiv. 6.

LIX. *Q.* Which day of the seven hath God appointed to be the weekly Sabbath?

A. From the beginning of the world to the resurrection of Christ, God appointed the seventh day of the week to be the weekly Sabbath; and the first day of the week ever since, to continue to the end of the world, which is the Christian Sabbath.

§ I.

1. *Q.* Was the Sabbath appointed from the beginning of the world?
A. Yes: God blessed the seventh day and sanctified it, when the heavens and the earth were finished. Gen. ii. 1—3.

2. *Q.* Was it in remembrance of the work of creation?

A. Yes: because that in it he rested from all his work. Gen. ii. 2.

3. *Q.* Was it observed, before the giving of the law, upon ount Sinai?

A. Yes: for, before that, it was said, To-morrow is the rest of the holy Sabbath to the Lord. Exod. xvi. 23.

4. *Q.* Was that appointed to be kept on the seveth day of the week?

A. Yes: for he spake of the seventh day on this wise. Heb. iv. 4.

§ II.

1. *Q.* Was the law of the Sabbath given more particularly to Israel?

A. Yes: I gave them my Sabbath to be a sign between me and them. Ezek. xx. 12.

2. *Q.* Was it religiously observed among them?

A. Yes: for their enemies did mock at their Sabbaths. Lam. i. 7.

3. *Q.* Did they sanctify the Sabbath, in solemn assemblies?

A. Yes: Moses of old time is read in the synagogues every Sabbath day. Acts xv. 21.

4. *Q.* Was the blessing confined to the seventh day?

A. No: for the Lord blessed the Sabbath day and hallowed it. Exod. xx. 11.

§ III

1. *Q.* Was the Sabbath to continue in gospel times?

A. Yes: for there remaineth the keeping of a Sabbath to the people of God. Heb. iv. 9. (marg.)

2. *Q.* Did Christ intend it should continue?

A. Yes: for he said, pray that your flight be not on the Sabbath day. Matt. xxiv. 20.

3. *Q.* Did he, in order to that, expound the fourth commandment?

A. Yes: for he shewed, that it is lawful to do well upon the Sabbath day. Matt. xii. 12.

4. *Q.* Is there the same need of Sabbaths now that ever there was?

A. Yes: for I gave them my Sabbaths, that they might know that I am the Lord. Ezek. xx. 12.

§ IV.

1. *Q.* Is the Sabbath changed, now, to the first day of the week?

A. Yes: for on the first day of the week the disciples came together to break bread. Acts xx. 7.

2. *Q.* Was it because, on that day of the week, our Lord Jesus rose from the dead?

A. Yes: for he rose as it began to dawn towards the first day of the week. Matt. xxviii. 1.

3. *Q.* And because on that day, the Spirit was poured out?

A. Yes: for that was when the day of Pentecost was fully come. Acts ii. 1.

4. *Q.* Was it fit there should be an alteration?

A. Yes: for it shall no more be said, the Lord liveth that brought up the children of Israel out of the land of Egypt; but the Lord liveth that brought them up from the land of the North. Jer. xvi. 14, 15.

§ v.

1. *Q.* Did the Apostles observe the first day of the week?

A. Yes: on the first day of the week, let every one lay by. 1 Cor. xvi. 2.

2. *Q.* Did the primitive church call it the Lord's day?

A. Yes: I was in the Spirit on the Lord's day. Rev. i. 10.

3. *Q.* In a thing of this nature, ought we to acquiesce?

A. Yes: for, if any man will be contentious, we have no such custom, neither the churches of God. 1 Cor. xi. 16.

LX. *Q.* How is the Sabbath to be sanctified?

A. The Sabbath is to be sanctified by a holy resting all that day, even from such worldly employments and recreations as are lawful on other days; and spending the whole time in the public and private exercises of God's worship, except so much as is to be taken up in the works of necessity and mercy.

§ i.

1. *Q.* Must we rest on the Sabbath day?

A. Yes: six days may work be done, but in the seventh is the Sabbath of rest. Exod. xxxi. 15.

2. *Q.* Must we rest from worldly employments?

A. Yes: ye shall hallow the Sabbath day, to do no work therein. Jer. xvii. 24.

3. *Q.* And from recreations?

A. Yes: not finding thine own pleasure. Isa. lviii. 13.

4. *Q.* Is this to signify our being dead to this world?

A. Yes: for he that is entered into his rest has ceased from his own works. Heb. iv. 10.

5. *Q.* And to awaken us to think of leaving it?

A. Yes: for here we have no continuing city. Heb. xiii. 14.

6. *Q.* Must this rest be dedicated to God?

A. Yes: It is a holy day, a Sabbath of rest to the Lord. Exod. xxxv. 2.

§ II.

1. *Q.* Must we spend time, on that day in the public exercises of God's worship?

A. Yes: for it is a holy convocation. Lev. xxiii. 3.

2. *Q.* Must we do so, every Sabbath, as we have opportunity?

A. Yes: from one Sabbath to another shall all flesh come to worship before me, saith the Lord. Isa. lxvi. 23.

3. *Q.* And must we not absent ourselves from public worship?

A. No: not forsaking the assembling of yourselves together. Heb. x. 25.

4. *Q.* Must we spend time, on that day in the private exercises of religion?

A. Yes: it is the Sabbath of the Lord, in all your dwellings. Lev. xxiii. 3.

5. *Q.* Did the disciples of Christ thus spend the first Lord's day?

A. Yes: for, on the first day of the week, the disciples were assembled. John xx. 19.

§ III.

1. *Q.* Must we prepare for the Sabbath day beforehand?

A. Yes: it was the preparation, and the Sabbath drew on. Luke xxiii. 54.

2. *Q.* Must the Sabbath be a day of holy joy?

A. Yes: we will rejoice and be glad in it. Ps. cxviii. 24.

3. *Q.* Must it be a day of praise?

A. Yes: the Psalm for the Sabbath day begins, "It is a good thing to give thanks to the Lord." Ps. xcii. 1.

4. *Q.* Must we be spiritual in the duties of the day?

A. Yes: I was in the spirit on the Lord's day. Rev. i. 10.

5. *Q.* And must we take pleasure in them?

A. Yes: call the Sabbath a delight. Isa. lviii. 13.

§ IV.

1. *Q.* Are works of mercy and charity proper for a Sabbath day?

A. Yes: ought not this woman to be loosed from this bond on the Sabbath day? Luke xiii. 16.

2. *Q.* And may works of necessity be done on that day?

A. Yes: do not you, on the Sabbath, lead your ox, or your ass to watering? Luke xiii. 13.

LXI. *Q.* What is forbidden in the fourth commandment?

A. The fourth commandment forbiddeth the omission, or careless performance, of the duties required; and the profaning the day, by idleness, or doing that which is in itself sinful, or by unnecessary thoughts, words or works, about our worldly employments or recreations.

§ I.

1. *Q.* Do we profane the Sabbath if we neglect the Sabbath work?

A. Yes: I came seeking fruit, but find none. Luke xiii. 7.

2. *Q.* Or if we perform carelessly?

A. Yes: ye brought that which was torn, and the lame, and the sick. Mal. i. 13.

3. *Q.* Or if we be weary of it?

A. Yes: they say, when will the Sabbath be gone? Amos viii. 5.

4. *Q.* Or if we idle away Sabbath time?

A. Yes; why stand ye here all the day idle? Matt. xx. 6.

5. *Q.* And much more if we do that which is, in itself, sinful?

A. Yes: they have defiled my sanctuary in the same day, and have profaned my Sabbaths. Ezek. xxiii. 38.

§ II.

1. *Q.* Do we profane the Sabbath by violating the Sabbath rest?

A. Yes: What evil thing is this that ye do, and profane the Sabbath day? Neh. xiii. 17.

2. *Q.* May we not buy and sell, on that day?

A. No: make not my father's house, a house of merchandize. John ii. 16.

3. *Q.* May we not work harvest work on that day?

A. No: in earing time, and in harvest, thou shalt rest. Exod. xxxiv. 21.

4. *Q.* May we not, however, think, and speak at our pleasure, on that day?

A. No: not doing thine own ways, nor speaking thine own words. Isa. lviii. 13.

§III.

1. *Q.* Was he punished, that gathered sticks, on the Sabbath?

A. Yes: they stoned him with stones, that he died. Numb. xv. 36.

2. *Q.* Are nations, sometimes punished, for Sabbath profanation?

A. Yes: if ye will not hallow the Sabbath day, I will kindle a fire in the gates of Jerusalem. Jer. xvii. 27.

3. *Q.* Is the contempt of the Sabbath, a contempt of God?

A. Yes: this man is not of God, because he keeepeth not the Sabbath day. John ix. 16.

LXII. *Q.* What are the reasons annexed to the fourth commandment?

A. The reasons annexed to the fourth commandment are, God's allowing us six days of the week for our own employments, his challenging a special propriety in the seventh, his own example, and his blessing the Sabbath day.

§I.

1. *Q.* Has God allowed us six days of the week?

A. Yes: six days shalt thou labour, and do all thy work. Exod. xx. 9.

2. *Q.* Has he reserved but one day in seven for himself?

A. Yes: for he hath not made us to serve with an offering, nor wearied us with increase. Isa. xliii. 23.

3. *Q.* Does he claim a special property in the seventh day?

A. Yes: it is the Sabbath of the Lord thy God. Exod. xx. 10.

4. *Q.* Has our Lord Jesus a property in it?

A. Yes: for the Son of man is Lord also of the Sabbath. Mark ii. 28.

5. *Q.* Ought we not, therefore, to devote it to his service?

A. Yes: for, will a man rob God? Mal. iii. 8.

§II.

1. *Q.* Did God, the Creator, set us an example of Sabbath rest?

A. Yes: for the seventh day he rested and was refreshed. Exod. xxxi. 17.

2. *Q.* Did God, the Redeemer, set us an example of Sabbath work?

A. Yes: for, as his custom was, he went into the synagogue on the Sabbath day. Luke iv. 16.

3. *Q.* And, has he given us encouragement in the work of the christian Sabbath?

A. Yes: for, when they were assembled on the first day of the week, Jesus stood in the midst. John xx. 19.

§III

1. *Q.* Has God blessed the Sabbath day, and so put an honour upon it?

A. Yes: the Lord blessed the Sabbath day, and hallowed it. Exod. xx. 11.

2. *Q.* Is it not an ill thing, then, for us, to put a slight upon it?

A. Yes: as they do that despise the holy things, and profane the Sabbath. Ezek xxii. 8.

3. *Q.* Has God appointed it to be a day of blessing to us?

A. Yes: there will I come to thee, and will bless thee. Exod. xx. 24.

4. *Q.* Are not they enemies to themselves then that neglect it?

A. Yes: they forsake their own mercy. Jonah ii. 8.

LXIII. *Q.* Which is the fifth commandment?

A. The fifth commandment is, Honour thy father and thy mother; that thy days may be long upon the land which the Lord thy God giveth thee.

§I.

1. *Q.* Do the six last commandments concern our duty to our neighbour?

A. Yes: for, this is his commandment, that we love one another. 1 John iii. 23.

2. *Q.* And must we mind that as well as our duty to God?

A. Yes: providing for honest things, not only in the sight of the Lord, but in the sight of men. 2 Cor. viii. 21.

3. *Q.* And are we concerned to be very careful in the second table duties?

A. Yes: that the name of God, and his doctrine, be not blasphemed. 1 Tim vi. 1.

4. *Q.* Will our devotions be acceptable without this?

A. No: When ye make many prayers I will not hear, for your hands are full of blood. Isa. i. 15.

§ II.

1. *Q.* Is religion toward God a branch of universal righteousness?

A. Yes: render to God the things that are God's. Matt. xxii. 21.

2. *Q.* And is righteousness towards men a branch of true religion?

A. Yes: for, pure religion and undefiled before God and the Father is this, to visit the fatherless and widows in their affliction. James i. 27.

3. *Q.* Does the law of God require both?

A. Yes: to do justly, and to love mercy, and to walk humbly with thy God. Mich. vi. 8.

4. *Q.* And does the grace of the gospel teach both?

A. Yes: to live soberly, righteously, and godly, in this present world. Tit. ii. 12.

5. *Q.* Must every godly man, then, be an honest man?

A. Yes: for we must live in all godliness and honesty. 1 Tim. ii. 2.

6. *Q.* And must he be a charitable man?

A. Yes: he is gracious and full of compassion and righteous. Ps. cxii. 4.

7. *Q.* And will the trial be by this, at the great day?

A. Yes: for, I was hungry, and ye gave me meat. Matt. xxv. 35.

§ III.

1. *Q.* Does the fifth commandment concern our duty to our relations?

A. Yes: for all ye are brethren. Matt. xxiii. 8.

2. *Q.* And must we be careful to do this duty?

A. Yes: that they who will not be won by the word, may be won by the conversation. 1 Pet. iii. 1.

LXIV. *Q.* What is required in the fifth commandment?

A. The fifth commandment requireth the preserving the honour, and performing the duties, belonging to every one in their several places and relations, as superiors, inferiors, or equals.

§ I.

1. *Q.* Is it the duty of children to reverence their parents?
A. Yes: Ye shall fear every man his mother and his father. Lev. xix. 3.

2. *Q.* And must they give honour to them?
A. Yes: if I be a father, where is my honour? Mal. i. 6.

3. *Q.* And may they, upon no account, despise them?
A. No: despise not thy mother when she is old. Prov. xxiii. 22.

4. *Q.* Ought they to carry themselves respectfully towards them?
A. Yes: King Solomon rose up to meet his mother, and bowed himself to her. 1 Kings ii. 19.

5. *Q.* And to speak honourably to them?
A. Yes: her children rise up and call her blessed. Prov. xxxi. 28.

§ II.

1. *Q.* Is it the duty of children to obey their parents?
A. Yes: children, obey your parents in the Lord. Ephes. vi. 1.

2. *Q.* And to receive their instructions?
A. Yes: hear the instruction of thy father, and forsake not the law of thy mother. Prov. i. 8.

3. *Q.* And to submit to their correction?
A. Yes: the fathers of our flesh corrected us, and we gave them reverence. Heb. xiii. 9.

4. *Q.* Should children labour to rejoice the hearts of their parents?
A. Yes: my son, if thy heart be wise, my heart shall rejoice. Prov. xxiii. 15.

5. *Q.* And to requite them?
A. Yes: let them shew piety at home, and requite their parents. 1 Tim. v. 4.

6. *Q.* And to have their consent, in disposing of themselves?
A. Yes: Jacob obeyed his father, and his mother, and went to Padanaram, for a wife. Gen. xxviii. 7.

7. *Q.* Is Christ an example of this subjection?
A. Yes: for he went with his parents to Nazareth, and was subject to them. Luke ii. 51.

§ III.

1. *Q.* Is it the duty of children to be respectful to the aged?
A. Yes: thou shalt rise up before the hoary head, and honour the face of the old man. Lev. xix. 32.

2. *Q.* And must they be observant of their teachers?

A. Yes: for they will mourn at the last, who obey not the the voice of their teachers, and incline not their ears to them that instruct them. Prov. v. 11, 13.

3. *Q.* And must they order themselves lowly and reverently to all their betters?

A. Yes: ye younger, submit yourselves to the elder. 1 Pet. v. 5.

§ IV.

1. *Q.* Is it the duty of parents to be tender of their children?

A. Yes: for, can a woman forget her sucking child? Isa. xlix. 15.

2. *Q.* And mild towards them?

A. Yes: for a father pities his children. Ps. ciii. 13.

3. *Q.* And to bear with them?

A. Yes: as a man spares his son that serves him. Mal. iii. 17.

4. *Q.* And yet, must they correct them when it is necessary?

A. Yes: for he that spares his rod, hates his son; but he that loves him, chastens him betimes. Prov. xiii. 24.

§ V.

1. *Q.* Is it the duty of parents to pray for their children?

A. Yes: Job offered for his sons burnt-offerings, according to the number of them all. Job. i. 5.

2. *Q.* And to bless God for them?

A. Yes: they are the children which God hath graciously given thy servant. Gen. xxxiii. 5.

3. *Q.* Are they to bless them in the name of the Lord?

A. Yes: by faith Isaac blessed Jacob and Esau. Heb. xi. 20.

4. *Q.* And are they to provide for them what is convenient?

A. Yes: if any provide not for his own, especially for those of his own house, he hath denied the faith, and is worse than an infidel. 1 Tim. v. 8.

§ VI.

1. *Q.* Is it the duty of parents to bring up their children in the fear of God?

A. Yes: bring them up in the nurture and admonition of the Lord. Ephes. vi. 4.

2. *Q.* And to teach them the things of God?

A. Yes: thou shalt teach them diligently unto thy children. Deut. vi. 7.

3. *Q.* And to oblige them to their duty?

A. Yes: I know Abraham, that he will command his children to keep the way of the Lord. Gen. xviii. 19.

4. *Q.* And ought they to set them a good example?

A. Yes: I will walk within my house with a perfect heart. Ps. ci. 2.

5. *Q.* And must they patiently part with their children when God calls for them?

A. Yes: thou hast not withheld thy son, thine only son. Gen. xxii. 16.

§ VII

1. *Q.* Is it the duty of servants to honour their masters and mistresses?

A. Yes: let as many servants as are under the yoke, count their own masters worthy of all honour. 1 Tim. vi. i.

2. *Q.* Is it their duty to obey them?

A. Yes: servants, be obedient to them that are your masters. Ephes. vi. 5.

3. *Q.* And to be just and true to them?

A. Yes: not purloining, but shewing all good fidelity. Tit. ii. 10.

4. *Q.* Ought they to be diligent in the duty of their place?

A. Yes: not with eye service, as men-pleasers, but in singleness of heart. Col. iii. 22.

5. *Q.* And to do it cheerfully?

A. Yes: whatsoever ye do, do it heartily and with good will, doing service. Col. iii. 23; and Ephes. vi. 7.

6. *Q.* Ought they to be patient under rebukes?

A. Yes: not answering again. Tit. ii. 9.

7. *Q.* What, though they suffer unjustly?

A. Yes: servants, be subject, not only to the good and gentle, but also to the froward. 1 Pet. ii. 18.

8. *Q.* And must they have an eye to God in all?

A. Yes: as to the Lord, and not to men. Col. iii. 23.

§ VIII.

1. *Q.* Is it the duty of masters to be just to their servants?

A. Yes: masters, give to your servants that which is just and equal. Col. iv. 1.

2. *Q.* And to be gentle towards them?

A. Yes: forbearing threatening. Ephes. vi. 9.

3. *Q.* Should all masters of families worship God with their families?

A. Yes: as for me and my house, we will serve the Lord. Josh. xxiv. 15.

4. *Q.* And should they restrain sin in their families?

A. Yes: thou shalt put away iniquity far from thy tabernacle. Job. xxii. 23.

§ IX.

1. *Q.* Is it the duty of wives to be respectful to their husbands?

A. Yes: let the wife see that she reverence her husband. Ephes. v. 33.

2. *Q.* And to love them?

A. Yes: they must love their husbands and love their children. Tit. ii. 4.

3. *Q.* Must they be submissive to their husbands?

A. Yes: wives, submit yourselves to your own husbands, as it is fit in the Lord. Col. iii. 18.

4. *Q.* Must they be faithful and obedient to them?

A. Yes: they must be chaste, keepers at home, obedient to their own husbands. Tit. ii. 5.

5. *Q.* Must they receive instruction from them?

A. Yes: if they will learn anything, let them ask their husbands at home. 1 Cor. xiv. 35.

6. *Q.* Must they be helpers to them in religion?

A. Yes: that they may be won by the conversation of the wives. 1 Pet. iii. 1.

§ X.

1. *Q.* Is it the duty of husbands to love their wives?

A. Yes: husbands, love your wives, and be not bitter against them. Col. iii. 19.

2. *Q.* Must they love them dearly?

A. Yes: let every one love his wife, even as himself. Ephes. v. 33.

3. *Q.* And delight in them?

A. Yes: rejoice, with the wife of thy youth. Prov. v. 18.

4. *Q.* And be tender of them?

A. Yes: giving honour to the wife, as unto the weaker vessel. 1 Pet. iii. 7.

§ XI.

1. *Q.* Is it the duty of husbands and wives to be pleasing, one to another?

A. Yes: he that is married careth how to please his wife, and she that is married how to please her husband. 1 Cor. vii. 33, 34.

2. *Q.* Is it their duty to live in the fear of God, and to pray together?

A. Yes: as heirs together of the grace of life, that your prayers be not hindered. 1 Pet. iii. 7.

3. *Q.* Should they promote the eternal salvation one of another?

A. Yes: what knowest thou, O wife, whether thou shalt save thy husband? Or how knowest thou, O man, whether thou shalt save thy wife? 1 Cor. vii. 16.

§ XII.

1. *Q.* Is it the duty of subjects to reverence their magistrates?
A. Yes: fear God, honour the king. 1 Pet. ii. 17.
2. *Q.* And to obey them in the Lord?
A. Yes: we must be subject to principalities and powers, and obey magistrates. Tit. iii. 1.
3. *Q.* And to be loyal to them?
A. Yes: for the powers that be are ordained of God. Rom. xiii. 1.
4. *Q.* Is it our duty to pray for magistrates?
A. Yes: for kings, and for all that are in authority. 1 Tim. ii. 2.
5. *Q.* And to pay them tribute?
A. Yes: tribute to whom tribute is due, custom to whom custom. Rom. xiii. 7.
6. *Q.* Must we be peaceable under their government?
A. Yes: that we under them may lead a quiet and peaceable life. 1 Tim. ii. 2.
7. *Q.* And all this conscientiously?
A. Yes: ye must needs be subject, not only for wrath, but also for conscience sake. Rom. xiii. 5.
8. *Q.* Ought magistrates to be as parents to their subjects?
A. Yes: kings shall be thy nursing fathers, and queens thy nursing mothers. Isa. xlix. 23.

§ XIII.

1. *Q.* Is it the duty of people to love and respect their ministers?
A. Yes: know them which labour among you, and esteem them very highly in love, for their work's sake. 1 Thess. v. 12, 13.
2. *Q.* Ought they to submit to their instructions?
A. Yes: obey your guides, and submit yourselves, for they watch for your souls. Heb. xiii. 17.
3. *Q.* And to provide for their comfortable subsistence?
A. Yes: let him that is taught in the word communicate to him that teacheth. Gal. vi. 6.
4. *Q.* And ought ministers to be as spiritual fathers to their people?
A. Yes: we exhorted, and comforted, and charged every one of you, as a father doth his children. 1 Thess. ii. 11.

§ XIV.

1. *Q.* Is it the duty of equals to be kind one to another?

A. Yes: be kindly affectioned one to another, with brotherly love. Rom. xii. 10.

2. *Q.* And to be respectful, one to another?

A. Yes: in honour, preferring one another. Rom. xii. 10.

3. *Q.* And to be submissive, one to another?

A. Yes: yea, all of you, be subject one to another. 1 Pet. v. 5.

LXV. *Q.* What is forbidden in the fifth commandment?

A. The fifth commandment forbiddeth the neglecting of, or doing anything against, the honour and duty which belongeth to every one in their several places and relations.

§ I.

1. *Q.* Is it a sin for children to despise their parents?

A. Yes: cursed be he that sets light by his father or mother. Deut. xxvii. 16.

2. *Q.* Or to disobey them?

A. Yes: the eye that mocks at his father, and despiseth to obey his mother, the ravens of the valley shall pick it out, and the young eagles shall eat it. Prov. xxx. 17.

3. *Q.* Is it a sin for children prodigally to spend their parent's substance?

A. Yes: he that wasteth his father, and chaseth away his mother, is a son that causeth shame. Prov. xix. 26.

4. *Q.* Or to grieve their parents?

A. Yes: a foolish son is the heaviness of his mother. Prov. x. 1.

§ II.

1. *Q.* Is it a sin for inferiors to be rude and undutiful to their superiors?

A. Yes: for a child to behave himself proudly against the ancient, and the base against the honourable. Isa. iii. 5.

2. *Q.* Is it a sin for superiors to be harsh and unkind to their inferiors?

A. Yes: fathers, provoke not your children to wrath, lest they be discouraged. Col. iii. 21.

§ III.

1. *Q.* Is it a sin to be vexatious to our relations?

A. Yes: her adversary provoked her to make her fret. 1 Sam. i. 6.

2. *Q.* And to be quarrelsome with our relations?

A. Yes: let there be no strife, I pray thee, between me and thee, and between my herdsmen, and thy herdsmen, for we be brethren. Gen. xiii. 8.

3. *Q.* And to be suspicious of our relations?

A. Yes: for charity thinketh no evil. 1 Cor. xiii. 4, 5.

LXVI. *Q.* What is the reason annexed to the fifth commandment?

A. The reason annexed to the fifth commandment, is a promise of long life and prosperity, (as far as it shall serve for God's glory and their own good) to all such as keep this commandment.

§ I.

1. *Q.* Is there a gracious promise made to those that honour their parents?

A. Yes: it is the first commandment with promise. Ephes. vi. 2.

2. *Q.* Is long life promised?

A. Yes: that thy days may be long in the land. Exod. xx. 12.

3. *Q.* Is outward prosperity promised?

A. Yes: that it may be well with thee. Ephes. vi. 3.

4. *Q.* Are temporal blessings promised to good people?

A. Yes: Godliness hath the promise of the life that now is. 1 Tim. iv. 8.

5. *Q.* And are they promised particularly to pious and dutiful children?

A. Yes: my son, forget not my law, but let thine heart keep my commandments; for length of days, and long life, and peace shall they add to thee. Prov. iii. 1, 2.

§ II.

1. *Q.* Do all good children prosper in this world?

A. No: for all things come alike to all. Eccl. ix. 2.

2. *Q.* But are they most likely to prosper?

A. Yes: for, by humility, and the fear of the Lord, are riches, honour and life. Prov. xxii. 4.

3. *Q.* Shall they prosper as far as is for God's glory?

A. Yes: I will deliver thee, and thou shalt glorify me. Ps. l. 15.

4. *Q.* And as far as is for their own good?

A. Yes: for we read of those whom God sent into captivity for their good. Jer. xxiv. 5.

5. *Q.* But shall good children live, however, in the Heavenly Canaan?

A. Yes: there, their inheritance shall be forever. Ps. xxxvii. 18.

6. *Q.* And are disobedient children often punished in this life?

A. Yes: as Absalom that was hanged in an oak. 2 Sam. xviii. 9.

LXVII. *Q.* Which is the sixth commandment?

A. The sixth commandment is, *Thou shalt not kill.*

§ I.

1. *Q.* Does the sixth commandment concern our own and our neighbour's life?

A. Yes: for the life is more than meat. Matt. vi. 25.

2. *Q.* Has God a tender regard to the life of men?

A. Yes: for he giveth to all life and breath. Acts xvii. 25.

3. *Q.* Has he, by this law, made a hedge about life?

A. Yes: that men might not be like the fishes of the sea. Hab. i. 14.

§ II.

1. *Q.* Did there need this law?

A. Yes: for men live in malice and envy, hateful, and hating one another. Tit. iii. 3.

2. *Q.* Is it a part of the law of nature?

A. Yes: for the barbarous people said of a murderer, that vengeance suffers him not to live. Acts xxviii. 4.

LXVIII. *Q.* What is required in the sixth commandment?

A. The sixth commandment requireth all lawful endeavours to preserve our own life, and the life of others.

§ I.

1. *Q.* Are we to take care of our own lives?

A. Yes: no man ever yet hated his own flesh, but nourisheth and cherisheth it. Ephes. v. 29.

2. *Q.* Must we endeavour the preservation of them?

A. Yes: skin for skin, and all that a man hath, will he give for his life. Job ii. 4.

3. *Q.* Are we to be careful of our diet?

A. Yes: hast thou found honey? Eat so much as is sufficient for thee. Prov. xxv. 16.

4. *Q.* Are we to use physic when we need it?

A. Yes: take a lump of figs and lay it upon the boil. Isa. xxxviii. 21.

5. *Q.* And are we to be cheerful?

A. Yes: for a merry heart doeth good like a medicine. Prov. xvii. 22.

§ II.

1. *Q.* But may we deny Christ, to save our lives?

A. No: for he that so saveth his life shall lose it. Matt. xvi. 25.

2. *Q.* May we commit any wilful sin, to save our lives?

A. No: we must do no evil that good may come. Rom. iii. 8.

3. *Q.* But, what we do for the preservation of our own lives, must it be with an eye to God's glory?

A. Yes: that I may live, and keep thy word. Ps. cxix. 17. Live and praise thee. v. 175.

§ III.

1. *Q.* Are we to be compassionate, even to the brute creatures?

A. Yes: a righteous man regardeth the life of his beast. Prov. xii. 10.

2. *Q.* Are we to be careful of the lives of others, as well as of our own?

A. Yes: it was Cain that said, am I my brother's keeper? Gen. iv. 9.

3. *Q.* Are we to do what we can, in our places, for the relief of those who are exposed to violence?

A. Yes: we must deliver them that are ready to be slain. Prov. xxiv. 11.

4. *Q.* Must we succour the distressed, like the good Samaritan?

A. Yes: go thou, and do likewise. Luke x. 37.

§ IV.

1. *Q.* Are we to support the lives of those who are in straits?

A. Yes: the blessing of him that was ready to perish, came upon me. Job xxix. 13.

2. *Q.* Are we to be meek towards those that provoke us?

A. Yes: shewing all meekness toward all men. Tit. iii. 2.

3. *Q.* And are we to be merciful toward those who need us?

A. Yes: put on, as the elect of God, bowels of mercy. Col. iii. 12.

LXIX. Q. What is forbidden in the sixth commandment?

A. The sixth commandment forbiddeth the taking away of our own life, or the life of our neighbour unjustly, or whatsoever tendeth thereunto.

§ I.

1. *Q.* May we dispose of our own lives at our pleasure?
A. No: for, surely, your blood of your lives will I require. Gen. ix. 5.

2. *Q.* Is it a sin, in any case, to kill ourselves?
A. Yes: do thyself no harm. Acts xvi. 28.

3. *Q.* Is it an exceeding sinful sin?
A. Yes: it was the sin of Saul and Judas. 1 Sam. xxxi. 4; Matt. xxvii. 5.

4. *Q.* Is it a sin, needlessly to expose our lives?
A. Yes: thou shalt not tempt the Lord thy God. Matt. iv. 7.

5. *Q.* But must we not expose our lives to keep a good conscience?
A. Yes: neither count I my life dear unto me, so that I might finish my course with joy. Acts xx. 24.

§ II.

1. *Q.* Is drunkenness a sin against our own lives?
A. Yes: take heed, lest your hearts be overcharged with surfeiting and drunkenness, and so that day come upon you unawares. Luke xxi. 34.

2. *Q.* Is uncleanness so?
A. Yes: he that commits fornication, sins against his own body. 1 Cor. vi. 18.

3. *Q.* Is immoderate care and grief a sin against our own lives?
A. Yes: for the sorrow of the world worketh death. 2 Cor. vii. 10.

§ III.

1. *Q.* Is it lawful for the magistrate to take away the life of a malefactor?
A. Yes: for he bears not the sword in vain. Rom. xiii. 4.

2. *Q.* May soldiers kill, in a lawful war?
A. Yes: cursed is he that keepeth back his sword from blood. Jer. xlviii. 10.

3. *Q.* But is wilful murder a great sin?

A. Yes: the voice of thy brother's blood cries. Gen. iv. 10.
4. *Q.* Is it an iniquity to be punished by the judge?
A. Yes: whoso sheddeth man's blood, by man shall his blood be shed. Gen. ix. 6.
5. *Q.* And ought the murderer to be put to death?
A. Yes: a man that doeth violence to the blood of any person shall flee to the pit; let no man stay him. Prov. xxviii. 17.

§ IV.

1. *Q.* Is murder a great affront to God?
A. Yes: for in the image of God made he man. Gen. ix. 6.
2. *Q.* Does it make men like the devil?
A. Yes: for he was a murderer from the beginning. John viii. 44.
3. Is it of dangerous consequence to the murderer?
A. Yes: for no murderer hath eternal life abiding in him. 1 John iii. 15.
4. *Q.* Ought we, therefore, to pray, that God would keep us from it?
A. Yes: deliver me from blood-guiltiness, O God of my salvation. Ps. li. 14.

§ V.

1. *Q.* Is malice heart-murder?
A. Yes: he that hateth his brother is a murderer. 1 John iii. 15.
2. *Q.* Is rash anger a breach of this commandment?
A. Yes: but I say unto you, whosoever is angry with his brother without cause, shall be in danger of the judgment. Matt. v. 22.
3. *Q.* Is giving foul language a breach of this commandment?
A. Yes: whosoever shall say to his brother, Raca, or thou fool, shall be in danger of hell fire. Matt. v. 22.
4. *Q.* Is revenge a breach of this commandment?
A. Yes: dearly beloved, avenge not yourselves. Rom. xii. 19.

LXX. *Q.* Which is the seventh commandment?

A. The seventh commandment is, *Thou shalt not commit adultery.*

§ I.

1. *Q.* Does this commandment concern our own and our neighbour's chastity?
A. Yes: for this is the will of God, even our sanctification. 1 Thess. iv. 3.

2. Q. Is it needful there should be such a commandment?

A. Yes: for since all are gone aside, they are all become filthy. Ps. xiv. 3.

3. Q. Is it agreeable to the light of nature?

A. Yes: for Abimelech called adultery a great sin. Gen. xx. 9.

4. Q. And is this command for the public good of mankind?

A. Yes: for whoredom and wine take away the heart. Hos. iv. 11.

LXXI. Q. What is required in the seventh commandment?

A. The seventh commandment requireth the preservation of our own and our neighbour's chastity, in heart, speech and behaviour.

§ I.

1. Q. Is it our duty to keep our bodies pure from all fleshly lusts?

A. Yes: we must possess our vessel in sanctification and honour, and not in the lust of concupiscence. 1 Thess. iv. 4, 5.

2. Q. Are we to present our bodies to God?

A. Yes: present your bodies unto God a living sacrifice. Rom. xii. 1.

3. Q. Are we to glorify him with them?

A. Yes: glorify God with your bodies. 1 Cor. vi. 20.

4. Q. Are we to use them for him?

A. Yes: for your body is the temple of the Holy Ghost, which is in you. 1 Cor. vi. 19.

5. Q. And to employ them in his service?

A. Yes: yield your members as instruments of righteousness unto God. Rom. vi. 13.

6. Q. May they, then, be used, in the service of our lusts?

A. No: for if any man defile the temple of God, him shall God destroy. 1 Cor. iii. 17.

§ II.

1. Q. Ought we to preserve our chastity in heart?

A. Yes; that we may be holy both in body and spirit. 1 Cor. vii. 34.

2. Q. And must we keep out all unclean thoughts and desires?

A. Yes: we must flee youthful lusts. 2 Tim. ii. 22.

3. Q. And is that the way to prevent the acts of uncleanness?

A. Yes: for, when lust hath conceived, it brings forth sin.

§ III.

1. *Q.* Ought we to preserve our chastity, in speech?
A. Yes: let your specch be always with grace, seasoned with salt. Col. iv. 6.

2. *Q.* Is it the character of good people to be modest?
A. Yes: I will turn to the people a pure language. Zeph. iii. 9.

§ IV.

1. *Q.* Ought we to preserve our chastity in behaviour?
A. Yes: we must have a chaste conversation coupled with fear. 1 Pet. iii. 2.

2. *Q.* And in our clothing?
A. Yes: women must adorn themselves in modest apparel, with shame-facedness and sobriety. 1 Tim. ii. 9.

3. *Q.* Must we abstain from all appearances of uncleanness?
A. Yes: hating, even the garment spotted with the flesh. Jude 23.

4. *Q.* And from all approaches to it?
A. Yes: come not nigh the door of her house. Prov. v. 8.

§ V.

1. *Q.* Must we resolve against wanton looks?
A. Yes: I made a covenant with mine eyes; why, then should I think upon a maid? Job xxxi. 1.

2. *Q.* Must we always keep our bodies in soberness and chastity?
A. Yes: we must cleanse ourselves from all filthiness both of flesh and spirit. 2 Cor. vii. 1.

3. *Q.* And must we crucify all the lusts of the flesh?
A. Yes: they that are Christ's have crucified the flesh. Gal. v. 24.

4. *Q.* Must the body be subdued?
A. Yes: I keep under my body, and bring it into subjection. 1 Cor. ix. 27.

5. *Q.* And must its sinful desires be denied?
A. Yes: if thy right eye offend thee, pluck it out, and cast it from thee. Matt. v. 29.

LXXII. *Q.* What is forbidden in the seventh commandment?

A. The seventh commandment forbiddeth all unchaste thoughts, words and actions.

§ I.

1. *Q.* Is adultery a very great sin?

A. Yes: how can I do this great wickedness, and sin against God? Gen. xxxix. 9.

2. *Q.* Is it an iniquity, to be punished by the judge?

A. Yes: the adulterer and the adulteress shall surely be put to death. Lev. xx. 10.

3. *Q.* Is fornication a very great sin?

A. Yes: fornication and all uncleanness, let it not be once named among you. Ephes. v. 3.

4. *Q.* Will these sins certainly shut men out of heaven, if they be not repented of, and forsaken?

A. Yes: for fornicators and adulterers shall not inherit the kingdom of God. 1 Cor. vi. 9, 10.

§ II.

1. *Q.* Are unclean thoughts sins?

A. Yes: for whosoever looketh on a woman, to lust after her, hath committed adultery with her already in his heart. Matt. v. 28.

2. *Q.* Are unclean reflections sins?

A. Yes: for some multiply their whoredoms by calling to remembrance the days of their youth. Ezek. xxiii. 19.

3. *Q.* Are unclean desires sins?

A. Yes: inordinate affection, and evil concupiscence, are to be mortified in us. Col. iii. 5.

4. *Q.* And must all fleshly lusts be shunned?

A. Yes: dearly beloved, I beseech you, as strangers and pilgrims, abstain from fleshly lusts. 1 Pet. ii. 11.

§ III.

1. *Q.* Are unclean words sin?

A. Yes: for there must be neither filthiness, nor foolish talking, nor jesting. Ephes. v. 4.

2. *Q.* Must we, therefore, take heed of speaking any filthy words?

A. Yes: let no corrupt communication proceed out of your mouth. Ephes. iv. 29.

3. *Q.* May we take delight in hearing filthy talk?

A. No: for evil communications corrupt good manners. 1 Cor. xv. 33.

§ IV.

1. *Q.* Are all unchaste actions forbidden in this commandment?

A. Yes: not only adultery and fornication, but uncleanness and lasciviousness, (Gal. v. 19.) chambering and wantonness. Rom. xiii. 13.

2. *Q.* Are the occasions of uncleanness here forbidden?
A. Yes: have no fellowship with the unfruitful works of darkness. Ephes. v. 11.

§ v.

1. *Q.* Is all uncleanness provoking to God?
A. Yes: for I, the Lord, am holy. Lev. xx. 26.
2. *Q.* Is it against our bodies?
A. Yes: for the body is not for fornication, but for the Lord. 1 Cor. vi. 13.
3. *Q.* Is it a wrong to our souls?
A. Yes: for, fleshly lusts war against the soul. 1 Pet. ii. 11.
4. *Q.* Is it wounding to conscience?
A. Yes: I find more bitter than death the woman whose heart is snares and nets. Eccl. vii. 26.

§ vi.

1. *Q.* Are idleness and gluttony occasions of uncleanness, and forbidden in this commandment?
A. Yes? for, this was the iniquity of Sodom, pride, fulness of bread, and abundance of idleness. Ezek. xvi. 49.
2. *Q.* And is drunkenness also a sin of dangerous consequences?
A. Yes: for drunkards shall not inherit the kingdom of God. 1 Cor. vi. 10.

LXXIII. *Q.* What is the eighth commandment?

A. The eighth commandment is, *Thou shalt not steal.*

§ I.

1. *Q.* Does the eighth commandment concern our own and our neighbour's wealth and outward estate?
A. Yes: for the earth God hath given to the children of men. Ps. cxv. 16.
2. *Q.* Is it necessary there should be such a command?
A. Yes: for every brother will utterly supplant. Jer. ix. 4.

§ II.

1. *Q.* Is robbing God the worst theft?
A. Yes: will a man rob God? Yet ye have robbed me. Mal. iii. 8.
2. *Q.* And is justice to God the highest justice?

A. Yes: render to God, the things that are God's. Matt. xxii. 21.

LXXIV. *Q.* What is required in the eighth commandment?

A. The eighth commandment requireth the lawful procuring and furthering the wealth and outward estate of ourselves and others.

§ I.

1. *Q.* Is religion a friend to outward prosperity?
A. Yes: for, in wisdom's left hand are riches and honour. Prov. iii. 16.

2. *Q.* Does it teach us to be diligent in our callings?
A. Yes: be thou diligent to know the state of thy flocks. Prov. xxvii. 23.

3. *Q.* And to keep close to them?
A. Yes: study to be quiet, and to do your own business. 1 Thess. iv. 11.

4. *Q.* And is that the way to thrive?
A. Yes: for, the hand of the diligent maketh rich. Prov. x. 4.

5. *Q.* Does religion teach us to be prudent, in our affairs?
A. Yes: the good man will guide his affairs with discretion. Ps. cxii. 5.

6. *Q.* And is that the way to thrive?
A. Yes: for, through wisdom is a house builded. Prov. xxiv. 3.

§ II.

1. *Q.* Must we serve God with our worldly estate?
A. Yes: honour the Lord with thy substance. Prov. iii. 9.

2. *Q.* And is that the way to thrive?
A. Yes: so shall thy barns be filled with plenty. Prov. iii. 10.

3. *Q.* Must we cheerfully use our estates?
A. Yes: for I know no good in them, but for a man to rejoice, and to do good in his life. Eccl. iii. 12.

4. *Q.* And must we cheerfully serve God with them?
A. Yes: we must serve the Lord our God with joyfulness and gladness of heart, in the abundance of all things. Deut. xxviii. 47.

§ III.

1. *Q.* Must we be just to all we deal with?
A. Yes: render, therefore, to all their due. Rom. xiii. 7.

2. *Q.* And must we give every body his own?

A. Yes: owe no man anything, but to love one another. Rom. xiii. 8.

3. *Q.* Must we be true to every trust reposed in us?
A. Yes: as the workmen who dealt faithfully. 2 Kings xii. 15.

4. *Q.* And is honesty the best policy?
A. Yes: for a little that a righteous man hath, is better than the riches of many wicked. Ps. xxxvii. 16.

5. *Q.* And shall we have the comfort of it in this world?
A. Yes: he that walketh righteously, and speaketh uprightly, that despiseth the gain of oppression, and shaketh his hands from holding of bribes, he shall dwell on high, his place of defence shall be in the munitions of rocks, bread shall be given him, and his waters shall be sure. Isa. xxxiii. 15, 16.

6. *Q.* If, therefore, we have done any wrong, must we make restitution?
A. Yes: Zaccheus stood and said, if I have wronged any man, I restore him four fold. Luke. xix. 8.

§ IV.

1. *Q.* Must we concern ourselves for the welfare of others?
A. Yes: look not every one on his own things, but every one also on the things of others. Philipp. ii. 4.

2. *Q.* And must we do all we can to promote the welfare of others?
A. Yes: if thy brother's ox or ass go astray, thou shalt bring him back. Deut. xxii. 1.

§ V.

1. *Q.* Must we relieve the poor, according to our ability?
A. Yes: if thy brother be waxen poor, and fallen into decay with thee, then thou shalt relieve him. Lev. xxv. 35.

2. *Q.* Must we be forward to relieve the poor?
A. Yes: we must be ready to distribute, willing to communicate. 1 Tim. vi. 18.

3. *Q.* Is that the way to thrive in this world?
A. Yes: for he that hath pity on the poor, lendeth to the Lord, and that which he hath given will he pay him again. Prov. xix. 17.

4. *Q.* And shall it be repaid in a future* world?
A. Yes: thou shalt be recompensed in the resurrection of the just. Luke xiv. 14.

5. *Q.* And must we make this use of what we have in the world?

---

* The author's language is "the other world."—EDITOR.

A. Yes: we must labour, that we may have to give to him that needeth. Ephes. iv. 28.

LXXV. Q. What is forbidden in the eighth commandment?

A. The eighth commandment forbiddeth whatsoever doth or may unjustly hinder our own or our neighbour's wealth or outward state.

§ I.

1. *Q.* May we do what we will with our own estates?
A. No: for we are but stewards of the manifold grace of God. 1 Pet. iv. 10.

2. *Q.* Is it a sin, then, to waste our estates in prodigality?
A. Yes: for, the drunkard and glutton shall come to poverty. Prov. xxiii. 21.

3. *Q.* Is luxury the way to beggary?
A. Yes: he that loveth pleasure shall be a poor man. Prov. xxi. 17.

4. *Q.* Is slothfulness a robbing of ourselves?
A. Yes: for he that is slothful in his work, is brother to him that is a great waster. Prov. xviii. 9.

5, *Q.* And is that the way to poverty?
A. Yes: for drowsiness shall clothe a man with rags. Prov. xxiii. 21.

§ II.

1. *Q.* Is keeping idle company the way to poverty?
A. Yes: for he that followeth after vain persons shall have poverty enough. Prov. xxviii. 19.

2. *Q.* Is fraud and injustice the way to poverty?
A. Yes: for wealth gotten by vanity shall be diminished. Prov. xiii. 11.

3. *Q.* Can any expect to prosper in a way of unjust gain?
A. No: for he that getteth riches, and not by right, shall leave them in the midst of his days, and at his end shall be a fool. Jer. xvii. 11.

4. *Q.* Do men rob themselves and their families by foolishness in their affairs?
A. Yes: for every wise woman buildeth her house, but the foolish plucketh it down with her hands. Prov. xiv. 1.

5. *Q.* And by rash suretyship?
A. Yes: for he that is surety for a stranger shall smart for it. Prov. xi. 15.

§ III.

1. *Q.* Is it a sin to rob ourselves of the comfort of that which God has given us?

A. Yes: if a man hath not power to eat of it, it is vanity, and an evil disease. Eccles. vi. 2.

2. *Q.* And is it a sin to deny it to our relations?

A. Yes: if any provide not for his own, especially for those of his own house, he hath denied the faith, and is worse than an infidel. 1 Tim. v. 8.

§ IV.

1. *Q.* Is it a great sin to steal from any body?

A. Yes: for every one that stealeth shall be cut off. Zech. v. 3.

2. *Q.* Is it a great sin for children to steal from their parents?

A. Yes: whoso robbeth his father or his mother, and saith it is no transgression, the same is the companion of a destroyer. Prov. xxviii. 24.

3. *Q.* And for the rich to oppress the poor?

A. Yes: rob not the poor because he is poor. Prov. xxii. 22.

4. *Q.* Will you, therefore, keep your hands from picking and stealing?

A. Yes: because of the fear of God. Neh. v. 15.

5. *Q.* Must those who have used themselves to it break it off?

A. Yes: let him that stole steal no more. Ephes. iv. 28.

6. *Q.* Must poor people especially watch and pray against this temptation?

A. Yes: lest I be poor and steal. Prov. xxx. 9.

§ V.

1. *Q.* Is it a sin to cheat any body in a bargain?

A. Yes: let no man go beyond or defraud his brother in any matter. 1 Thess. iv. 6.

2. *Q.* Is it a sin to use false weights and measures?

A. Yes: a false balance is abomination to the Lord. Prov. xi. 1.

3. *Q.* Is it a sin to give assistance or countenance to any fraud?

A. Yes: whoso is partner with a thief hateth his own soul. Prov. xxix. 24.

§ VI.

1. *Q.* Is it a sin to deny relief to the poor?

A. Yes: whoso hath this world's goods, and seeth his brother have need, and shutteth up the bowels of his compassion from him, how dwelleth the love of God in that man? 1 John iii. 17.

2. *Q.* Is it a sin to deny the payment of a just debt?

A. Yes: for the wicked borroweth and payeth not again. Ps. xxxvii. 21.

3. *Q.* Or withhold wages that is due?

A. Yes: the hire of the labourer kept back by fraud, crieth. James v. 4.

4. *Q.* And is the love of money the cause of all these sins?

A. Yes: the love of money is the root of all evil. 1 Tim. vi. 10.

LXXVI. *Q.* Which is the ninth commandment?

A. The ninth commandment is, *Thou shalt not bear false witness against thy neighbour.*

§ I.

1. *Q.* Does this commandment concern our own and our neighbour's good name?

A. Yes: for a good name is better than precious ointment. Eccl. vii. 1.

2. *Q.* Is there need of this commandment?

A. Yes: for every neighbour will walk with slanders. Jer. ix. 4.

LXXVII. *Q.* What is required in the ninth commandment?

A. The ninth commandment requireth the maintaining and promoting of truth between man and man, and of our own and our neighbour's good name, especially in witness bearing.

§ I.

1. *Q.* Is it our duty to govern our tongues?

A. Yes: I said I will take heed to my ways, that I sin not with my tongue. Ps. xxxix. 1.

2. *Q.* Is he a good Christian that does not?

A. No: for if any man among you seem to be religious, and bridleth not his tongue, that man's religion is vain. James i. 26.

3. *Q.* Must we, therefore, pray to God, to keep us from tongue sins?

A. Yes: set a watch, O Lord, before my mouth. Ps. cxli. 3.

§ II.

1. *Q.* Is it our duty to speak truth?

A. Yes: speak ye every man the truth to his neighbour. Zech. viii. 16.

2. *Q.* Is there good reason for it?
A. Yes: for we are members, one of another. Ephes. iv. 25.
3. *Q.* And is this the character of a good man?
A. Yes: that he speaketh the truth in his heart. Ps. xv. 2.
4. *Q.* Are all truths to be spoken at all times?
A. No: for there is a time to keep silence, and a time to speak. Eccl. iii. 7.
5. *Q.* But may an untruth be spoken at any time?
A. No: for God's people are children that will not lie. Isa. lxiii. 8.

§ III.

1. *Q.* Is it our duty, especially in witness bearing, to speak truth?
A. Yes: for a faithful witness will not lie. Prov. xiv. 5.
2. *Q.* And the whole truth?
A. Yes: Samuel told Eli every whit, and hid nothing from him. 1 Sam. iii. 18.
3. *Q.* And nothing but the truth?
A. Yes: for a lying tongue is but for a moment. Prov. xii. 19.

§ IV.

1. *Q.* Is it our duty to strive to have a good name with God?
A. Yes: for, not he that commendeth himself is approved, but whom the Lord commendeth. 2 Cor. x. 8.
2. *Q.* And should we endeavour to have a good name with good people?
A. Yes: let those that fear thee turn unto me. Ps. cxix. 79.
3. *Q.* And, if possible, a good name with all people?
A. Yes: Demetrius hath a good report of all men. 3 John 12.
4. *Q.* Must we abound in those things that are of good report?
A. Yes: if there be any virtue, if there be any praise, think on those things. Philipp. iv. 8.

§ V.

1. *Q.* In order to our getting a good name, must we live by faith?
A. Yes: for by it the Elders obtained a good report. Heb. xi. 2.
2. *Q.* Must we walk wisely?
A. Yes: for a man's wisdom makes his face to shine. Eccl. viii. 1.
3. *Q.* Must we do justly?
A. Yes: having your conversation honest among the Gentiles. 1 Pet. ii. 12.

4. *Q.* And be humble?

A. Yes: for, before honour is humility. Prov. xviii. 12.

5. *Q.* And must we abound in good works?

A. Yes: let your light so shine before men. Matt. v. 16.

6. *Q.* But can good people expect to have every one's good word?

A. No: woe unto you when all men speak well of you. Luke vi. 26.

7. *Q.* May we hazard a good conscience to preserve our reputation?

A. No: for our praise is not of men, but of God. Rom. ii. 29.

§ VI.

1. *Q.* Ought we to be very tender of the good names of others?

A. Yes: we must honour all men. 1 Pet. ii. 17.

2. *Q.* Must we give them the praise of that in them which is good?

A. Yes: we also bear record. 3 John 12.

3. *Q.* But may we flatter them?

A. No: he that speaketh flattery to his friends, even the eyes of his children shall fail. Job. xvii. 5.

4. *Q.* Must we charitably conceal their faults?

A. Yes: for charity covereth a multitude of sins. 1 Pet. iv. 8.

5. *Q.* Must we discourage slandering and censoriousness?

A. Yes: we must, with an angry countenance, drive away a back-biting tongue, Prov. xxv. 23.

LXXVIII. *Q.* What is forbidden in the ninth commandment?

A. The ninth commandment forbiddeth whatsoever is prejudicial to truth, or injurious to our own or our neighbour's good name.

§ I.

1. *Q* Is lying a great sin?

A. Yes: lie not one to another, seeing ye have put off the old man. Col. iii. 9.

2. *Q.* Is it a sin that God hates?

A. Yes: lying lips are abomination to the Lord. Prov. xii. 22.

3. *Q.* And is it a sin that all good men hate?

A. Yes: I hate and abhor lying. Ps. cxix. 163.

4. *Q.* Does it make men like the devil?

A. Yes: for he is a liar and the father of it. John viii. 44.

5. *Q.* And will it bring them to hell?

A. Yes: for all liars have their part in the lake that burns with fire and brimstone. Rev. xxi. 8.

§ II.

1. *Q.* Is it lawful to tell a lie to make sport?

A. No: for as a madman who casteth fire-brands, arrows and death, so is he that deceiveth his neighbour, and saith, am not I in sport? Prov. xxvi. 18, 19.

2. *Q.* Is it lawful to tell a lie to excuse a fault?

A. No: for Gehazi for doing so had a leprosy entailed on him and his seed forever. 2 Kings v. 37.

3. *Q.* May we tell a lie with intention to do good?

A. No: we must not do evil that good may come. Rom. iii. 8.

4. *Q.* Will what is got by lying do us any good?

A. No: the getting of treasures by a lying tongue is vanity, tossed to and fro of them that seek death. Prov. xxi. 6.

5. *Q.* Should we, therefore, pray against this sin?

A. Yes: remove from me the way of lying. Ps. cxix. 29.

§ III.

1. *Q.* Is it a sin to belie ourselves?

A. Yes: as there is that maketh himself poor, yet hath great riches. Prov. xiii. 7.

2. *Q.* May we be careless of our own good name?

A. No: if I should say I know him not, I should be a liar like unto you. John viii. 55.

§ IV.

1. *Q.* Is it a sin to belie our neighbour?

A. Yes: they laid to my charge things that I know not. Ps. xxxv. 11.

2. *Q.* Is it folly?

A. Yes: he that uttereth slander is a fool. Prov. x. 18.

3. *Q.* Is it a sin to speak evil of any?

A. Yes: put them in mind to speak evil of no man. Tit. iii. 1, 2.

4. *Q.* And to be censorious of our brethren?

A. Yes: judge not, that ye be not judged. Matt. vii. 1.

5. *Q.* Is it a great offence to God to do this?

A. Yes: he that speaks evil of his brother, and judgeth his brother, speaketh evil of the law and judgeth the law. James iv. 11.

6. *Q.* Does it make us like the devil?

A. Yes: for he is the accuser of the brethren. Rev. xii. 10.

§ V.

1. *Q.* Is it a sin to raise a false report?
A. Yes: thou shalt not raise a false report. Exod. xxiii. 1.
2. *Q.* And a sin to spread it?
A. Yes: thou shalt not go up and down as a tale-bearer. Lev. xix. 16.
3. *Q.* May we proclaim our brethren's faults?
A. No: for charity rejoiceth not in iniquity. 1 Cor. xiii. 6.
4. *Q.* Is it a sin to speak ill of magistrates?
A. Yes: thou shalt not speak evil of the ruler of thy people. Acts. xxiii. 5.
5. *Q.* Is it a sin to be abusive to the poor?
A. Yes: for he that mocketh the poor, reproacheth his maker, Prov. xvii. 5.
6. *Q.* May we speak ill of those who speak ill of us?
A. No: we must not render railing for railing. 1 Pet. iii. 9.

LXXIX. *Q.* What is the tenth commandment?

A. The tenth commandment is, *Thou shalt not covet thy neighbour's house, thou shalt not covet thy neighbour's wife, nor his man-servant, nor his maid-servant, nor his ox, nor his ass, nor any thing that is thy neighbours.*

§ I.

1. *Q.* Does this commandment lay a restraint upon the heart?
A. Yes: for the law is spiritual. Rom. vii. 14.
2. *Q.* Does the heart need this restraint?
A. Yes: for the inward part is very wickedness. Ps. v. 9.
3. *Q.* Does the light of nature discover this?
A. No: I had not known lust except the law had said, thou shalt not covet. Rom. vii. 6.

§ II.

1. *Q.* Are we forbidden to covet another man's house?
A. Yes: as they that covet houses and take them away. Mic. ii. 2.
2. *Q.* Or another man's wife?
A. Yes: for her husband is to her a covering of the eyes Gen. xx. 16.
3. *Q.* Or another man's goods?

A. Yes: I have coveted no man's silver, or gold, or apparel. Acts xx. 33.

LXXX. *Q.* What is required in the tenth commandment?

A. The tenth commandment required full contentment with our own condition, with a right and charitable frame of spirit toward our neighbour, and all that is his.

§ I.

1. *Q.* Has God the disposal of our outward condition?
A. Yes: my times are in thy hand. Ps. xxxi. 15.
2. *Q.* And does he order all events concerning us?
A. Yes: He performeth the thing that is appointed for us. Job xxiii. 14.
3. *Q.* Ought we, therefore, to be content with our condition?
A. Yes: be content with such things as ye have. Heb. xiii. 5.
4. *Q.* Ought we to be content in every condition?
A. Yes: I have learned, in whatsoever state I am, therewith to be content. Philipp. iv. 11.
5. *Q.* Must we be content with a little?
A. Yes: having food and raiment, let us be therewith content. 1 Tim. vi. 8.

§ II.

1. *Q.* Can we expect that our condition should be in every thing brought to our mind?
A. No: for all is vanity. Eccl. i. 14.
2. *Q.* Is it, therefore, our wisdom, to bring our mind to our condition?
A. Yes: I know how to be abased, and I know how to abound. Philipp. iv. 12.
3. *Q.* Is anything got by this?
A. Yes: godliness, with contentment, is great gain. 1 Tim. vi. 6.
4. *Q.* And is this the way to be easy?
A. Yes: in your patience possess ye your souls. Luke xxi. 19.

§ III.

1. *Q.* Is that best which is?
A. Yes: It is the Lord, let him do what seemeth him good. 1 Sam. iii. 18.

2. *Q.* Must we therefore make the best of it?

A. Yes: for, wherefore should a living man complain? Sam. iii. 39.

3. *Q.* And must we acknowledge it is better than we deserve?

A. Yes: I am not worthy of the least all thy mercies. Gen. xxxii. 10.

§ IV.

1. *Q.* Ought we to desire the welfare of our neighbours?

A. Yes: let no man seek his own, but every man another's wealth. 1 Cor. x. 24.

2. *Q.* And to pray for it?

A. Yes: supplications, and prayers must be made for all men. 1 Tim. ii. 1.

3. *Q.* And to be well pleased with it?

A. Yes: rejoice with them that do rejoice. Rom. xii. 15.

4. *Q.* And to lay to heart our neighbour's troubles?

A. Yes: remember them that are in bonds, as bound with them. Heb. xiii. 3.

5. *Q.* And is this a charitable frame of spirit?

A. Yes: for, charity suffereth long, and is kind. 1 Cor. xiii. 4.

LXXXI. *Q.* What is forbidden in the tenth commandment?

A. The tenth commandment forbiddeth all discontentment with our own estate, envying or grieving at the good of our neighbour, and all inordinate motions and affections to anything that is his.

§ I.

1. *Q.* Is it a sin to fret at the disposals of God's Providence?

A. Yes: for, shall we receive good of the hand of the Lord, and shall we not receive evil also? Job ii. 10.

2. *Q.* Is it a sin to quarrel with them?

A. Yes: for, they that murmured were destroyed of the destroyer. 1 Cor. x. 10.

3. *Q.* Is it an evil thing to undervalue the mercies we have?

A. Yes: as the Israelites that said, there is nothing besides this manna. Numb. xi. 6.

4. *Q.* And to aggravate the afflictions we are under?

A. Yes: as they that said, we die, we perish, we all perish. Numb. xvii. 12.

5. *Q.* May we, in any thing, be discontented?

A. No: for, we must, in every thing, give thanks. 1 Thess. v. 18.

§ II.

1. *Q.* Is it a sin against this commandment, to envy our neighbour's welfare?

A. Yes: for charity envieth not. 1 Cor. xiii. 4.

2. *Q.* Is envy an offence to God?

A. Yes: for, is our eye evil because his is good. Matt. xx. 15.

3. *Q.* Is it hurtful to ourselves?

A. Yes: for envy is the rottenness of the bones. Prov. xiv. 30.

4. *Q.* Is it the cause of much mischief?

A. Yes: for where envy is, there is confusion, and every evil work. James iii. 16.

5. *Q.* Is it a sin to be pleased with our neighbour's hurt or loss?

A. Yes: he that is glad at calamities shall not be unpunished. Prov. xvii. 5.

§ III.

1. *Q.* Is it a sin to desire to sin?

A. Yes: lust not after evil things as they also lusted. 1 Cor. x. 6.

2. *Q.* Does all sin begin in the lustings of the heart?

A. Yes: for lust, when it hath conceived, bringeth forth sin. James i. 15.

3. *Q.* Is it a sin to desire any temporal good inordinately?

A. Yes: as Rachel, that said, give me children, or else I die. Gen. xxx. 1.

4. *Q.* And is it a sin to lust after the delights of sense?

A. Yes: as the Israelites who wept again, saying, who will give us flesh to eat? Numb. xi. 4.

5. *Q.* Must we, therefore, suppress all sinful desires?

A. Yes: and make no provision for the flesh, to fulfil the lusts thereof. Rom. xiii. 14.

§ IV.

1. *Q.* Is it a sin to set our hearts upon worldly wealth?

A. Yes: love not the world, nor the things that are in the world. 1 John ii. 15.

2. *Q.* Is covetousness an offence to God?

A. Yes: for, it is idolatry. Col. iii. 5.

3. *Q.* Will it be a vexation to ourselves?

A. Yes: for he that loveth silver shall not be satisfied with silver. Eccl. v. 10.

4. *Q.* Will it be a vexation to our families?

A. Yes: for, he that is greedy of gain troubles his own house. Prov. xv. 27.

§ v.

1. *Q.* And injurious to our neighbour?

A. Yes: for they that lay house to house and field to field, would be placed alone in the midst of the earth. Isa. v. 8.

2. *Q.* Is covetousness the cause of much sin?

A. Yes: for they that will be rich, fall into temptation and a snare. 1 Tim. vi. 9.

3. *Q.* Must we, therefore, watch against it?

A. Yes: take heed, and beware of covetousness. Luke xii. 15.

4. *Q.* and must we abstain from all the practices of it?

A. Yes: let your conversation be without covetousness. Heb. xiii. 5.

5. *Q.* And must we pray earnestly against it?

A. Yes: incline my heart unto thy testimonies, and not to covetousness. Ps. cxix. 36.

LXXXII. Q. Is any man able, perfectly, to keep the commandments of God?

A. No mere man, since the fall, is able, in this life, perfectly, to keep the commandments of God, but doth daily break them in thought, word, and deed.

§ I.

1. *Q.* Are any in this world perfectly free from sin?

A. No: for there is no man that sinneth not. 2 Chron. vi. 36.

2. *Q.* Was Christ, who was not a mere man, perfect?

A. Yes: he knew no sin. 2 Cor. v. 21.

3. *Q.* Was Adam, before the fall, perfect?

A. Yes: for, God made man upright. Eccl. vii. 29.

4. *Q.* Are the saints in the other life, perfect?

A. Yes: the glorious church, is without spot, or wrinkle. Ephes. v. 27.

5. *Q.* But is any mere man, since the fall, in this life, perfect?

A. No: for there is not a just man upon earth, that doeth good, and sinneth not. Eccl. vii. 20.

§ II.

1. *Q.* Are self-justifiers self-deceivers?

A. Yes: if we say we have no sin, we deceive ourselves. 1 John i. 8.

2. *Q.* And do they put a great affront upon God?
A. Yes: for, if we say we have not sinned, we make him a liar. 1 John i. 10.

§ III.

1. *Q.* Are not we able to keep God's commandments better than we do?
A. Yes: if I have done iniquity, I will do no more. Job xxxiv. 32.

2. *Q.* But, are we able, perfectly to keep them?
A. No: for, when I would do good, evil is present with me. Rom. vii. 21.

3. *Q.* Though Noah was said to be perfect, yet, did not he sin?
A. Yes: for, he drank of the wine, and was drunk. Gen. ix. 21.

4. *Q.* And Job?
A. Yes: for he cursed his day. Job iii. 1.

5. *Q.* And Hezekiah?
A. Yes: for, his heart was lifted up. 2 Chron. xxxii. 25.

6. *Q.* Was St. Paul himself perfect?
A. No: not as though I had already attained, either were already perfect. Philipp. iii. 12.

§ IV.

1. *Q.* Do we sin daily?
A. Yes: in many things, we offend all. James iii. 2.

2. *Q.* Do we daily sin in thought?
A. Yes: for the imagination of man's heart is evil from his youth. Gen. viii. 21.

3. *Q.* Are we guilty of many tongue-sins?
A. Yes: in the multitude of words, there wanteth not sin. Prov. x. 19.

4. *Q.* Are the best guilty of many defects?
A. Yes: for when the spirit is willing, the flesh is weak. Matt. xxvi. 41.

5. *Q.* And of many inadvertencies?
A. Yes: they are overtaken in a fault. Gal. vi. 1.

6. *Q.* Can we tell how often we offend?
A. No: who can understand his errors? Ps. xix. 12.

7. *Q.* Should we not, therefore, have recourse to Christ daily by faith and repentance?
A. Yes: if any man sin, we have an advocate with the Father. 1 John ii. 1.

LXXXIII. Q. Are all transgressions of the law equally heinous?

A. Some sins in themselves, and, by reason of several aggravations, are more heinous in the sight of God than others.

§ I.

1. *Q.* Is every sin done in God's sight?
A. Yes: I did this evil in thy sight. Ps. li. 4.

2. *Q.* Is it heinous, in God's sight?
A. Yes: for he is of purer eyes than to behold iniquity. Heb. i. 13.

3. *Q.* But is every sin alike heinous?
A. No: he that delivered me unto thee hath the greater sin. John xix. 11.

4. *Q.* Are some sins, in themselves, more heinous than others?
A. Yes: if a man sin against the Lord, who shall entreat for him? 1 Sam. ii. 25.

5. *Q.* Are presumptuous sins more heinous than others?
A. Yes: the soul that doeth aught presumptuously, that soul reproacheth the Lord. Numb. xv. 30.

6. *Q.* Was ever any sin so heinous as not to be forgiven?
A. Yes: the Pharisee's blasphemy against the Holy Ghost was so. Matt. xii. 32.

§ II.

1. *Q.* Are sins against knowledge aggravated sins?
A. Yes: that servant that knew his Lord's will and did it not, shall be beaten with many stripes. Luke xii. 47.

2. *Q.* And sins against mercies?
A. Yes: do ye thus requite the Lord, O foolish people and unwise? Deut. xxxii. 6

3. *Q.* Especially against spiritual mercies?
A. Yes: as Solomon, who turned from the Lord God of Israel, which had appeared unto him twice. 1 Kings xi. 9.

4. *Q.* Are sins against reproof aggravated sins?
A. Yes: he that, being often reproved, hardeneth his neck, shall suddenly be destroyed. Prov. xxix. 1.

5. *Q.* And sins against our vows and covenants?
A. Yes: thou saidst, I will not transgress. Jer. ii. 20.

§ III.

1. *Q.* Are the sins of great professors aggravated sins?
A. Yes: for the name of God is blasphemed through them. Rom. ii. 24.

2. *Q.* And the sins of ministers?

A. Yes: thou that preachest a man should not steal, dost thou steal? Rom. ii. 21.

3. *Q.* May the place be an aggravation of the sin?

A. Yes: they provoked him at the sea, even at the Red Sea. Ps. cvi. 7.

4. *Q.* And the time?

A. Yes: they turned aside quickly. Exod. xxxii. 8.

§ IV.

1. *Q.* Is it an aggravation of sin, if it be done with contrivance?

A. Yes: woe to them that devise iniquity. Mic. ii. 1.

2. *Q.* And if it be done with delight?

A. Yes: they rejoice to do evil. Prov. ii. 14.

3. *Q.* And without blushing?

A. Yes: they declare their sin as Sodom. Isa. iii. 9.

4. *Q.* And if it be boasted of?

A. Yes: whose glory is in their shame. Philipp. iii. 19.

5. *Q.* And if it be often repeated?

A. Yes: they have tempted me now these ten times. Numb. xiv. 22.

6. *Q.* Should we take notice of these aggravations, in our confessions?

A. Yes: Aaron shall confess the iniquity of the children of Israel, and all their transgressions in all their sins. Lev. xvi. 21.

LXXXIV. *Q.* What doth every sin deserve?

A. Every sin deserveth God's wrath and curse, both in this life, and that which is to come.

§ I.

1. *Q.* Does sin provoke God?

A. Yes: Ephraim provoked him to anger most bitterly. Hos. xii. 14.

2. *Q.* Does it deserve his wrath?

A. Yes: according to their deserts will I judge them. Ezek. vii. 27.

3. *Q.* Does that wrath rest upon impenitent sinners?

A. Yes: the wrath of God abideth on them. John iii. 36.

4. *Q.* And is it just it should?

A. Yes: for when God renders to every man according to his work, he renders indignation and wrath, tribulation and anguish to every soul of man that doeth evil. Rom. ii. 6, 8, 9.

§ II.

1. *Q.* Does sin deserve God's curse?
A. Yes: cursed is every one that continueth not in all things written in the book of the law to do them. Gal. iii. 10.
2. *Q.* Can any avoid that curse?
A. No: for all these curses shall come upon thee, and overtake thee. Deut. xxviii. 15.
3. *Q.* Can a man bear up under that curse?
A. No: for it shall come into his bowels like water and like oil into his bones. Ps. cix. 18.
4. *Q.* Can a man fortify himself against that curse?
A. No: for it shall consume the house with the timber thereof, and the stones thereof. Zech. v. 4.

§ III.

1. *Q.* Does sin deserve God's wrath and curse, in this life?
A. Yes: for these things' sake cometh the wrath of God upon the children of disobedience. Col. iii. 6.
2. *Q.* And in the life to come?
A. Yes: for wrath is treasured up against the day of wrath. Rom. ii. 5.
3. *Q.* Does every sin deserve God's wrath?
A. Yes: for the wages of sin is death. Rom. vi. 23.
4. *Q.* Is any sin venial in its own nature?
A. No: for the blood of Christ is that which must cleanse from all sin. 1 John i. 7.
5. *Q.* Does your sin deserve this wrath and curse?
A. Yes: if I be wicked woe to me. Job. x. 15.

LXXXV. *Q.* What doth God require of us, that we may escape his wrath and curse due to us for sin?

A. To escape the wrath and curse of God due to us for sin, God requireth of us faith in Jesus Christ, repentance unto life, with the diligent use of all the outward means whereby Christ communicateth to us the benefits of redemption.

§ I.

1. *Q.* Is the wrath and curse of God due to us for sin?
A. Yes: we are, by nature, children of wrath. Ephes. ii. 3.

2. *Q.* Has God provided a way of escape from that wrath?

A. Yes: I have found a ransom. Job. xxxiii. 24.

3. *Q.* Does the gospel shew us that way?

A. Yes: he shall tell the words whereby thou mayest be saved. Acts xi. 14.

4. *Q.* Is it through Christ that we may escape this wrath?

A. Yes: it *is* Jesus that delivereth us from the wrath to come. 1 Thess. i. 10.

5. *Q.* Is any thing to be done by us in order to our escape?

A. Yes: work out your own salvation with fear and trembling; for it is God that worketh in you. Philipp. ii. 12, 13.

§ II.

1. *Q.* Are we concerned to inquire what is to be done by us in order to our escape?

A. Yes: wherewithal shall I come before the Lord? Mic. vi. 6.

2. *Q.* Will a convinced conscience put us upon this inquiry?

A. Yes: when they were pricked to the heart they said, men and brethren what shall we do? Acts ii. 37.

3. *Q.* Must we be serious and solicitous in this inquiry?

A. Yes: as the gaoler that came trembling and said, Sirs, what must I do to be saved? Acts xvi. 30.

4. *Q.* Must we be speedy in this inquiry?

A. Yes: the morning cometh and also the night: if ye will inquire, inquire ye. Isa. xxi. 12.

5. *Q.* Must we make this inquiry with resolution?

A. Yes: they shall ask the way to Zion, with their faces thitherward. Jer. l. 5.

6. *Q.* Must we apply ourselves to Christ with this inquiry?

A. Yes: good Master, what good thing shall I do that I may have eternal life? Matt. xix. 16.

§ III.

1. *Q.* Is that which is to be done by us for our salvation required of us?

A. Yes: this is his commandment, that we believe. 1 John iii. 23.

2. *Q.* And are we called upon to do it?

A. Yes: turn ye, turn ye, why will ye die, O house of Israel? Ezek. xxxiii. 11.

§ IV.

1. *Q.* Is faith in Jesus Christ required that we may escape this wrath?

A. Yes: believe in the Lord Jesus Christ, and thou shalt be saved. Acts xvi. 31.

2. *Q.* Is repentance required?

A. Yes: repent and be converted, that your sins may be blotted. Acts iii. 19.

3. *Q.* Did our Lord Jesus preach these as the two great commandments of the gospel?

A. Yes: the kingdom of God is at hand; repent ye, and believe the gospel. Mark i. 15.

4. *Q.* Did the Apostles preach them?

A. Yes: testifying both to the Jews and also to the Greeks, repentance towards God, and faith towards our Lord Jesus Christ. Acts xx. 21.

5. *Q.* And is it required that we diligently use the means of grace?

A. Yes: teaching them to observe all things whatsoever I have commanded you. Matt. xxvii. 20.

LXXXVI. *Q.* What is faith in Jesus Christ?

A. Faith in Jesus Christ is a saving grace, whereby we receive and rest upon him alone for salvation, as he is offered to us in the gospel.

§ I.

1. *Q.* Are we to believe in Jesus Christ?

A. Yes: ye believe in God, believe also in me! John xiv. 1

2. *Q.* Is Christ in the word the object of our faith?

A. Yes: for the word is nigh thee. Rom. x. 8.

3. *Q.* Is faith in Christ a grace?

A. Yes: it is not of ourselves, it is the gift of God. Ephes. ii. 8.

4. *Q.* Is it free grace?

A. Yes: to you it is given on the behalf of Christ to believe in him. Philipp. i. 29.

5. *Q.* Is it a saving grace?

A. Yes: for we believe to the saving of the soul. Heb. x. 39.

6. *Q.* Is it that by which we live?

A. Yes: the just shall live by faith. Rom. i. 17.

7. *Q.* Is unbelief the great damning sin?

A. Yes: they could not enter in because of unbelief. Heb. iii. 19.

§ II.

1. *Q.* Do we by faith assent to gospel truths?

A. Yes: he that hath received his testimony hath set to his seal that God is true. John iii. 33.

2. *Q.* Do we by faith consent to gospel terms?

A. Yes: take my yoke upon you, and learn of me. Matt. xi. 29.

3. *Q.* Must both these go together?

A. Yes: he said, Lord, I believe; and he worshipped him. John ix. 38.

4. *Q.* Is there good reason for both?

A. Yes: for it is both a faithful saying, and worthy of all acceptation. 1 Tim. i. 15.

§ III.

1. *Q.* Is this receiving Christ?

A. Yes: ye have received Christ Jesus the Lord. Col. ii. 6.

2. *Q.* Is it applying the righteousness of Christ to ourselves?

A. Yes: who loved me, and gave himself for me. Gal. ii. 20.

3. *Q.* And consenting to it?

A. Yes: we have now received the atonement. Rom. v. 11.

4. *Q.* Must we receive Christ, to rule us as well as to save us.

A. Yes: for him hath God exalted, to be both a Prince and a Saviour. Acts v. 31.

5. *Q.* And is it enough only to receive him?

A. No: as we have received him, so we must walk in him. Col. ii. 6.

§ IV.

1. *Q.* Do we by faith rest on Christ alone for salvation?

A. Yes: in his name shall the Gentiles trust. Matt. xii. 21.

2. *Q.* And rely on his righteousness?

A. Yes: that I may win Christ, and be found in him, not having on my own righteousness, which is of the law, but that which is through the faith of Christ. Philipp. iii. 8, 9.

3. *Q.* And do we rejoice in him?

A. Yes: for we are the circumcision that rejoice in Christ Jesus. Philipp. iii. 3.

§ V.

1. *Q.* Will faith in Christ produce good affections?

A. Yes: for it works by love. Gal. v. 6.

2. *Q.* Will it purify the heart?

A. Yes: purifying their hearts by faith. Acts xv. 9.

3. *Q.* Will it overcome the world?

A. Yes: this is the victory overcoming the world, even your faith. 1 John v. 4.

4. *Q.* Will it resist the temptation of Satan?

A. Yes: the shield of faith quenches the fiery darts of the wicked. Ephes. vi. 16.

5. *Q.* Does it exert itself in obedience?

A. Yes: for the gospel is made known to all nations for the obedience of faith. Rom. xvi. 26.

6. *Q.* And does it subject the soul to the grace and government of the Lord Jesus?

A. Yes: my Lord and my God. John xx. 28.

LXXXVII. *Q.* What is repentance unto life?

A. **Repentance unto life is a saving grace, whereby a sinner, out of a true sense of his sin, and apprehension of the mercy of God in Christ, doth, with grief and hatred of his sin, turn from it unto God, with full purpose of, and endeavour after, new obedience.**

§ I.

1. *Q.* Is true repentance, repentance unto life?

A. Yes: God hath to the Gentiles granted repentance unto life. Acts xi. 18.

2. *Q.* Is it a grace?

A. Yes: if God, peradventure will give them repentance. 2 Tim. ii. 25.

3. *Q.* Is it a saving grace?

A. Yes: godly sorrow worketh repentance unto salvation. 2 Cor. vii. 10.

§ II.

1. *Q.* Is repentance required of every one of us?

A. Yes: God commandeth all men every where to repent. Acts xvii. 30.

2. *Q.* Is it necessary to our pardon?

A. Yes: for repentance and remission of sins are preached to all nations. Luke xxiv. 47.

3. *Q.* Is it given, to qualify us for pardon?

A. Yes: God hath exalted his Son Christ Jesus, to give repentance and remission of sins. Acts v. 31.

4. *Q.* Can we be saved without it?

A. No: except ye repent, ye shall all likewise perish. Luke xiii. 3.

§ III.

1. *Q.* Is it necessary to repentance, that there be a sense of sin?

A. Yes: cause Jerusalem to know her abominations. Ezek. xvi. 2.

2. *Q.* Must there be an acknowledgment of sin ?

A. Yes: I acknowledge my transgressions, and my sin is ever before me. Ps. li. 3.

3. *Q.* Must we acknowledge the fact of sin ?

A. Yes: thus and thus have I done. Josh. vii. 20.

4. *Q.* And the fault ?

A. Yes: I have done this evil in thy sight. Ps. li. 4.

5. *Q.* And the folly of it ?

A. Yes: O God, thou knowest my foolishness. Ps. lxix. 5.

6. *Q.* Must we acknowledge the original of sin ?

A. Yes: behold I was shapen in iniquity. Ps. li. 5.

7. *Q.* Must we acknowledge ourselves odious to God's holiness, because of sin ?

A. Yes: behold I am vile. Job. xl. 4.

8. *Q.* And obnoxious to his justice ?

A. Yes: if thou, Lord, shouldest mark iniquities, O Lord, who shall stand ? Ps. cxxx. 3.

§ IV.

1. *Q.* Must there be an apprehension of the mercy of God in Christ ?

A. Yes: there is forgiveness with thee, that thou mayest be feared. Ps. cxxx. 4.

2. *Q.* Must that invite us to repent ?

A. Yes: the goodness of God leadeth thee to repentance. Rom. ii. 4.

3. *Q.* Is that evangelical repentance which flows from a hope of that mercy ?

A. Yes: repent, for the kingdom of Heaven is at hand. Matt. iii. 2.

4. *Q.* Can there be true repentance where there is a despair of mercy ?

A. No: thou saidst there is no hope; no, I have loved strangers, and after them will I go. Jer. ii. 25.

5. *Q.* Have we reason to hope for that mercy ?

A. Yes: turn to the Lord, and he will have mercy. Is. lv. 7.

§ V.

1. *Q.* Must there be contrition for sin ?

A. Yes: when they heard this they were pricked to the heart. Acts ii. 37.

2. *Q.* Must we turn from sin ?

A. Yes: every one mourning for his iniquities. Ezek. vii. 16.

3. *Q.* Must we mourn greatly for sin?

A. Yes: Peter went out and wept bitterly. Matt. xxvi. 75.

4. *Q.* Must we mourn after a godly sort?

A. Yes: ye were made sorry after a godly manner.* 2 Cor. vii. 9.

5. *Q.* Must we mourn for sin with an eye to Christ?

A. Yes: they shall look on him whom they have pierced, and mourn. Zech. xii. 10.

§ VI.

1. *Q.* Must we hate sin?

A. Yes: I hate every false way. Ps. cxix. 128.

2. *Q.* Must we loathe ourselves because of sin?

A. Yes: I abhor myself, and repent in dust and ashes. Job xlii. 6.

3. *Q.* Must we be ashamed of ourselves before God?

A. Yes: I am ashamed, and blush to lift up my face to thee, my God. Ezra ix. 6.

4. *Q.* And must we humble ourselves greatly in his presence?

A. Yes: as the publican that stood afar off, and would not lift up so much as his eyes to heaven. Luke xviii. 13.

§ VII.

1. *Q.* Must we confess our sins?

A. Yes: for, he that covereth his sins shall not prosper. Prov. xxviii. 13.

2. *Q.* And must we aggravate them?

A. Yes: I have sinned against Heaven, and before thee. Luke xv. 18.

3. *Q.* And must we judge ourselves because of them?

A. Yes: if we would judge ourselves, we should not be judged. 1 Cor. xi. 31.

4. *Q.* And must we cry, earnestly to God, for pardon, in the blood of Christ?

A. Yes: God be merciful to me, a sinner, Luke xviii. 13.

§ VIII.

1. *Q.* Must we turn from sin?

A. Yes: repent, and turn yourselves from all your transgressions. Ezek. xviii. 30.

2. *Q.* From our own sin?

A. Yes: return ye, now, every one, from his evil way. Jer. xviii. 11.

---

* Mr. Henry here, adopted the marginal reading " ye sorrowed according to God," but the Editor supposes the reading of the text sufficiently correct and plain, and preferred retaining it.

3. *Q.* And must we turn to God?

A. Yes: if thou wilt return, O Israel, return unto me. Jer. iv. 1.

4. *Q.* Are back sliders invited to return?

A. Yes: return, ye back-sliding children. Jer. iii. 22.

5. *Q.* And should they accept the invitation?

A. Yes: behold, we come unto thee, for thou art the Lord, our God. Jer. iii. 22.

§ IX.

1. *Q.* In repentance, must there be a change of the mind?

A. Yes: make ye a new heart. Ezek. xviii. 31.

2. *Q.* Must there be a change of the way?

A. Yes: cease to do evil, learn to do well. Is. i. 16, 17.

3. *Q.* Must there be a full resolution against all sin?

A. Yes: Ephraim shall say, what have I to do any more with idols? Hos. xiv. 8.

4. *Q.* And a full resolution of new obedience?

A. Yes: the Lord our God will we serve, and his voice will we obey. Josh. xxiv. 24.

5. *Q.* And must we be serious in our endeavours accordingly?

A. Yes: bring forth, therefore, fruits meet for repentance. Matt. iii. 8.

LXXXVIII. *Q.* What are the outward means whereby Christ communicateth to us the benefits of redemption?

A. The outward and ordinary means whereby Christ communicateth to us the benefits of redemption, are his ordinances, especially the word, sacraments, and prayer; all which are made effectual to the elect for salvation.

§ I.

1. *Q.* Does Christ communicate the benefits of redemption?

A. Yes: for, of his fulness have all we received. John i. 16.

2. *Q.* Does he ordinarily communicate them by means?

A. Yes: I will, for this, be inquired of. Ezek. xxxvi. 37.

3. *Q.* Is he tied to those means?

A. No: for, the Spirit, as the wind, bloweth where it listeth. John iii. 8.

4. *Q.* But are we tied to the use of them?

A. Yes: where I record my name, I will come to thee, and will bless thee. Exod. xx. 24.

5. *Q.* Are the ordinances the outward and ordinary means of grace?

A. Yes: I the Lord do sanctify Israel, when my sanctuary shall be in the midst of them. Ezek. xxxvii. 28.

§ II.

1. *Q.* Are the words, sacraments, and prayer, the great gospel ordinances?

A. Yes: then they that gladly received his word were baptized, and they continued stedfastly in the apostle's doctrine and fellowship, and in breaking of bread, and in prayers. Acts ii. 41, 42.

2. *Q.* Is singing of psalms also a gospel ordinance?

A. Yes: speaking to yourselves in psalms, and hymns, and spiritual songs. Ephes. v. 19.

3. *Q.* Is it appointed for our own consolation?

A. Yes: is any merry? let him sing psalms. James v. 13.

4. *Q.* And for mutual instruction?

A. Yes: teaching and admonishing one another in psalms. Col. iii. 16.

5. *Q.* And for God's glory?

A. Yes: singing with grace in your heart to the Lord. Col. iii. 16.

§ III.

1. *Q.* Has Christ appointed ministers of the gospel?

A. Yes: He hath given pastors and teachers, for the edifying of the body of Christ. Ephes. iv. 11, 12.

2. *Q.* Is the administration of ordinances committed to them?

A. Yes: for they are the stewards of the mysteries of God. 1 Cor. iv. 1.

3. *Q.* And must they attend to that service?

A. Yes: we will give ourselves to prayer, and to the ministry of the word. Acts vi. 4.

§ IV.

1. *Q.* Are gospel ordinances made effectual to all for salvation?

A. No: for, with many of them, God was not well pleased. 1 Cor. x. 5.

2. *Q.* But are they made effectual to the elect?

A. Yes: as many as were ordained to eternal life believed. Acts xiii. 48.

LXXXIX. *Q.* How is the word made effectual to salvation?

A. The Spirit of God maketh the reading, but especially the preaching of the word, an effectual means of convincing and converting sinners, and of building them up in holiness and comfort, through faith, unto salvation.

§ I.

1. *Q.* Is the word to be read by us?
A. Yes: I charge you that this epistle be read unto all the holy brethren. 1 Thess. v. 27.
2. *Q.* Is it to be read in solemn assemblies?
A. Yes: Moses is read in the synagogues every Sabbath day. Acts xv. 21.
3. *Q.* Is it profitable to expound the scriptures?
A. Yes: they that read in the law of God, gave the sense, and caused them to understand the reading. Neh. viii. 8.
4. *Q.* Is the word of God to be preached?
A. Yes: preach the word, be instant in season, and out of season, reprove, rebuke, exhort. 2 Tim. iv. 2.
5. *Q.* Is it the duty of all to hear the word?
A. Yes: he that hath an ear, let him hear what the Spirit saith unto the churches. Rev. ii. 7.
6. *Q.* Will the bare reading and hearing of the word profit?
A. No: the letter kills, but the Spirit gives life. 2 Cor. iii. 6.

§ II.

1. *Q.* But is the reading and hearing of the word the ordinary means of convincing sinners?
A. Yes: for it is mighty through God, to the pulling down of strong holds. 2 Cor. x. 4.
2. *Q.* And of startling the secure?
A. Yes: by them is thy servant warned. Ps. xix. 11.
3. *Q.* Is it the ordinary means of conversion?
A. Yes: if the prophets had stood in my counsel, they should have turned people from their evil way. Jer. xxiii. 22.
4. *Q.* And has it been the conversion of many?
A. Yes: when the law of truth was in his mouth, he did turn many away from iniquity. Mal. ii. 6.
5. *Q.* Is it the ordinary means of working faith?
A. Yes: for, faith cometh by hearing. Rom. x. 17.
6. *Q.* And of the renewing of the heart?
A. Yes: for, the seed is the word of God. Luke viii. 11.
7. *Q.* And of reforming the life?

A. Yes: by the words of thy lips I have kept me from the paths of the destroyer. Ps. xvii. 4.

§ III.

1. *Q.* Is the reading and hearing of the word needful to those who are regenerate?
A. Yes: for, they are nourished up in the words of faith, and of good doctrine. 1 Tim. iv. 6.
2. *Q.* Is it a means of building them up in holiness?
A. Yes: it is for the perfecting of the saints. Ephes. iv. 12.
3. *Q.* Will it furnish them for all good?
A. Yes: that the man of God may be perfect, thoroughly furnished to all good works. 2 Tim. iii. 17.
4. *Q.* Will it fortify them against all evil?
A. Yes: for, the sword of the Spirit is the word of God. Ephes. vi. 17.
5. *Q.* Is it a means of building them up in comfort?
A. Yes: that we through patience and comfort of the scriptures might have hope. Rom. xv. 4.

§ IV.

1. *Q.* Does the Spirit of God make the word effectual for all these good purposes?
A. Yes: when the hand of the Lord was with them, a great number believed, and turned to the Lord. Acts xi. 21.
2. *Q.* Is it effectual through faith unto salvation?
A. Yes: it is the power of God unto salvation to every one that believeth. Rom. i. 16.
3. *Q.* Is it not a great mercy, then, to have plenty of the word of God?
A. Yes: blessed is the people that know the joyful sound. Ps. lxxxix. 15.
4. *Q.* And should we not welcome those that bring it?
A. Yes: blessed is he that cometh in the name of the Lord. Ps. cxviii. 26.

XC. *Q.* How is the word to be read and heard, that it may become effectual to salvation?

A. That the word may become effectual to salvation, we must attend thereunto with diligence, preparation, and prayer, receive it with faith and love, lay it up in our hearts, and practice it in our lives.

§ I.

1. *Q.* Must we read the word of God with seriousness?
A. Yes: we must give attendance to reading. 1 Tim. iv. 13.
2. *Q.* And not read it as a common book?
A. No: it is not a vain thing, for it is your life. Deut. xxxii. 47.

§ II.

1. *Q.* Must we be diligent to hear the word?
A. Yes: watching daily at wisdom's gates, waiting at the posts of her doors. Prov. viii. 34.
2. *Q.* Must we prepare for hearing it?
A. Yes: lay aside all malice, and guile, and hypocrisy, and filthiness, and superfluity of naughtiness. 1 Pet. ii. 1, and James i. 21.
3. *Q.* Must we come to it with a spiritual appetite?
A. Yes: as new born babes, desire the sincere milk of the word. 1 Pet. ii. 2.
4. *Q.* Must we set ourselves to receive it?
A. Yes: as Mary sat at Jesus' feet to hear his word. Luke x. 39.
5. *Q.* Must we bow our souls before it?
A. Yes: speak, Lord, for thy servant heareth. 1 Sam. iii. 9.
6. *Q.* Must we diligently hearken to it?
A. Yes: be swift to hear. James i. 19.

§ III.

1. *Q.* Must we hear the word with reverence?
A. Yes: when Ezra opened the book, all the people stood up. Neh. viii. 5.
2. *Q.* Must we hear it with care?
A. Yes: take heed how ye hear. Luke viii. 18.
3. *Q.* And with meekness?
A. Yes: receive, with meekness, the ingrafted word. James i. 21.
4. *Q.* And with delight?
A. Yes: how sweet are thy words unto my taste! Ps. cxix. 103.
5. *Q.* And with a holy fear?
A. Yes: we must tremble at the word. Isa. lxvi. 2.
6. *Q.* Must we receive it, as the word of men?
A. No: but as it is, in truth, the word of God. 1 Thess. ii. 13.

§ IV.

1. *Q.* Must we take heed of sleeping under the word?

A. Yes: could ye not watch, with me, one hour? Matt. xxvi. 40.

2. *Q.* Must we pray for a blessing upon the word?

A. Yes: open thou mine eyes, that I may behold wondrous things out of thy law. Ps. cxix. 18.

3. *Q.* Must we receive the word with faith?

A. Yes: for it will not profit if it be not mixed with faith. Heb. iv. 2.

4. *Q.* Must we receive men's words, with an implicit faith?

A. No: believe not every spirit, but try the spirits. 1 John iv. 1.

5. *Q.* But, must we receive God's word, with an implicit faith?

A. Yes: for every word of God is pure. Prov. xxx. 5.

6. *Q.* Must we receive it with love?

A. Yes: I have esteemed the words of his mouth more than my necessary food. Job xxiii. 12.

§ v.

1. *Q.* Must we remember the word we read and hear?

A. Yes: lest, at any time, we let it slip. Heb. ii. 1.

2. *Q.* Must we lay it up in our hearts?

A. Yes: thy word have I hid in my heart. Ps. cxix. 11.

3. *Q.* Must we meditate on it?

A. Yes: in that law doth he meditate day and night. Ps. i. 2.

4. *Q.* Must we practice it in our lives?

A. Yes: be ye doers of the word, and not hearers only. James i. 22.

5. *Q.* Will it suffice to hear, though we do not practice?

A. No: if ye know these things, happy are ye if ye do them. John xiii. 17.

XCI. *Q.* How do the sacraments become effectual means of salvation?

A. The sacraments become effectual means of salvation, not from any virtue in them, or in him that doth administer them; but only by the blessing of Christ, and the working of his Spirit in them that by faith receive them.

§ i.

1. *Q.* Do the sacraments certainly save all that partake of them?

A. No: they who were rejected of Christ could say, we have eaten and drunk in thy presence. Luke xiii. 26.

2. *Q.* Are they, then, effectual, by any virtue, in themselves?
A. No: for bodily exercise profiteth little. 1 Tim. iv. 8.

3. *Q.* Do they, of themselves, confer grace?
A. No: for if thou be a breaker of the law, thy circumcision is made uncircumcision. Rom. ii. 25.

4. *Q.* Is the thing signified of greater consequence than the sign?
A. Yes: for circumcision is that of the heart, in the spirit, and not in the letter. Rom. ii. 29.

§ II.

1. *Q.* Does the efficacy of the sacraments depend upon the minister?
A. No: for, who is Paul, and who is Apollos, but ministers by whom ye believed? 1 Cor. iii. 5.

2. *Q.* Does the goodness of the minister invigorate the sacrament?
A. No: for Philip baptized Simon, who yet was in the gall of bitterness. Acts viii. 13, 23.

3. *Q.* Does the badness of the minister invalidate the sacrament?
A. No: for Judas was numbered with us, and obtained part of this ministry. Acts i. 17.

§ III.

1. *Q.* Does the efficacy of sacraments depend upon the blessing of Christ?
A. Yes: lo, I am with you alway. Matt. xxviii.

2. *Q.* And upon the working of the Spirit?
A. Yes: for it is the Spirit that quickeneth. John vi. 63.

3. *Q.* And are they effectual to those only who by faith receive them?
A. Yes: he that beleveth and is baptized, shall be saved. Mark xvi. 16.

XCII. *Q.* What is a sacrament?
A. A sacrament is an holy ordinance instituted by Christ; wherein, by sensible signs, Christ, and the benefits of the new covenant, are represented, sealed, and applied to believers.

§ I.

1. *Q.* Is a sacrament a holy ordinance?

A. Yes: for we minister about holy things. 1 Cor. ix. 13.

2. *Q.* Must they, therefore, be holy that attend them?

A. Yes: be ye clean that bear the vessels of the Lord. Is. lii. 11.

3. *Q.* Are sacraments instituted by Christ?

A. Yes: the Lord himself shall give you a sign. Isa. vii. 14.

4. *Q.* May men institute sacraments?

A. No: Jeroboam, that ordained a feast which he had devised of his own heart, sinned, and made Israel to sin. 1 Kings xii. 33.

§ II.

1. *Q.* Is there, in a sacrament, an outward and visible sign?

A. Yes: behold the blood of the covenant. Exod. xxiv. 8.

2. *Q.* Is there an inward and spiritual grace?

A. Yes: for that rock was Christ. 1 Cor. x. 4.

3. *Q.* Are outward signs of use to inform our understanding?

A. Yes: for, in them, Christ is evidently set forth crucified among us. Gal. iii. 1.

4. *Q.* Are they of use to refresh our memories?

A. Yes: these stones shall be for a memorial. Josh. iv. 7.

5. *Q.* And to stir up our affections?

A. Yes: they shall look on him whom they have pierced, and mourn. Zech. xii. 10.

6. *Q.* Are they of use to transmit the things of God from generation to generation?

A. Yes: for your children shall ask you, what mean you by this service? Exod. xii. 26.

§ III.

1. *Q.* Is a sacrament a seal?

A. Yes: circumcision was a seal of the righteousness which is by faith. Rom. iv. 11.

2. *Q.* A seal of the covenant?

A. Yes: he gave him the covenant of circumcision. Acts vii. 8.

3. *Q.* Is a sacrament an oath?

A. Yes: they entered into an oath to walk in God's law. Neh. x. 29.

4. *Q.* Is it an encouragement to our faith?

A. Yes: reach hither thy hand, and thrust it into my side, and be not faithless, but believing. John xx. 27.

5. *Q.* Is it an engagement to obedience?

A. Yes: that henceforth we should not serve sin. Rom. vi. 6.

6. *Q.* Is Christ applied to us in sacraments?

A. Yes: as many of you as have been baptized into Christ, have put on Christ. Gal. iii. 27.

7. *Q.* Are the benefits of the new covenant applied to us?

A. Yes: to be a God to thee, and to thy seed after thee. Gen. xvii. 7.

XCIII. *Q.* Which are the sacraments of the New Testament?

A. The sacraments of the New Testament are, Baptism, and the Lord's Supper.

§ I.

1. *Q.* Were there sacraments in innocency?

A. Yes: the tree of life in the midst of the garden, and the tree of the knowledge of good and evil. Gen. ii. 9.

2. *Q.* Were there sacraments under the law?

A. Yes: for the law had a shadow of good things to come. Heb. x. 1.

3. *Q.* Was circumcision a sacrament?

A. Yes: he received the sign of circumcision. Rom. iv. 11.

4. *Q.* Was the passover a sacrament?

A. Yes: Christ our passover is sacrificed for us. 1 Cor. v. 7.

§ II.

1. *Q.* Have we sacraments now, under the gospel?

A. Yes: for unto us was the gospel preached, as well as unto them. Heb. iv. 2.

2. *Q.* Are Baptism and the Lord's Supper our two sacraments?

A. Yes: for we are baptized into one body, and all drink into one spirit. 1 Cor. xii. 13.

3. *Q.* May men add any more sacraments?

A. No: add thou not unto his words, lest he reprove thee. Prov. xxx. 6.

XCIV. *Q.* What is Baptism?

A. Baptism is a sacrament, wherein the washing with water in the name of the Father, and of the Son, and of the Holy Ghost, doth signify and seal our ingrafting into Christ, and partaking of the benefits of the covenant of grace, and our engagement to be the Lord's.

§ I.

1. *Q.* Is washing with water the outward sign in Baptism?

A. Yes: I am come baptizing with water. John i. 31.

2. *Q.* Is that well done by sprinkling?

A. Yes: for so shall he sprinkle many nations. Isa. lii. 15; Ezek. xxxvi. 25.

3. *Q.* Is that sign significant?

A. Yes: if ye are washed, ye are sanctified, ye are justified. 1 Cor. vi. 11.

4. *Q.* But, is the outward sign alone sufficient?

A. No: baptism saves us, not as it is the putting away the filth of the flesh, but the answer of a good conscience toward God. 1 Pet. iii. 21.

§ II.

1. *Q.* Must Baptism be in the name of the Father, Son, and Holy Ghost?

A. Yes: go ye, therefore, and teach all nations, baptizing them in the name of the Father, and of the Son, and of the Holy Ghost. Matt. xxviii. 19.

2. *Q.* And not in the minister's name?

A. No: were ye baptized in the name of Paul? 1 Cor. i. 13.

3. *Q.* Is it, therefore, one?

A. Yes: for there is one Lord, one faith, one baptism. Ephes. iv. 5.

§ III.

1. *Q.* Is Baptism a door of admission into the visible church?

A. Yes: there were added to the church daily. Acts ii. 47.

2. *Q.* Are we thereby entered into Christ's school?

A. Yes: Jesus made and baptized disciples. John iv. 1.

3. *Q.* And listed under his banner?

A. Yes: as good soldiers of Jesus Christ. 2 Tim. ii. 3.

§ IV.

1. *Q.* Is Baptism a seal of our ingrafting into Christ?

A. Yes: for being baptized into Jesus Christ, we are baptized into his death. Rom. vi. 3.

2. *Q.* And of our partaking of the benefits of the new covenant?

A. Yes: be baptized for the remission of sins, and ye shall receive the gift of the Holy Ghost. Acts ii. 38.

3. *Q.* And of our engagement to be the Lord's?

A. Yes: I entered into a covenant with thee, saith the Lord God, and thou becamest mine. Ezek. xvi. 8.

4. *Q.* Is the covenant sealed in the Baptism, a mutual covenant?

A. Yes: ye shall be my people, and I will be your God. Jer. xxx. 22.

SCRIPTURE CATECHISM. 193

§ v.

1. *Q.* Are we bound, by our Baptism, to renounce the devil, and all his works?

A. Yes: for the Son of God was manifested, to destroy the works of the devil. 1 John iii. 8.

2. *Q.* And to renounce the pomps and vanities of this wicked world?

A. Yes: for we must not be conformed to this world. Rom. xii. 2.

3. *Q.* And all the sinful lusts of the flesh?

A. Yes: for we are not in the flesh, but in the Spirit. Rom. viii. 9.

4. *Q.* Are we bound to believe all the articles of the Christian faith?

A. Yes: we must hold fast the form of sound words. 2 Tim. i. 13.

5. *Q.* And to keep God's holy will and commandments?

A. Yes: that we also should walk in newness of life. Rom. vi. 4.

6. *Q.* And to walk in the same all the days of our life?

A. Yes: if ye continue in my word, then are ye my disciples indeed. John viii. 31.

XCV. *Q.* To whom is Baptism to be administered?

A. Baptism is not to be administered to any that are out of the visible church, till they profess their faith in Christ, and obedience to him; but the infants of such as are members of the visible church are to be baptized.

§ I.

1. *Q.* Are Jews and Pagans to be baptized, upon their believing?

A. Yes: if thou believest with all thy heart, thou mayest. Acts viii. 37.

2. *Q.* Will their justifiable profession warrant the administering of Baptism to them?

A. Yes: Simon Magus himself believed also, and was baptized. Acts viii. 13.

§ II.

1. *Q.* Are the children of believing parents to be baptized in their infancy?

A. Yes: for a seed shall serve him, it shall be accounted to the Lord for a generation. Ps. xxii. 30.

2. *Q.* Is it possible, that they may be in covenant with God?

A. Yes: for you have not chosen me, but I have chosen you. John xv. 16.

3. *Q.* Is it probable they should be in covenant?

A. Yes: for, when Israel was a child, then I loved him. Hos. xi. 1.

4. *Q.* Is it certain they were in covenant?

A. Yes: I will be a God to thee, and to thy seed. Gen. xvii. 7.

5. *Q.* Is it, therefore, certain they are in covenant?

A. Yes: for the blessing of Abraham comes upon the Gentiles. Gal. iii. 14.

6. *Q.* Does the seal of the covenant, therefore, belong to them?

A. Yes: every man-child among you shall be circumcised. Gen. xvii. 10.

§ III.

1. *Q.* Are the children of Christians members of Christ's visible church?

A. Yes: for, of such is the kingdom of God. Mark x. 14.

2. *Q.* Do the promises belong to them?

A. Yes: the promise is to you and to your children. Acts ii. 39.

3. *Q.* Does the promise of the Spirit belong to them?

A. Yes: I will pour my Spirit upon thy seed. Isa. xliv. 3.

4. *Q.* Are they capable of receiving it?

A. Yes: John was filled with the Holy Ghost from his mother's womb. Luke i. 15.

5. *Q.* Are they, then, to be baptized?

A. Yes: for who can forbid water to them which have received the Holy Ghost as well as we. Acts x. 47.

§ IV.

1. *Q.* Are the children of believers federally holy?

A. Yes: else were your children unclean, but now are they holy. 1 Cor. vii. 14.

2. *Q.* Are they so in their parent's right?

A. Yes: if the root be holy, so are the branches. Rom. xi. 16.

3. *Q.* Are they disciples?

A. Yes: for the yoke of circumcision was put upon the neck of the disciples. Acts xv. 1. 10.

4. *Q.* Are they to be received, in Christ's name?

A. Yes: whosoever receiveth one such little child in my name, receiveth me. Matt. xviii. 5.

5. *Q.* Are they born unto God?

A. Yes: thou hast taken thy sons and thy daughters, whom thou hast born unto me. Ezek. xvi. 20.

6. *Q.* Are they bound by relation to be his servants?

A. Yes: I am thy servant, the son of thine hand-maid. Ps. cxvi. 16.

7. *Q.* Ought they, then, to be presented to him?

A. Yes: the first-born of thy sons shalt thou give unto me. Exod. xxii. 29.

§ v.

1. *Q.* Do children need to be cleansed from the pollutions of sin?

A. Yes: for they are shapen in iniquity. Ps. li. 5.

2. *Q.* Is there provision made for their cleansing?

A. Yes: for there is a fountain opened to the house of David. Zech. xiii. 1.

§ vi.

1. *Q.* Are the nations to be discipled by Baptism?

A. Yes: go ye and disciple all nations, baptizing them. Matt. xxviii. 19.

2. *Q.* Are children a part of the nations?

A. Yes: your little ones stand here this day, to enter into covenant with God. Deut. xxix. 11, 12.

3. *Q.* And has Christ excepted them?

A. No: suffer little children to come unto me, and forbid them not. Matt. xix. 14.

4. *Q.* Were the families of believers baptized by the Apostles?

A. Yes: Lydia was baptized, and her household. Acts xvi. 15.

5. *Q.* Did Christ himself receive the seal of the covenant, in his infancy?

A. Yes: when he was eight days old, he was circumcised. Luke ii. 21.

§ vii.

1. *Q.* Is infant baptism useful, for preserving the church?

A. Yes: that our children may not cease from fearing the Lord. Josh. xxii. 25.

2. *Q.* Was it a great mercy to you, that you were baptized?

A. Yes: for we are the children of the covenant. Acts iii. 25.

§ VIII.

1. Q. Must we be careful to improve our baptism?
A. Yes: be ye mindful always of his covenant. 1 Chron. xvi. 15.
2. Q. Is it a good argument against sin?
A. Yes: how shall we that are dead to sin live any longer therein? Rom. vi. 2.
3. Q. And for holiness?
A. Yes: for we also should walk in newness of life. Rom. vi. 4.
4. Q. Is it a great encouragement to faith?
A. Yes: thou art my God, from my mother's belly. Ps. xxii. 10.
5. Q. Is it a good plea in prayer?
A. Yes: save the son of thy hand-maid. Ps. lxxxvi. 16.
6. Q. Is it a strong inducement to brotherly love?
A. Yes: for we all are baptized into one body. 1 Cor. xii. 13.

XCVI. Q. What is the Lord's Supper?
A. The Lord's Supper is a sacrament, wherein, by giving and receiving bread and wine, according to Christ's appointment, his death is shewed forth; and the worthy receivers are, not after a corporal and carnal manner, but by faith, made partakers of his body and blood, with all his benefits, to their spiritual nourishment, and growth in grace.

§ I.

1. Q. Was the Lord's Supper instituted by Christ himself?
A. Yes: I received of the Lord that which I delivered unto you. 1 Cor. xi. 23.
2. Q. Did he leave it, as a legacy, to his church?
A. Yes: it was in the night in which he was betrayed. 1 Cor. xi. 23.
3. Q. Did he intend it should continue?
A. Yes: till he come. 1 Cor. xi. 26.

§ II.

1. Q. Is bread to be used in this sacrament?
A. Yes: for he took bread. Matt. xxvi. 26.
2. Q. And does that signify it to be a strengthening ordinance?

A. Yes: for bread strengthens man's heart. Ps. civ. 15.

3. *Q.* Is the cup to be used in this sacrament?
A. Yes: He took the cup when he had supped. 1 Cor. xi. 25.

4. *Q.* Does that signify it to be a refreshing ordinance?
A. Yes: for wine makes glad the heart. Ps. civ. 15.

5. *Q.* Must these be given and received?
A. Yes: Jesus took bread, and gave to them,—took the cup, and gave it to them. Mark xiv. 22, 23.

6. *Q.* Are the people to partake of the cup?
A. Yes: drink ye all of it. Matt. xxvi. 27.

7. *Q.* Is this ordinance doubled?
A. Yes: because the thing is established. Gen. xli. 32.

§ III.

1. *Q.* Does the bread signify the body of Christ?
A. Yes: this is my body which is broken for you. 1 Cor. xi. 24.

2. *Q.* Does the wine signify the blood of Christ?
A. Yes: this cup is the New Testament in my blood. Luke xxii. 20.

3. *Q.* Are they turned into the very body and blood of Christ?
A. No: for it is the spirit that quickens, the flesh profits nothing. John vi. 63.

4. *Q.* But is the doctrine of Christ crucified meat and drink to a believing soul?
A. Yes: My flesh is meat indeed, and my blood is drink indeed. John vi. 55.

5. *Q.* And are we to feed upon that doctrine?
A. Yes: he that eateth me, even he shall live by me. John vi. 57.

§ IV.

1. *Q.* Is the Lord's Supper a commemorating ordinance?
A. Yes: do this in remembrance of me. Luke xxii. 19.

2. *Q.* Is it a confessing ordinance?
A. Yes: ye do shew the Lord's death. 1 Cor. xi. 26.

3. *Q.* Is it a communicating ordinance?
A. Yes: the cup of blessing which we bless, is it not the communion of the blood of Christ? And the bread which we break, is it not the communion of the body of Christ? 1 Cor. x. 16.

4. *Q.* Is it a covenanting ordinance?
A. Yes: for it is the New Testament. 1 Cor. xi. 25.

5. *Q.* Is it a confirming ordinance?

A. Yes: for Christ, in it, is evidently set forth. Gal. iii. 1.

6. *Q.* Is it an ordinance of communion with all Christians?

A. Yes: for we have been all made to drink into one spirit. 1 Cor. xii. 13.

§ v.

1. *Q.* Is the pardon of sin sealed to believers in this sacrament?

A. Yes: it is the blood of the New Testament, which is shed for many for the remission of sins. Matt. xxvi. 28.

2. *Q.* Is the gift of the Holy Ghost sealed to them?

A. Yes: receive ye the Holy Ghost. John xx. 22.

3. *Q.* Is the promise of eternal life sealed to them?

A. Yes: that ye may eat and drink at my table in my kingdom. Luke xxii. 30; and Matt. xxvi. 28.

4. *Q.* Do we, by receiving this sacrament, bind ourselves out from all sin?

A. Yes: for we reckon ourselves to be dead indeed unto sin. Rom. vi. 11.

5. *Q.* And do we bind ourselves up to all duty?

A. Yes: for, being made free from sin, we become the servants of righteousness. Rom. vi. 18.

§ vi.

1. *Q.* Is the Lord's Supper a spiritual feast?

A. Yes: a feast of fat things, of wines on the lees. Isa. xxv. 6.

2. *Q.* Is it a marriage feast?

A. Yes: a certain king made a marriage for his son. Matt. xxii. 2.

3. *Q.* Is it a feast upon a sacrifice?

A. Yes: Christ is sacrificed for us: Let us keep the feast. 1 Cor. v. 7, 8.

4. *Q.* Is it a feast upon a covenant?

A. Yes: as Isaac made a feast for Abimelech when they sware one to another. Gen. xxvi. 30, 31.

5. *Q.* Are all good Christians invited to this feast?

A. Yes: come; for all things are now ready. Luke xiv. 17.

6. *Q.* Are they often to partake of it?

A. Yes: as often as ye eat this bread. 1 Cor. xi. 26.

XCVII. *Q.* What is required to the worthy receiving of the Lord's Supper?

A. It is required of them that would worthily partake of the Lord's Supper, that they examine themselves of their knowledge to discern the Lord's body, of their faith to feed upon him, of their repentance, love, and new obedience; lest, coming unworthily, they eat and drink judgment to themselves.

§ I.

1. Q. Are the ignorant to be admitted to the Lord's Supper?
A. No: for they discern not the Lord's body. 1 Cor. xi. 29.
2. Q. Are those to be admitted to it who are openly profane?
A. No: for what concord hath Christ with Belial? 2 Cor. vi. 15.
3. Q. But must all visible adult believers be admitted to it?
A. Yes: all the congregation of Israel shall keep the passover. Exod. xii. 47.

§ II.

1. Q. Must those who come to the Lord's Supper prepare for it?
A. Yes: we must prepare our heart to seek God, the Lord God of our Fathers. 2 Chron. xiii. 18.
2. Q. Must we put away every sin?
A. Yes: purge out the old leaven. 1 Cor. v. 7.
3. Q. And must we cleanse ourselves from all pollutions?
A. Yes: I will wash my hands in innocency, so will I compass thine altar, O Lord. Ps. xxvi. 6.
4. Q. Must we sequester ourselves from the world?
A. Yes: tarry ye here, while I go yonder and worship. Gen. xxii. 5.
5. Q. And must we apply ourselves seriously to this service?
A. Yes: we must engage the heart to approach unto God. Jer. xxx. 21.

§ III.

1. Q. When we come to this ordinance, must we examine ourselves?
A. Yes: let a man examine himself, and so let him eat of that bread and drink of that cup. 1 Cor. xi. 28.
2. Q. Must we examine our spiritual state?
A. Yes: examine yourselves, whether ye be in the faith. 2 Cor. xiii. 5.
3. Q. Must we examine our particular ways?

A. Yes: let us search and try our ways. Sam. iii. 40.

4. *Q.* Must we renew our repentance for sin?

A. Yes: for if we would judge ourselves, we should not be judged. 1 Cor. xi. 31.

5. *Q.* And our faith in Christ crucified?

A. Yes: who loved me, and gave himself for me. Gal. ii. 20.

6. *Q.* Must we steadfastly purpose to lead a new life?

A. Yes: I have sworn, and I will perform it, that I will keep thy righteous judgments. Ps. cxix. 106.

7. *Q.* And must we be in charity with all men?

A. Yes: first be reconciled to thy brother, and then come and offer thy gift. Matt. v. 24.

8. *Q.* And must we stir up desires towards Christ?

A. Yes: let him that is athirst come. Rev. xxii. 17.

§ IV.

1. *Q.* Must we receive this sacrament, with great reverence?

A. Yes: in thy fear will I worship towards thy holy temple. Ps. v. 7.

2. *Q.* And with fixedness of thought?

A. Yes: bind the sacrifice with cords unto the horns of the altar. Ps. cxviii. 27.

3. *Q.* Must we receive it with godly sorrow for sin?

A. Yes: they shall look on me whom they have pierced and mourn. Zech. xii. 10.

4. *Q.* And with holy joy in the Lord?

A. Yes: they did eat their meat with gladness, praising God. Acts ii. 46, 47.

5. *Q.* Must we receive it with an affectionate remembrance of the love of Christ?

A. Yes: we will remember thy love more than wine. Song of Solomon i. 4.

6. *Q.* And with an earnest desire of mercy from God?

A. Yes: I will take the cup of salvation, and call upon the name of the Lord. Ps. cxvi. 13.

§ V.

1. *Q.* Must those who have received this sacrament be very watchful against all sin?

A. Yes: He will speak peace to his people, and to his saints, but let them not turn again to folly. Ps. lxxxv. 8.

2. *Q.* Must they abound in all duty?

A. Yes: I will pay my vows unto the Lord. Ps. cxvi. 14.

3. *Q.* And must they ever preserve a sense of their engagements?

A. Yes: thy vows are upon me, O God. Ps. lvi. 12.

§ VI.

1. Q. Do those who wilfully resolve to continue in sin receive unworthily?
A. Yes: for what hast thou to do to take my covenant in thy mouth, seeing thou hatest instruction? Ps. l. 16, 17.

2. Q. And do those receive unworthily who have no regard to Christ in what they do?
A. Yes: for they say the table of the Lord is contemptible. Mal. i. 7.

3. Q. Are they that do so guilty of a great sin?
A. Yes: they are guilty of the body and blood of the Lord. 1 Cor. xi. 27.

4. Q. And are they in great danger?
A. Yes: for they eat and drink judgment to themselves. 1 Cor. xi. 29.

5. Q. But shall weak believers, who bewail their unworthness, be encouraged?
A. Yes: for he will not break the bruised reed. Matt. xii. 20.

XCVIII. Q. What is prayer?
A. Prayer is an offering up of our desires unto God, for things agreeable to his will, in the name of Christ, with confession of our sins, and thankful acknowledgment of his mercies.

§ I.

1. Q. Is it every one's duty to pray?
A. Yes: men ought always to pray. Luke xviii. 1.

2. Q. Can a man be a good man, who lives without prayer?
A. No: every one that is godly shall pray. Ps. xxxii. 6.

3. Q. Are we to pray daily?
A. Yes: morning, and evening, and at noon, will I pray. Ps. lv. 17.

4. Q. Are we to pray continually?
A. Yes: pray, without ceasing. 1 Thess. v. 17.

5. Q. Are we to pray in secret?
A. Yes: thou, when thou prayest, enter into thy closet, and shut thy door. Matt. vi. 6.

6. Q. Are we to pray, when we are in affliction?
A. Yes: is any among you afflicted? Let him pray. James v. 13.

§ II.

1. Q. Are we to pray to God only?

A. Yes: for He only knows the hearts of all the children of men. 1 Kings viii. 39.

2. *Q.* May we pray to departed saints to pray for us?
A. No: for Abraham is ignorant of us. Isa. lxiii. 16.

3. *Q.* Is prayer the soul's ascent to God?
A. Yes: unto thee, O Lord, do I lift up my soul. Ps. xxv. 1.

4. *Q.* Is it the soul's converse with God?
A. Yes: pour out your hearts before him. Ps. lxii. 8.

5. *Q.* Are we, in prayer, to ascribe glory to God?
A. Yes: give unto the Lord glory and strength. 1 Chron. xvi. 28.

6. *Q.* And to ask mercy of God?
A. Yes: ask, and it shall be given you; seek, and ye shall find. Matt. vii. 7.

§ III.

1. *Q.* Are we to pray to God for things agreeable to his will?
A. Yes: if we ask anything according to his will, he heareth us. 1 John v. 14.

2. *Q.* Must we pray for pardoning mercy and sanctifying grace?
A. Yes: let us come boldly to the throne of grace, that we may obtain mercy, and find grace to help in time of need. Heb. iv. 16.

3. *Q.* Are God's promises to be the guide of our desires in prayer?
A. Yes: remember thy word unto thy servant. Ps. cxix. 49.

4. *Q.* And the ground of our faith?
A. Yes: for I hope in thy word. Ps. cxix. 81.

§ IV.

1. *Q.* Must we pray in the name of Christ?
A. Yes: whatsoever ye shall ask in my name, that will I do. John xiv. 13.

2. *Q.* Relying on his righteousness alone?
A. Yes: for we have boldness to enter into the holiest by the blood of Jesus. Heb. x. 19.

3. *Q.* Must we pray in faith?
A. Yes: let him ask in faith, nothing wavering. James i. 6

4. *Q.* Depending on the assistance of the Holy Spirit?
A. Yes: for the Spirit helpeth our infirmities. Rom. viii. 26.

§ V.

1. *Q.* Must we, in prayer, make confession of sin?
A. Yes: I prayed to the Lord my God, and made my confession. Dan. ix. 4.

2. *Q.* And must we give thanks for mercies received?
A. Yes: enter into his gates with thanksgiving. Ps. c. 4.

§ VI.

1. *Q.* Must we be constant in prayer?
A. Yes: I give myself unto prayer. Ps. cix. 4.
2. *Q.* And humble in prayer?
A. Yes: for we are but dust and ashes. Gen. xviii. 27.
3. *Q.* And earnest in prayer?
A. Yes: always labouring fervently in prayer. Col. iv. 12.
4. *Q.* Must we in sincerity, set God before us, in prayer?
A. Yes: let us draw near, with a true heart. Heb. x. 22.
5. *Q.* Must we pray in charity?
A. Yes: lifting up pure hands, without wrath. 1 Tim. ii. 8.

§ VII.

1. *Q.* Will God hear and accept those who thus pray to him?
A. Yes: he never said to the seed of Jacob, seek ye me in vain. Isa. xlv. 19.
2. *Q.* But will the love of sin spoil the success of prayer?
A. Yes: if I regard iniquity in my heart, God will not hear me. Ps. lxvi. 18.

XCIX. *Q.* What rule hath God given for our direction in prayer?

A. The whole word of God is of use to direct us in prayer; but the special rule of direction is that form of prayer which Christ taught his disciples, commonly called "The Lord's Prayer."

§ I.

1. *Q.* Do we need direction in prayer?
A. Yes: for we know not what we should pray for as we ought. Rom. viii. 26.
2. *Q.* Should we pray to God for direction?
A. Yes: Lord, teach us to pray. Luke xi. 1.
3. *Q.* Hath he given us direction in prayer?
A. Yes: take with you words and turn to the Lord. Hos. xiv. 2.

§ II.

1. *Q.* Is the whole word of God of use to direct us?
A. Yes: I will shew thee that which is noted in the scripture of truth. Dan. x. 21, compared with 2 Chron. ix. 22.

2. *Q.* Is the Lord's prayer to be used as a directory for prayer?
A. Yes: after this manner, therefore pray ye. Matt. vi. 9.
3. *Q.* And is it to be used, as a form of prayer?
A. Yes: when ye pray, say, Our Father. Luke xi. 2.

C. *Q.* What doth the preface of the Lord's prayer teach us?

A. The preface of the Lord's Prayer (which is, *Our Father which art in Heaven,*) teacheth us to draw near to God with all holy reverence and confidence, as children to a father, able and ready to help us; and that we should pray with and for others.

§ I.

1. *Q.* Is God our Father?
A. Yes: doubtless thou art our Father. Isa. lxiii. 16.
2. *Q.* Does he appoint us to call him so?
A. Yes: wilt thou not from this time, cry unto me, My Father, thou art the guide of my youth? Jer. iii. 4.
3. *Q.* Is he our Father by creation?
A. Yes: have we not all one Father? Hath not one God created us? Mal. ii. 10.
4. *Q.* And by redemption?
A. Yes: is not he thy Father that bought thee? Deut. xxxii. 6.
5. *Q.* And by adoption?
A. Yes: I will be a Father to them. 2 Cor. vi. 18.

§ II.

1. *Q.* Is God a wise Father?
A. Yes: the Father of lights. James i. 17.
2. *Q.* Is he a gracious Father?
A. Yes: the Father of mercies. 2 Cor. i. 3.
3. *Q.* Is he our soul's Father?
A. Yes: the Father of spirits. Heb. xii. 9.
4. *Q.* Is he the Father of our Lord Jesus Christ?
A. Yes: I bow my knee to the Father of our Lord Jesus Christ. Ephes. iii. 14.
5. *Q.* Is he, in him, our Father?
A. Yes: I ascend to my Father, and your Father. John xx. 17.

§ III.

1. *Q.* Are we in prayer, to call God Father?

A. Yes: crying Abba, Father. Gal. iv. 6.

2. *Q.* And to esteem him as a Father?

A. Yes: I will arise and go to my father, and say unto him, Father. Luke xv. 18.

3. *Q.* And is this comfortable in prayer?

A. Yes: for with thee the fatherless findeth mercy. Hos. xiv. 3.

§ IV.

1. *Q.* Is God our Father in Heaven?

A. Yes: for the Lord's throne is in Heaven. Ps. xi. 4.

2. *Q.* Is Heaven a high place?

A. Yes: and we must lift up our hearts with our hands to God in the Heavens. Sam. iii. 41.

3. *Q.* Is it a holy place?

A. Yes: and we must lift up holy hands. 1 Tim. ii. 8.

4. *Q.* Is it a place of prospect?

A. Yes: and therefore our father seeth in secret. Matt. vi. 5.

5. *Q.* Is it a place of power?

A. Yes: and therefore, he is able to do above all that we ask or think. Ephes. iii. 20.

§ V.

1. *Q.* Ought we, therefore, to pray with reverence?

A. Yes: for God is in Heaven, and we upon earth. Eccl. v. 2.

2. *Q.* And with holy confidence?

A. Yes: for we have boldness and access with confidence. Ephes. iii. 12.

3. *Q.* For is God a father, who is able to help us?

A. Yes: my father is greater than all. John x. 29.

4. *Q.* Does he know our wants?

A. Yes: your Heavenly Father knows that ye have need of all these things. Matt. vi. 32.

5. *Q.* Is he willing to help?

A. Yes: for the Father himself loveth you. John xvi. 27.

§ VI.

1. *Q.* Must we pray with others?

A. Yes: there were many gathered together praying. Acts xii. 12.

2. *Q.* Must we pray for others?

A. Yes: we must make supplication for all saints. Ephes. vi. 18.

CI. *Q.* What do we pray for in the first petition?

A. In the first petition (which is *hallowed be thy name,*) we pray, that God would enable us and others to glorify him in all that whereby he maketh himself known, and that he would dispose all things to his own glory.

§ I.

1. *Q.* Ought we to desire the glory of God in the first place?
A. Yes: that God, in all things, may be glorified. 1 Pet. iv. 11.

2. *Q.* Is God glorified when his name is glorified?
A. Yes: they shall worship before thee, O Lord, and shall glorify thy name. Ps. lxxxvi. 9.

3. *Q.* Is God's name glorified, when it is sanctified or hallowed?
A. Yes: for he is glorious in holiness. Exod. xv. 11.

4. *Q.* Ought we, therefore, to sanctify it?
A. Yes: sanctify the Lord God in your hearts. 1 Pet. iii. 15.

§ II.

1. *Q.* Are we to pray that we ourselves may be enabled to glorify God?
A. Yes: open thou my lips, and my mouth shall shew forth thy praise. Ps. li. 15.

2. *Q.* And that we may live for that end?
A. Yes: let my soul live, and it shall praise thee. Ps. cxix. 175.

3. *Q.* And be delivered for that end?
A. Yes: bring my soul out of prison, that I may praise thy name. Ps. cxlii. 7.

4. *Q.* And are we to pray that others also may be enabled to glorify him?
A. Yes: that they may glorify our Father which is in Heaven. Matt. v. 16.

§ III.

1. *Q.* Do we here pray for the propagating of the knowledge of God?
A. Yes: that thy way may be known upon earth, thy saving health among all nations. Ps. lxvii. 2.

2. *Q.* And for the conversion of souls to him?
A. Yes: let the people praise thee, O God, let all the people praise thee! Ps. lxvii. 3.

3. *Q.* And for the success of the gospel?

A. Yes: that the word of the Lord may have free course, and be glorified. 2 Thess. iii. 1.

4. *Q.* Do we pray for the faithfulness of Christians?

A. Yes: that they may be filled with fruits of righteousness, which are by Jesus Christ, to the glory and praise of God. Philipp. i. 11.

5. *Q.* And for the flourishing of the churches of Christ?

A. Yes: that they may be called the trees of righteousness, the planting of the Lord, that he might be glorified. Isa. lxi. 3.

§ IV.

1. *Q.* Do we pray, that God would glorify himself?

A. Yes: Father, glorify thy name. John xii. 28.

2. *Q.* And are we sure he will do it?

A. Yes: for there came a voice from Heaven, saying, I have both glorified it, and I will glorify it yet again. John xii. 28.

3. *Q.* Do we pray that he would exalt his own name?

A. Yes: be thou exalted, O Lord, in thine own strength. Ps. xxi. 13.

4. *Q.* And are we sure he will do it?

A. Yes: I will be exalted among the heathen, I will be exalted in the earth. Ps. xlvi. 10.

5. *Q.* May we plead this with him. Ps. lxxvi. 10.

A. Yes: what wilt thou do to thy great name? Josh. vii. 9.

§ V.

1. *Q.* Do we pray that God would bring glory to himself out of all events?

A. Yes: to thy name give glory. Ps. cxv. 1.

2. *Q.* Even out of those events that seem contrary?

A. Yes: that the wrath of man may praise him. Ps. lxxvi. 10.

3. *Q.* Must we desire it concerning ourselves?

A. Yes: that we may be unto him for a name, and for a praise, and for a glory. Jer. xiii. 11.

4. *Q.* And concerning all our affairs?

A. Yes: that Christ may be magnified in my body both by life and death. Philipp. i. 20.

CII. *Q.* What do we pray for in the second petition?

A. In the second petition (which is, *Thy kingdom come,*) we pray, that Satan's kingdom may be destroyed; and that the kingdom of grace may be advanced, ourselves and others brought into it, and kept in it, and that the kingdom of glory may be hastened.

§ I.

1. Q. Must we acknowledge our Heavenly Father's kingdom?
A. Yes: the Lord is king forever and ever. Ps. x. 16.
2. Q. And must we admire it?
A. Yes: we must speak of the glory of his kingdom. Ps. cxlv. 11.
3. Q. Must we own him to be our king?
A. Yes: thou art my king, O God. Ps. xliv. 4.
4. Q. Must we heartily wish well to his kingdom?
A. Yes: seek ye first the kingdom of God. Matt. vi. 33.

§ II.

1. Q. Has Satan a kingdom in opposition to God's kingdom?
A. Yes: for he is the prince of this world. John xii. 31.
2. Q. Does he rule where sin rules?
A. Yes: for he works in the children of disobedience. Ephes. ii. 2.
3. Q. Must we pray that that kingdom may be destroyed?
A. Yes: The Lord rebuke thee, O Satan, even the Lord that has chosen Jerusalem, rebuke thee. Zech. iii. 2.
4. Q. Must we pray that the dominion of sin may be broken?
A. Yes: O, let the wickedness of the wicked come to an end. Ps. vii. 9.
5. Q. And that the power of the church's enemies may be crushed?
A. Yes: so let all thine enemies perish, O Lord. Judges v. 31.
6. Q. And their policies blasted?
A. Yes: Lord, turn the counsel of Ahithopel into foolishness. 2 Sam. xv. 31.
7. Q. And their projects defeated?
A. Yes: O my God, make them like a wheel. Ps. lxxxiii. 13.

§ III.

1. Q. Have we reason to hope that Satan's kingdom shall be destroyed in the hearts of believers?
A. Yes: for the God of peace shall tread Satan under your feet shortly. Rom. xvi. 20.

2. *Q.* And that it shall be destroyed in the world?
A. Yes: for, I beheld Satan as lightning fall from Heaven. Luke x. 18.

3. *Q.* So destroyed that it shall not destroy the church?
A. Yes: for the church is built upon a rock, and the gates of Hell shall not prevail against it. Matt. xvi. 18.

§ IV.

1. *Q.* Is the kingdom of Christ our Father's kingdom?
A. Yes: I have set my king upon my holy hill of Zion. Ps. ii. 6.

2. *Q.* Must we pray that that may be advanced?
A. Yes: prayer shall be made for him continually. Ps. lxxii. 15.

3. *Q.* That we and others may be brought into it?
A. Yes: that Christ may dwell in your heart by faith. Ephes. iii. 17.

4. *Q.* And kept in it?
A. Yes: that we may be preserved blameless to the coming of our Lord Jesus Christ. 1 Thess. v. 23.

§ V.

1. *Q.* Are we to pray for converting grace?
A. Yes: turn thou me and I shall be turned. Jer. xxxi. 18.

2. *Q.* And that others may partake of that grace?
A. Yes: that sinners may be converted unto thee. Ps. li. 13.

3. *Q.* Are we to pray for confirming grace?
A. Yes: that God would comfort your hearts, and establish you in every good word and work. 2 Thess. ii. 17.

4. *Q.* Are we to pray for the strengthening of faith?
A. Yes: Lord increase our faith. Luke xvii. 5.

5. *Q.* And the increase of love?
A. Yes: this I pray, that your love may abound yet more and more. Philipp. i. 9.

§ VI.

1. *Q.* Are we to pray for the advancement of the kingdom of light?
A. Yes: O send out thy light and thy truth. Ps. xliii. 3.

2. *Q.* And the kingdom of holiness?
A. Yes: the God of peace sanctify you wholly. 1 Thess. v. 23.

3. *Q.* And the kingdom of love?
A. Yes: that they all may be one. John xvii. 21.

4. *Q.* Must we pray for the sending forth of ministers in order hereunto?

A. Yes: pray the Lord of the harvest that he would send forth labourers unto his harvest. Matt. ix. 38.

5. *Q.* And for the presence of God with them?

A. Yes: that utterance may be given to them. Ephes. vi. 19.

§ VII.

1. *Q.* Are we to pray for the prosperity of the church?

A. Yes: pray for the peace of Jerusalem. Ps. cxxii. 6.

2. *Q.* And for the welfare of all who belong to it?

A. Yes: let all those that seek thee rejoice and be glad in thee. Ps. lxx. 4.

3. *Q.* And for the comfort of all good christians?

A. Yes: grace be with all them that love our Lord Jesus Christ in sincerity. Ephes. vi. 24.

4. *Q.* Must we pray for the enlargement of the church?

A. Yes: my heart's desire and prayer to God for Israel, is that they may be saved. Rom. x. 1.

5. *Q.* And for the reformation of it?

A. Yes: turn us again, O Lord God of Hosts. Ps. lxxx. 19.

6. *Q.* And for the defence of it?

A. Yes: build thou the walls of Jerusalem. Ps. li. 18.

7. *Q.* And for the deliverance of it?

A. Yes: command deliverance for Jacob. Ps. xliv. 4.

§ VIII.

1. *Q.* May we pray in faith for the advancement and continuance of Christ's kingdom.

A. Yes: for of the increase of his government and peace there shall be no end. Isa. ix. 7.

2. *Q.* And have we reason to triumph in this?

A. Yes: hallelujah, for the Lord God omnipotent reigneth. Rev. xix. 6.

§ IX.

1. *Q.* Is the kingdom of glory yet to come?

A. Yes: when the mystery of God shall be finished. Rev. x. 7.

2. *Q.* Are we to pray that that may be hastened?

A. Yes: looking for and hastening unto the coming of the day of God. 2 Pet. iii. 12.

3. *Q.* Are we to desire our own removal to that glory at death?

A. Yes: desiring to be clothed upon with our house which is from Heaven. 2 Cor. v. 2.

4. *Q.* Are we to pray that we may be ready for it?

A. Yes: watch, therefore, and pray always. Luke xxi. 36.

5. *Q.* And then that it may be hastened?

A. Yes: Lord, now lettest thou thy servant depart in peace. Luke ii. 29.

6. *Q.* Are we to pray for Christ's second coming at the end of time?

A. Yes: Amen, even so come, Lord Jesus. Rev. xxii. 20.

CIII. *Q.* What do we pray for in the third petition?

A. In the third petition (which is, *Thy will be done in earth as it is in Heaven,*) we pray, that God by his grace, would make us able and willing to know, obey, and submit to his will in all things, as the angels do in Heaven.

§ I.

1. *Q.* Is the will of God's commands the rule of our action?

A. Yes: we must understand what the will of the Lord is. Ephes. v. 17.

2. *Q.* Are we to pray that we may conform to this rule?

A. Yes: that we may prove what is the good, and acceptable, and perfect will of God. Rom. xii. 2.

3. *Q.* Must we pray that God would give us to know his will?

A. Yes: give me understanding, and I will keep thy law. Ps. cxix. 34.

4. *Q.* And to know it fully?

A. Yes: that ye may be filled with the knowledge of his will. Col. i. 9.

5. *Q.* And to know it, in doubtful cases?

A. Yes: teach me thy way, O Lord, lead me in a plain path. Ps. xxvii. 11.

6. *Q.* Do all who are sanctified truly desire to know God's will?

A. Yes: what saith my Lord unto his servant? Josh. v. 14.

§ II.

1. *Q.* When we know God's will, are we able, of ourselves, to do it?

A. No: we are not sufficient, of ourselves. 2 Cor. iii. 5.

2. *Q.* Must we, therefore, pray to God to make us able?

A. Yes: now, therefore, O God, strengthen my hands. Neh. vi. 9.

3. *Q.* And must we depend upon his grace?

A. Yes: I will go in the strength of the Lord God. Ps. lxxi. 16.

4. *Q.* Must we pray to God to make us willing?

A. Yes: incline my heart unto thy testimonies. Ps. cxix. 36.

5. *Q.* And to make us entirely willing?

A. Yes: unite my heart to fear thy name. Ps. lxxxvi. 11.

§ III.

1. *Q.* Must we pray that we may be sincere in our obedience?

A. Yes: let my heart be sound in thy statutes. Ps. cxix. 80.

2. *Q.* And that we may be exact in our obedience?

A. Yes: O that my ways were directed to keep thy commandments! Ps. cxix. 5.

3. *Q.* And that we may be universal in our obedience?

A. Yes: that we may stand complete in all the will of God. Col. iv. 12.

4. *Q.* And that we may be armed against that which would divert us from our obedience?

A. Yes: turn away mine eyes from beholding vanity, and quicken thou me in thy way. Ps. cxix. 37.

5. *Q.* And must we pray that others also may do God's will?

A. Yes: that they may be perfect in every good work to do his will. Heb. xiii. 21.

§ IV.

1. *Q.* Is the will of God's counsel the rule of his actions?

A. Yes: for he worketh all according to the counsel of his own will. Ephes. i. 11.

2. *Q.* Must we desire that this may be done?

A. Yes: the will of the Lord be done. Acts xxi. 14.

3. *Q.* Rather than our own will?

A. Yes: not as I will, but as thou wilt. Matt. xxvi. 39.

4. *Q.* And must we acquiesce in it?

A. Yes: it is the Lord, let him do what seemeth him good. 1 Sam. iii. 18.

5. *Q.* And must we pray that he will enable us to do so?

A. Yes: that we may be strengthened with all might, unto all patience and long-suffering, with joyfulness. Col. i. 11.

§ V.

1. *Q.* Do the angels in Heaven do the will of God?

A. Yes: they do his commandments, hearkening to the voice of his word. Ps. ciii. 20.

2. *Q.* Do they do it readily?

A. Yes: they fly swiftly. Dan. ix. 21.

3. *Q.* Do they do it zealously?
A. Yes: for they are a flaming fire. Ps. civ. 4.
4. *Q.* Do they do it with an eye to God?
A. Yes: for they always behold the face of our Father. Matt. xviii. 10.
5. *Q.* And are we to pray that God's will may so be done on earth?
A. Yes: that the kingdoms of this world may become the kingdoms of our Lord, and of his Christ. Rev. xi. 15.

CIV. *Q.* What do we pray for in the fourth petition?

A. In the fourth petition (which is, *Give us this day our daily bread,*) we pray, that of God's free gift we may receive a competent portion of the good things of this life, and enjoy his blessings with them.

§ I.

1. *Q.* Are we to pray for the good things of this life?
A. Yes: for the Lord is for the body. 1 Cor. vi. 13.
2. *Q.* Must we go to God for them?
A. Yes: for he giveth to all life and breath, and all things. Acts xvii. 25.
3. *Q.* Must we go to him for the comfort of them?
A. Yes: for he gives us richly all things to enjoy. 1 Tim. vi. 17.
4. *Q.* Do we deserve the good things of this life?
A. No: we are less than the least of all God's mercies. Gen. xxxii. 10.
5. *Q.* Must we, therefore, beg them of God as a free gift?
A. Yes: God gives thee the dew of Heaven. Gen. xxvii. 28.

§ II.

1. *Q.* Are we to pray for riches?
A. No: lest we be full, and say, who is the Lord? Prov. xxx. 9.
2. *Q.* Are we to pray for dainties?
A. No: be not desirous of dainties, for they are deceitful meat. Prov. xxiii. 3.
3. *Q.* Are we to be content with such a competent portion of these things as God sees fit for us?

A. Yes: having food and raiment, let us be therewith content. 1 Tim. vi. 8.

4. *Q.* Are we to pray for that?

A. Yes: feed me with food convenient for me. Prov. xxx. 8.

5. *Q.* And need we desire any more?

A. No: if God will be with me and keep me in the way that I go, and will give me bread to eat, and raiment to put on, so that I come to my Heavenly Father's house in peace, then the Lord shall be my God. Gen. xxviii. 20, 21.

§ III.

1. *Q.* Are we to pray each day for the bread of the day?

A. Yes: for the morrow shall take thought for the things of itself. Matt. vi. 34.

2. *Q.* And must we pray for our bread honestly gotten?

A. Yes: for with quietness we must work and eat our own bread. 2 Thess. iii. 12.

3. *Q.* And have we encouragement to pray for this?

A. Yes: for godliness hath the promise of the life that now is. 1 Tim. iv. 8.

§ IV.

1. *Q.* Do we herein pray for health?

A. Yes: for God is our life, and the length of our days. Deut. xxx. 20.

2. *Q.* And for success in our callings?

A. Yes: establish thou the work of our hands upon us. Ps. xc. 17.

2. *Q.* And for sleep?

A. Yes: for so he giveth his beloved sleep. Ps. cxxvii. 2

4. *Q.* And for seasonable weather?

A. Yes: ask ye of the Lord rain. Zech. x. 1.

§ V.

1. *Q.* Must we pray for God's blessing on what we have?

A. Yes: for man liveth not by bread alone, but by every word that proceedeth out of the mouth of God. Matt. iv. 4.

2. *Q.* And is it then comfortable to us?

A. Yes: for it is sanctified by the word of God and prayer. 1 Tim. iv. 5.

3. *Q.* Must we pray most earnestly for bread for our souls?

A. Yes: Lord, evermore give us that bread. John vi. 34.

4. *Q.* Are we to pray for other's prosperity, as well as for our own?

A. Yes: I wish that thou mayest prosper, and be in health, even as thy soul prospereth. 3 John 2.

5. *Q.* And for the supply of the poor and needy?
A. Yes: that he will abundantly bless our provision, and satisfy our poor with bread. Ps. cxxxii. 15.

CV. *Q.* What do we pray for in the fifth petition?

A. In the fifth petition (which is, *And forgive us our debts as we forgive our debtors,*) we pray that God, for Christ's sake, would freely pardon all our sins; which we are the rather encouraged to ask, because by his grace we are enabled from the heart to forgive others.

§ I.

1. *Q.* Are our sins our debts to God?
A. Yes: there was a certain creditor that had two debtors, &c. Luke vii. 41.
2. *Q.* Are they great debts?
A. Yes: ten thousand talents. Matt. xviii. 24.
3. *Q.* Can we discharge these debts ourselves?
A. No: we have nothing to pay. Luke vii. 42.
4. *Q.* Are we liable to the prison of Hell then?
A. Yes: not to depart thence till we have paid the last mite. Luke xii. 58, 59.
5. *Q.* Is it possible to obtain the forgiveness of this debt?
A. Yes: there is forgiveness with thee. Ps. cxxx. 4.

II.

1. *Q.* Are we to pray for the forgiveness of these sins?
A. Yes: enter not into judgment with thy servant, O Lord. Ps. cxliii. 2.
2. *Q.* And to pray earnestly for it?
A. Yes: for thy name's sake, O Lord, pardon mine iniquity. Ps. xxv. 11.
3. *Q.* Must we plead God's mercies?
A. Yes: according to the multitude of thy tender mercies blot out my transgressions. Ps. li. 1.
4. *Q.* And Christ's merits?
A. Yes: through the redemption that is in Jesus. Rom. iii. 24.
5. *Q.* Must we pray for it every day?
A. Yes: when we pray, give us our daily bread, we must pray, forgive us our debts.

§ III.

1. Q. Must we pray that God would ease us of the burthen of sin?

A. Yes: take away all iniquity. Hos. xiv. 2.

2. Q. And that he would cleanse us from the filth of sin?

A. Yes: wash me thoroughly from mine iniquity. Ps. li. 2.

3. Q. And cure us of the wounds of sin?

A. Yes: heal my soul, for I have sinned against thee. Ps. xli. 4.

4. Q. And save us from the punishment of sin?

A. Yes: I will say unto God, do not condemn me. Job x. 2.

§ IV.

1. Q. Must we pray to God to give us that grace which will qualify us for pardon?

A. Yes: for Christ is exalted to give repentance and remission. Acts v. 31.

2. Q. And that he would give us the comfort of our pardon?

A. Yes: make me to hear joy and gladness. Ps. li. 8.

3. Q. And must we, in order hereunto, be particular in confessing sin?

A. Yes: declare that thou mayest be justified. Is. xliii. 26.

§ V.

1. Q. Must we forgive those who have provoked us?

A. Yes: forbearing one another, and forgiving one another, if any man have a quarrel against any. Col. iii. 13.

2. Q. Must we bear them no malice?

A. No: grudge not one against another, brethren, lest ye be condemned. James v. 9.

3. Q. Must we be ready to be reconciled to them?

A. Yes: when ye stand praying, forgive if ye have aught against any. Mark xi. 25.

4. Q. Should we be merciful to those that we have advantage against?

A. Yes: thou shouldst have had compassion on thy fellow-servant, as I had pity on thee. Matt. xviii. 33.

5. Q. Is this required to qualify us for the pardon of sin?

A. Yes: if ye forgive men their trespasses, your heavenly Father will also forgive you. Matt. vi. 14.

6. Q. Will God forgive those that do not forgive?

A. No: if ye forgive not men their trespasses, neither will your Father forgive yours. Matt. vi. 15.

CVI. Q. What do we pray for in the sixth petition?

A. In the sixth petition (which is, *And lead us not into temptation but deliver us from evil,*) we pray that God would either keep us from being tempted to sin, or support and deliver us when we are tempted.

§ I.

1. *Q.* Must we pray that we may not be tempted?
A. Yes: watch and pray that ye enter not into temptation. Matt. xxvi. 41.
2. *Q.* And that temptations may be removed?
A. Yes: I besought the Lord thrice that it might depart from me. 2 Cor. xii. 8.
3. *Q.* And that we may not be overcome by them?
A. Yes: let no iniquity have dominion over me. Ps. cxix. 133.

§ II.

1. *Q.* Must we pray that God would not leave us to ourselves?
A. Yes: incline not my heart to any evil thing. Ps. cxli. 4.
2. *Q.* And that he would not withdraw the assistance of his grace?
A. Yes: take not thy Holy Spirit away from me. Ps. li. 11.
3. *Q.* But that he would strengthen us against every temptation?
A. Yes: uphold me with thy free spirit. Ps. li. 12.
4. *Q.* And that he would preserve us through it?
A. Yes: that our faith fail not. Luke. xxii. 32.
5. *Q.* Have we encouragement to pray against temptation?
A. Yes: for God is faithful, who will not suffer us to be tempted above what we are able. 1 Cor. x. 13.
6. *Q.* And is prayer a part of our spiritual armor?
A. Yes: Praying always. Ephes. vi. 13, 18.

§ III.

1. *Q.* Must we dread sin as the worst evil?
A. Yes: that I should be afraid and do so and sin. Neh vi. 13.
2. *Q.* And must we pray to be kept from it?
A. Yes: to be delivered from every evil work. 2 Tim. iv. 18.
3. *Q.* And from all occasions of it?
A. Yes: turn away mine eyes from beholding vanity. Ps. cxix. 37.

§ IV.

1. *Q.* Must we pray against pride?
A. Yes: that he may hide pride from man. Job xxxiii. 17.
2. *Q.* And against lying?
A. Yes: remove from me the way of lying. Ps. cxix. 29.
3. *Q.* And against sensuality?
A. Yes: let me not eat of their dainties. Ps. cxli. 4.
4. *Q.* And against uncleanness?
A. Yes: create in me a clean heart, O God. Ps. li. 10.
5. *Q.* And against covetousness?
A. Yes: incline my heart to thy testimonies, and not to covetousness. Ps. cxix. 36.
6. *Q.* And against all tongue sins?
A. Yes: set a watch, O Lord, before the door of my mouth, keep the door of my lips. Ps. cxli. 3.
7. *Q.* Must we pray especially against wilful sin?
A. Yes: keep back thy servant from presumptuous sins. Ps. xix. 13.
8. *Q.* Must we pray that others also may be kept from sin?
A. Yes: I pray to God that ye do no evil. 2 Cor. xiii. 7.

§ V.

1. *Q.* Must we pray to be delivered from other evil?
A. Yes: keep me from evil that it may not grieve me. 1 Chron. iv. 10.
2. *Q.* Must our eye be to God for our preservation?
A. Yes: hide me under the shadow of thy wings. Ps. xvii. 8.
3. *Q.* May we take encouragement in this prayer from God's power?
A. Yes: for he is able to keep that which we have committed to him. 2 Tim. i. 12.
4. *Q.* And from his promise?
A. Yes: there shall no evil befall thee. Ps. xci. 10.
5. *Q.* And from our own experience?
A. Yes: he that has delivered, does deliver, in whom we trust that he will yet deliver. 2 Cor. i. 10.

CVII. *Q.* What doth the conclusion of the Lord's Prayer teach us?

A. The conclusion of the Lord's Prayer (which is, *For thine is the kingdom, and the power, and the glory forever, Amen,*) teacheth us to take our encouragement in prayer from

God only, and in our prayers to praise him, ascribing kingdom, power, and glory to him. And in testimony of our desire, and assurance to be heard, we say, Amen.

§ I.

1. Q. Are we in prayer to plead with God?
A. Yes: I would order my cause before him, and fill my mouth with arguments. Job. xxiii. 4.
2. Q. Are our pleadings to move God?
A. No: for he is in one mind, and who can turn him? Job. xxiii. 13.
3. Q. Are they to move ourselves?
A. Yes: that we may stir up ourselves to take hold on God. Isa. lxiv. 7.

§ II.

1. Q. Can we, in prayer, plead any merit of our own?
A. No: we do not present our supplications before thee for our righteousness. Dan. ix. 18.
2. Q. Must we, therefore, take our encouragement from God only?
A. Yes: defer not, for thine own sake, O my God. Dan. ix. 19.
3. Q. And must we depend on that encouragement?
A. Yes: now, Lord, what wait I for? My hope is in thee. Ps. xxxix. 7.

§ III.

1. Q. May we plead that his is the kingdom?
A. Yes: art not thou God in heaven? and rulest not thou over all the kingdoms of the heathen? 2. Chron. xx. 6.
2. Q. And that his is the power?
A. Yes: there is nothing too hard for thee. Jer. xxxii. 17.
3. Q. And that his is the glory?
A. Yes: help us, O God of our salvation, for the glory of thy name. Ps. lxxix. 9.

§ IV.

1. Q. May we also plead his mercy?
A. Yes: save me for thy mercy's sake, Ps. vi. 4.
2. Q. And his promise?
A. Yes: remember thy word unto thy servant. Ps. cxix. 49.
3. Q. And our own experience of his goodness?

...ast delivered my soul from death: wilt thou ..y feet from falling? Ps. lvi. 13.

..Q. But must we especially plead the mediation of his son?

A. Yes: look upon the face of thine anointed. Ps. lxxxiv. 9.

5. Q. And may we hope to prevail in these pleadings?

A. Yes: for the effectual fervent prayer of a righteous man availeth much. James, v. 16.

6. Q. Is it God's grace in us which alone qualifies us for his favour?

A. Yes: thou wilt prepare their heart, and then thou wilt cause thine ear to hear. Ps. x. 17.

§ v.

1. Q. Are we, in prayer, to praise God?

A. Yes: every day will I bless thee. Ps. cxlv. 2.

2. Q. Are we to ascribe kingdom, power and glory to him?

A. Yes: blessing, and honour, and glory, and power, be unto him that sitteth upon the throne. Rev. v. 13.

3. Q. Must we acknowledge them to be his?

A. Yes: thine, O Lord, is the greatness, and the power, and the glory, and the victory, and the majesty. 1. Chron. xxix. 11.

4. Q. Must we acknowledge them to be his forever?

A. Yes: thy kingdom is an everlasting kingdom. Ps. cxlv. 13.

5. Q. And must we desire to be forever praising him?

A. Yes: I will sing praise to my God while I have my being. Ps. civ. 33.

6. Q. Is the work of praise good work?

A. Yes: It is pleasant, and praise is comely. Ps. cxlvii. 1.

§ vi.

1. Q. Does Amen signify our desire to be heard?

A. Yes: so be it, O Lord. Jer. xi. 5.

2. Q. And our hope that we shall be heard?

A. Yes: we know that we have the petitions that we desired of him. 1 John v. 15.

3. Q. Is it, therefore, proper to conclude our prayers and praises with Amen?

A. Yes: let all the people say, Amen, Hallelujah! Ps. cvi. 48

THE END.

www.ingramcontent.com/pod-product-compliance
Lightning Source LLC
Chambersburg PA
CBHW062204080426
42734CB00010B/1786